Teach Yourself VISUALLY™

Dreamweaver® MX 2004

Janine Warner and Susannah Gardner

Visual™

From

maranGraphics®

&

Wiley Publishing, Inc.

Teach Yourself VISUALLY™
Dreamweaver® MX 2004

Published by
Wiley Publishing, Inc.
111 River Street
Hoboken, NJ 07030-5774

Published simultaneously in Canada

Copyright © 2004 by Wiley Publishing, Inc., Indianapolis, Indiana

Certain designs, text, and illustrations Copyright © 1992-2004 maranGraphics, Inc., used with maranGraphics' permission.

maranGraphics, Inc.
5755 Coopers Avenue
Mississauga, Ontario, Canada
L4Z 1R9

Library of Congress Control Number: 2001099317

ISBN: 0-7645-4335-0

Manufactured in the United States of America

10 9 8 7 6 5 4 3 2 1

1K/RT/QS/QU/IN

Trademark Acknowledgments

Important Numbers

For U.S. corporate orders, please call maranGraphics at 800-469-6616 or fax 905-890-9434.

For general information on our other products and services or to obtain technical support please contact our Customer Care Department within the U.S. at 800-762-2974, outside the U.S. at 317-572-3993 or fax 317-572-4002.

Permissions

maranGraphics

Certain text and Illustrations by maranGraphics, Inc., used with maranGraphics' permission.

Permissions Granted

Desi Aragon

Suzanne Berg

Jaclyn Easton

Philip Gardner

Susannah Gardner

Caryl Levy

Kathryn Lord

Anita Malik

Ken Milburn

Marilyn Pittman

Michael Overing

Patti Rayne

Wiley Publishing, Inc.

U.S. Corporate Sales	U.S. Trade Sales
Contact maranGraphics at (800) 469-6616 or fax (905) 890-9434.	Contact Wiley at (800) 762-2974 or fax (317) 572-4002.

Some comments from our readers...

"I have to praise you and your company on the fine products you turn out. I have twelve of the *Teach Yourself VISUALLY* and *Simplified* books in my house. They were instrumental in helping me pass a difficult computer course. Thank you for creating books that are easy to follow."

— *Gordon Justin (Brielle, NJ)*

"I commend your efforts and your success. I teach in an outreach program for the Dr. Eugene Clark Library in Lockhart, TX. Your *Teach Yourself VISUALLY* books are incredible, and I use them in my computer classes. All my students love them!"

— *Michele Schalin (Lockhart, TX)*

"Like a lot of other people, I understand things best when I see them visually. Your books really make learning easy and life more fun."

— *John T. Frey (Cadillac, MI)*

"I have quite a few of your Visual books and have been very pleased with all of them. I love the way the lessons are presented!"

— *Mary Jane Newman (Yorba Linda, CA)*

"I write to extend my thanks and appreciation for your books. They are clear, easy to follow, and straight to the point. Keep up the good work!"

— *Seward Kollie (Dakar, Senegal)*

"I am an avid fan of your Visual books. If I need to learn anything, I just buy one of your books and learn the topic in no time. Wonders! I have even trained my friends to give me Visual books as gifts."

— *Illona Bergstrom (Aventura, FL)*

"Thank you for making it so clear. I appreciate it. I will buy many more Visual books."

— *J.P. Sangdong (North York, Ontario, Canada)*

"I was introduced to maranGraphics about four years ago and YOU ARE THE GREATEST THING THAT EVER HAPPENED TO INTRODUCTORY COMPUTER BOOKS!"

— *Glenn Nettleton (Huntsville, AL)*

"Compliments to the chef!! Your books are extraordinary! Or, simply put, extra-ordinary, meaning way above the rest! THANK YOU THANK YOU THANK YOU! for creating these."

— *Christine J. Manfrin (Castle Rock, CO)*

"I just purchased my third Visual book (my first two are dog-eared now!) and, once again, your product has surpassed my expectations. The expertise, thought, and effort that go into each book are obvious, and I sincerely appreciate your efforts. Keep up the wonderful work!"

— *Tracey Moore (Memphis, TN)*

"Thank you, thank you, thank you...for making it so easy for me to break into this high-tech world. I now own four of your books. I recommend them to anyone who is a beginner like myself. Now...if you could just do one for programming VCR's, it would make my day!"

— *Gay O'Donnell (Calgary, Alberta, Canada)*

"You're marvelous! I am greatly in your debt."

— *Patrick Baird (Lacey, WA)*

maranGraphics is a family-run business located near Toronto, Canada.

At **maranGraphics**, we believe in producing great computer books — one book at a time.

maranGraphics has been producing high-technology products for over 25 years, which enables us to offer the computer book community a unique communication process.

Our computer books use an integrated communication process, which is very different from the approach used in other computer books. Each spread is, in essence, a flow chart — the text and screen shots are totally incorporated into the layout of the spread.

Introductory text and helpful tips complete the learning experience.

maranGraphics' approach encourages the left and right sides of the brain to work together — resulting in faster orientation and greater memory retention.

Above all, we are very proud of the handcrafted nature of our books. Our carefully-chosen writers are experts in their fields, and spend countless hours researching and organizing the content for each topic. Our artists rebuild every screen shot to provide the best

clarity possible, making our screen shots the most precise and easiest to read in the industry. We strive for perfection, and believe that the time spent handcrafting each element results in the best computer books money can buy.

Thank you for purchasing this book. We hope you enjoy it!

Sincerely,

Robert Maran
President
maranGraphics
Rob@maran.com
www.maran.com

CREDITS

Project Editor
Jade L. Williams

Acquisitions Editor
Jody Lefevere

Product Development Manager
Lindsay Sandman

Technical Editor
Wendy V. Williams

Editorial Manager
Robyn Siesky

Permissions Editor
Laura Moss

Manufacturing
Allan Conley
Linda Cook
Paul Gilchrist
Jennifer Guynn

Screen Artist
Jill A. Proll

Illustrators
Karl Brandt
Ronda David-Burroughs
Kelly Emkow
David E. Gregory
Rashell Smith

Book Design
maranGraphics®

Production Coordinator
Nancee Reeves

Layout
Joyce Haughey
LeAndra Hosier
Kristin McMullan
Heather Pope

Proofreader
Debbye Butler

Quality Control
John Greenough
Susan Moritz

Indexer
Richard T. Evans

Special Help
Macromedia, Inc.

Vice President and Executive Group Publisher
Richard Swadley

Vice President and Publisher
Barry Pruett

Composition Director
Debbie Stailey

ABOUT THE AUTHORS

Janine Warner is a best-selling author, professional speaker, syndicated columnist, and consultant. She is the author of several books about the Internet, including *Managing Web Projects For Dummies, Dreamweaver For Dummies, 50 Fast Dreamweaver Techniques,* and *Contribute For Dummies.*

Janine has been a featured guest on numerous television and radio programs, among them NBC's evening news and ZDTV's Screensavers. Her syndicated newspaper column, "Beyond the Net," appears in print and online, including in *The Miami Herald.*

Janine has also been a part-time lecturer at the University of Southern California Annenberg School for Communication and at the University of Miami. She currently has a contract to develop online multimedia training programs for the Western Knight Center, which serves both the UC Berkeley and USC.

As a consultant, Janine has served a broad range of clients from Internet companies to bricks-and-mortar businesses in the United States and abroad. Her expertise in multimedia, technology, and education have taken her on consulting assignments from Miami to Mexico and speaking engagements from New York to New Delhi.

An award-winning former reporter, she earned a degree in journalism from the University of Massachusetts, Amherst, and worked for several years in Northern California as a reporter and editor. She speaks fluent Spanish.

To learn more, visit www.JCWarner.com

Susannah Gardner is the founder and creative director for Hop Studios Internet Consultants (www.hopstudios.com), a Web design company specializing in custom Web solutions.

Susannah is also a freelance writer, coauthor of *"Dreamweaver MX 2004 For Dummies,"* and a part-time faculty member at the University of Southern California School For Communication.

Prior to running Hop Studios, Susannah worked in the Online Program at the University of Southern California, writing curriculum, teaching, and conducting research in the intersection of technology and journalism.

Susannah spent four years at *The Los Angeles Times.* She was one of the first designers to work on the newspaper's Web site, before being promoted to multimedia director.

Susannah earned bachelor's degrees in Print Journalism and American literature at USC. Today she is pursuing a master's degree in Public Art Studies. Susannah loves cats, food, books and travel, but not all at once.

To learn more about her Web design company, visit www.hopstudios.com.

AUTHORS' ACKNOWLEDGMENTS

Janine Warner:

I've always thanked many people in my books — former teachers, mentors, friends — but I have been graced by so many wonderful people now that no publisher will give me enough pages to thank them all. So I focus here on the people who made *this* book possible.

Above all others, I have to thank my wonderful coauthor Susannah Gardner, who has worked with me on two books now and surpassed my expectations both times. Even on a tight deadline, she never misses a beat, and her beautiful Web design work graces brings these pages to life with real-world examples of her great design work (see her portfolio online at www.hopstudios.com).

Thanks also to Frank Vera, whose programming skills helped ensure that the most technical aspects of this book were revised by a real expert

Thanks to Jade Williams for her attention to detail and helping make sure all the final pieces came together in this book. Thanks also Jody Lefevere for taking this project through the development process.

I've written acknowledgements for so many books now I think my parents have lost count, but I always send them copies and I always thank them. I love you all — Malinda, Janice, Helen, and Robin. Thank you for your love, support, and understanding.

And finally, let me thank the beautiful stars that this book is finally done. Complete. Finished. This is it. (And don't even tell me those aren't complete sentences.)

Susannah Gardner:

My thanks go first to Janine Warner, friend and colleague, who gave me the opportunity to work on this book with her. She has shared her expertise and advice at all hours of the day and night. Life would be a sad and dreary thing without friends like Janine.

My heart and my thanks go to my husband Travis Smith. Travis' love of all things technical, journalistic and computer-related is inspiring during those (very few, of course) moments of discouragement. He is a wonderful partner in life and in work.

I want also to say thanks to the many clients and friends who allowed me to use their photos and Web sites in this book and who have let me come back to do work for them once, twice, sometimes even three times! My thanks go to Deborah Nathanson, Tracy Dominick, Suzanne Berg, Ted Gest, Jaclyn Easton, Anita Malik, Kathryn Lord, and Patti Rayne.

I have my smart and ambitious parents to thank for my love of books and reading. Thanks, Mom and Dad (Jan and Phil Gardner)! My family would be incomplete without the humor of my brother Matt Gardner (his site is shown in this book) and the sheer grit of my sister Debbie Gardner (whose site I hope to do whenever she needs one).

I have some friends to thank for assistance with technology and simple common sense: Lance Watanabe, Jae Sung, Karin Sung and Elaine Zinngrabe. For pure inspiration and great conversation, my thanks go to Julie Thompson, Mike Lathrop and Zipporah Lax.

It was great to work with the fine people at Wiley. Their pinpoint attention and solid editing improved this book immeasurably.

Thanks, finally, to everyone out there who buys this book. (Any mistakes are all Janine's fault.)

TABLE OF CONTENTS

Chapter 1

GETTING STARTED WITH DREAMWEAVER

Introduction to the World Wide Web 4

Parts of a Web Page 6

Plan Your Web Site 8

Start Dreamweaver on a PC 10

Start Dreamweaver on a Macintosh 11

Tour the Dreamweaver Interface on a PC 12

Tour the Dreamweaver Interface on a Macintosh 13

Show or Hide a Window 14

Exit Dreamweaver 15

Get Help 16

Chapter 2

SETTING UP YOUR WEB SITE

Set Up a New Web Site 20

Create a New Web Page 22

Add a Title to a Web Page 23

Save a Web Page 24

Preview a Web Page in a Browser 26

Chapter 3

EXPLORING THE DREAMWEAVER INTERFACE

Customize the Document Window 30

Format Content with the Properties Inspector 32

Add an E-Mail Link from the Insert Panel 34

Correct Errors with the History Panel 35

Open a Panel 36

Create and Apply a Custom Command 38

Set Preferences .40

Chapter 4

WORKING WITH HTML

```
<HTML>

<HEAD>
<TITLE>Castle Beach Club Realty - Reservation
Request Form</TITLE>
```

Introduction to HTML 44

Work in Design View and Code View 46

Explore Head and Body Tags 48

Explore Block-Formatting Tags 49
Explore Text-Formatting Tags 50
Explore Image and Hyperlink Tags 51
Clean Up HTML Code .52
View and Edit Head Content 54
Access Reference Information about HTML Tags 56

Chapter 5

FORMATTING AND STYLING TEXT

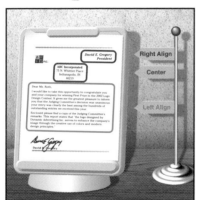

Create a Heading 60
Create Paragraphs 62
Create Line Breaks 64
Indent Paragraphs 65
Create Lists 66
Insert Special Characters 68
Change the Font Face .70
Change the Font Size .72
Change the Font Color 73
Change the Font Size and Color of a Page 74
Import Text from Another Document 76

Chapter 6

WORKING WITH IMAGES AND MULTIMEDIA

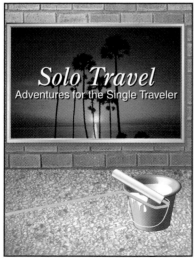

Insert an Image into a Web Page 80
Wrap Text Around an Image 82
Align an Image 84
Crop an Image 86
Resize an Image 88
Resample an Image 90
Add Space Around an Image 92
Add a Background Image 94
Change the Background Color 96
Add Alternate Text to an Image 97
Insert a Flash File 98
Insert Other Multimedia Files 100
Create a Rollover Image 102
Insert a Navigation Bar 104

TABLE OF CONTENTS

Chapter 7

CREATING HYPERLINKS TO CONNECT INFORMATION

Link to Pages in Your Site 108
Link to Another Web Site 110
Use an Image as a Link 112
Create a Jump Link Within a Page 114
Create a Link to Another File Type 116
Create an Image Map 118
Create a Link Using the Files Panel 120
Open a Linked Page in a New Browser Window . .121
Create an E-Mail Link 122
Check Links 123
Change the Color of Links on a Page 124

Chapter 8

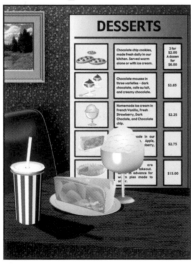

USING TABLES TO DESIGN A WEB PAGE

Insert a Table into a Web Page 128
Insert Content into a Table 130
Change the Background of a Table 132
Change the Cell Padding in a Table 134
Change the Cell Spacing in a Table 135
Change the Alignment of a Table 136
Change the Alignment of Cell Content 137
Insert or Delete a Row or Column 138
Split or Merge Table Cells 140
Change the Dimensions of a Cell 142
Change the Dimensions of a Table 143
Create a Layout Table 144
Rearrange a Table 146
Adjust the Width of a Table 148

Chapter 9

CREATING FRAMES

Introduction to Frames 152
Insert a Predefined Frameset 153
Save a Frameset .154
Divide a Page into Frames 156

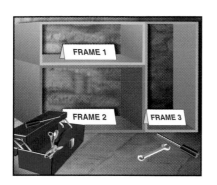

Create a Nested Frame .157

Change the Attributes of a Frame 158

Add Content to a Frame 160

Delete a Frame 162

Name a Frame 163

Create a Link to a Frame 164

Format Frame Borders 166

Control Scroll Bars in Frames 168

Control Resizing in Frames 169

Chapter 10

CREATING WEB-BASED FORMS

Introduction to Forms 172

Define a Form 173

Add a Text Field to a Form 174

Add a Check Box to a Form 176

Add a Radio Button to a Form 178

Add a Menu or List to a Form 180

Add a Password Field to a Form 182

Add a Submit or Reset Button to a Form 183

Chapter 11

USING LIBRARY ITEMS AND TEMPLATES

Introduction to Library Items and Templates 186

View Library Items and Templates 187

Create a Library Item 188

Insert a Library Item .190

Edit and Update a Library Item to Your Web Site . . .192

Detach Library Content for Editing 194

Create a Template 196

Set an Editable Region in a Template 198

Create a Page from a Template 200

Edit a Template and Update Your Web Site 202

TABLE OF CONTENTS

Chapter 12

CREATING AND APPLYING STYLE SHEETS

Introduction to Cascading Style Sheets 206
Customize an HTML Tag 208
Create a Custom Style 210
Apply a Style 212
Edit a Style 214
Create Custom Link Styles 216
Create an External Style Sheet 218
Attach an External Style Sheet 220
Edit an External Style Sheet 222

Chapter 13

USING LAYERS TO INCREASE USER INTERACTION

Introduction to Layers 226
Create a Layer with Content 228
Resize and Reposition Layers 230
Change the Stacking Order of Layers 232
Drag a Layer 233
Show and Hide Layers Behavior 234
Create a Nested Layer 236

Chapter 14

PUBLISHING A WEB SITE

Publish Your Web Site 240
Use the Site Window 241
Test Your Work in Different Browsers 242
Organize Your Files and Folders 244
Set Up a Remote Site 246
Connect to a Remote Site 248
Upload Files to a Web Server 250
Download Files from a Web Server 252
Synchronize Your Local and Remote Sites 254

Chapter 15

MAINTAINING A WEB SITE

View the Site Map 258
Manage Site Assets 260
Add Content with the Assets Panel 262
Specify Favorite Assets 264
Check a Page In or Out 266
Make Design Notes 268
Run a Site Report 270
Change a Link Sitewide 271
Find and Replace Text 272

Chapter 16

BUILDING A DATABASE-DRIVEN WEB SITE

The Power of Dynamic Web Sites 276
Install a Testing Server 278
Create a Database Connection 282
Configure a Dynamic Web Site 286
Create a Recordset 288
Add a Record 292
Update a Record 293
Add Recordset Paging 294
Create a Site Search .296

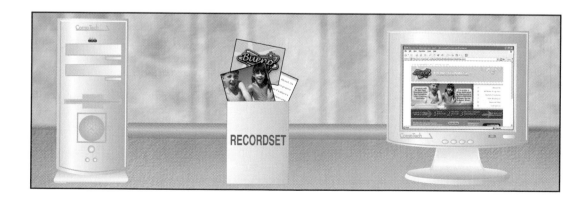

RECORDSET

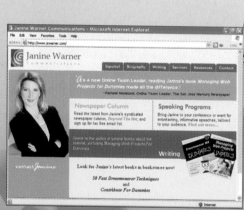

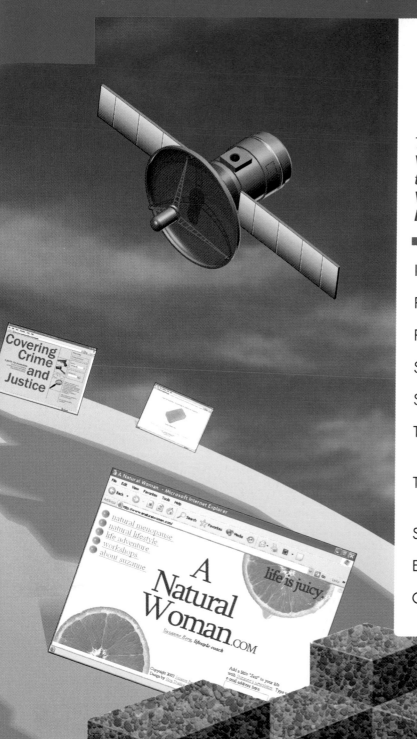

CHAPTER 1

Getting Started with Dreamweaver

This chapter describes the World Wide Web, introduces the different types of information you can put on a Web site, and tells you how to start Dreamweaver.

Introduction to the World Wide Web 4

Parts of a Web Page 6

Plan Your Web Site............................8

Start Dreamweaver on a PC 10

Start Dreamweaver on a Macintosh 11

Tour the Dreamweaver Interface
on a PC 12

Tour the Dreamweaver Interface on
a Macintosh 13

Show or Hide a Window 14

Exit Dreamweaver 15

Get Help 16

INTRODUCTION TO THE WORLD WIDE WEB

You can use Dreamweaver to create and
publish pages on the World Wide Web.

World Wide Web

The *World Wide Web* (Web) is a global collection
of documents located on Internet-connected
computers that you can access by using a Web
browser. Web pages are connected to one
another through clickable hyperlinks.

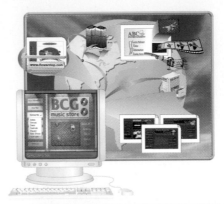

Web Site

A *Web site* is a collection of linked Web pages
stored on a Web server. Most Web sites have a
home page that describes the information
located on the Web site and provides a place
where people can start their exploration of the
site. The pages of a good Web site are intuitively
organized and have a common theme.

Dreamweaver

Dreamweaver is a program that enables you to
create Web pages with links, text, images, and
multimedia. You create your Web pages on your
computer and then use Dreamweaver to transfer
the finished files to a Web server where others
can view them on the Web.

HTML

Hypertext Markup Language (HTML) is the formatting language used to create Web pages. You can use Dreamweaver to create Web pages without knowing HTML because Dreamweaver writes the HTML for you behind the scenes.

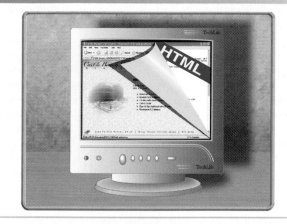

Web Server

A *Web server* is a computer that is connected to the Internet and has software that serves Web pages to visitors. Each Web page that you view in a browser on the World Wide Web resides on a Web server somewhere on the Internet. When you are ready to publish your pages on the Web, you can use Dreamweaver to transfer your files to a Web server.

Web Browser

A *Web browser* is a program that can download Web documents from the Internet, interpret HTML, and then display the Web page text and any associated images and multimedia. Two popular Web browsers are Microsoft Internet Explorer and Netscape Navigator.

PARTS OF A WEB PAGE

You can communicate your message on the Web in a variety of ways. The following are some of the common elements found on Web pages.

Text

Text is the simplest type of content you can publish on the Web. Dreamweaver enables you to change the size, color, and font of Web-page text and organize it into paragraphs, headings, and lists. Perhaps the best thing about text is that practically everyone can view it, no matter what type of browser or Internet connection a person may have, and it downloads very quickly.

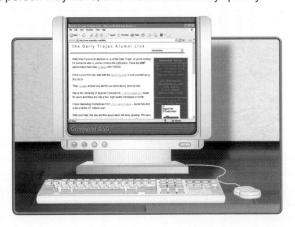

Images

For your Web site, you can take photos with a digital camera, and you can scan drawings, logos, or other images for the Web by using a scanner. You can also create and edit images in a graphics program, such as Adobe Photoshop or Macromedia Fireworks, and then place them on Web pages with Dreamweaver.

Links

Usually called simply a *link*, a *hyperlink* is text or an image that has been associated with another file. You can open the other file in a browser by clicking the hyperlink. Hyperlinks usually link to other Web pages or other Web sites, but they can also link to other locations on the same page or to other types of files.

Tables

Tables organize information in columns and rows on your Web page, and they are used for much more than just organizing financial data. Tables provide one of the best ways to create complex Web designs. By turning off a table's borders and setting it to span an entire page, you can use a table to organize the entire layout of a page. For more about tables, see Chapter 8.

Forms

Forms reverse the information flow on Web sites, enabling visitors to your site to send information back to you. With Dreamweaver, you can create forms that include text fields, drop-down menus, radio buttons, and other elements.

Frames

In a framed Web site, the browser window is divided into several rectangular frames, and a different Web page is loaded into each frame. Users can scroll through content in each frame, independently of the content in the other frames. Dreamweaver offers visual tools for building frame-based Web sites.

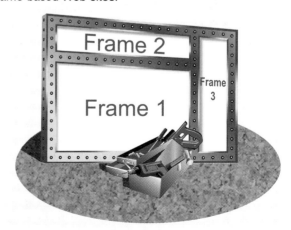

PLAN YOUR WEB SITE

Carefully planning your pages before you build them can help ensure that your finished Web site looks great and is well organized. Before you start building your site, take a little time to organize your ideas and gather the materials you will need.

Organize Your Ideas

Build your Web site on paper before you start building it in Dreamweaver. Sketching out a site map, with rectangles representing Web pages and arrows representing links, can help you visualize the size and scope of your project. Use sticky notes if you want to move pages around as you plan your site.

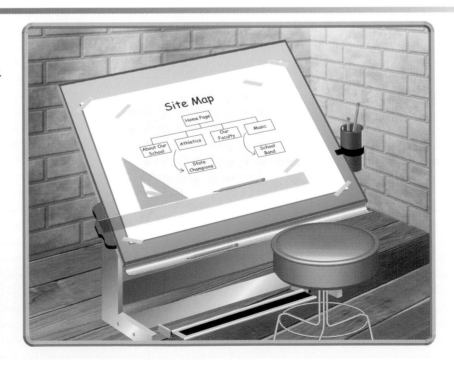

Gather Your Content

Before you start building your Web site, gather all the elements you want to use. This process may require writing text, taking photos, and designing graphics. It can also involve producing multimedia content such as audio and video files. Gathering all your material together in the beginning makes it easier to organize your Web site once you start building it in Dreamweaver.

Define Your Audience

Identifying your target audience can help you decide what kind of content to offer on your Web site. For example, you might create a very different design for children than for adults. It is important to know if visitors are using the latest browser technology and how fast they can view advanced features, such as multimedia.

Host Your Finished Web Site

To make your finished site accessible on the Web, you need to store, or *host*, it on a Web server. Most people have their Web sites hosted on a Web server at a commercial *Internet service provider (ISP)* or at their company or university.

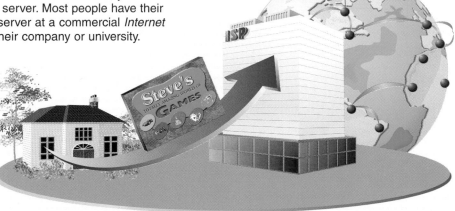

START DREAMWEAVER ON A PC

You can start Dreamweaver on a PC and begin building pages that you can publish on the Web. You will need to purchase and install Dreamweaver if you do not have it already.

START DREAMWEAVER ON A PC

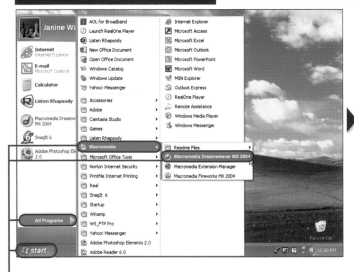

1 Click **Start**.

2 Click **All Programs**.

3 Click **Macromedia**.

4 Click **Macromedia Dreamweaver MX 2004**.

Note: Your path to the Dreamweaver application may be different, depending on how you installed your software and your operating system.

■ The Dreamweaver Start screen appears.

You can start Dreamweaver on a Macintosh and begin building pages that you can publish on the Web. You will need to purchase and install Dreamweaver if you do not have it already.

START DREAMWEAVER ON A MACINTOSH

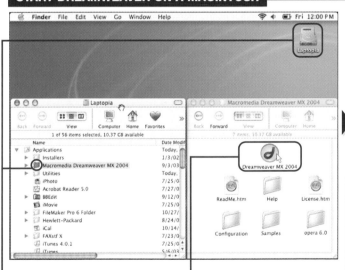

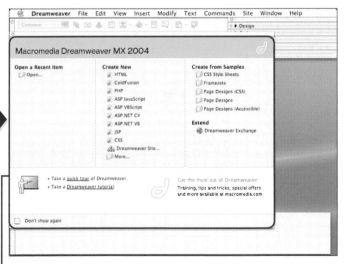

1 Double-click your hard drive.

2 Double-click the Macromedia Dreamweaver MX 2004 folder ( ).

3 Double-click the Dreamweaver MX 2004 icon ( ).

Note: The exact location of the Dreamweaver folder will depend on how you installed your software.

■ The Dreamweaver Start screen appears.

TOUR THE DREAMWEAVER INTERFACE ON A PC

Dreamweaver MX 2004 on a PC
features a variety of windows,
panels, and inspectors.

Menus

Contains the commands for
using Dreamweaver. Many of
these commands are duplicated
within the windows, panels, and
inspectors of Dreamweaver.

Insert Bar

Used to implement page elements and
technology. There are several different
Insert bars that you can select,
depending on what type of element
you want to insert in your page.

Toolbar

Contains
shortcuts to
preview and
display features,
and a text field
where you can
specify the title
of a page.

Panels

Provide access
to the Design,
Code,
Application, Tag
Inspector, Files,
Layers,
and History
panels.

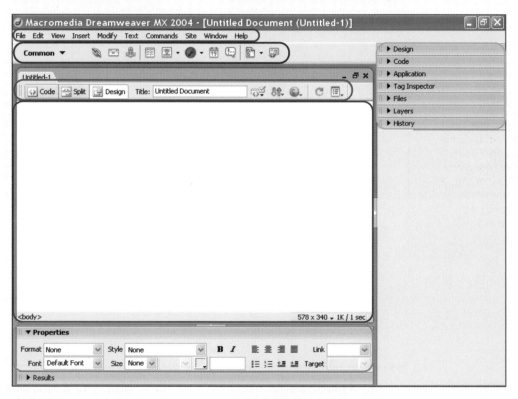

Properties Inspector

This window is used to edit
attributes. It changes to feature the
attributes of any element selected
in the Document window.

Document Window

This is the main workspace
where you insert and arrange
the text, images, and other
elements of your Web page.

TOUR THE DREAMWEAVER INTERFACE ON A MACINTOSH

Dreamweaver MX 2004 on a Macintosh features a variety of windows, panels, and inspectors.

Toolbar

Contains shortcuts to preview and display features, and a text field where you can specify the title of a page.

Document Window

This is the main workspace where you insert and arrange the text, images, and other elements of your Web page.

Insert Bar

Used to implement page elements and technology. There are several different Insert bars that you can select, depending on what type of element you want to insert in your page.

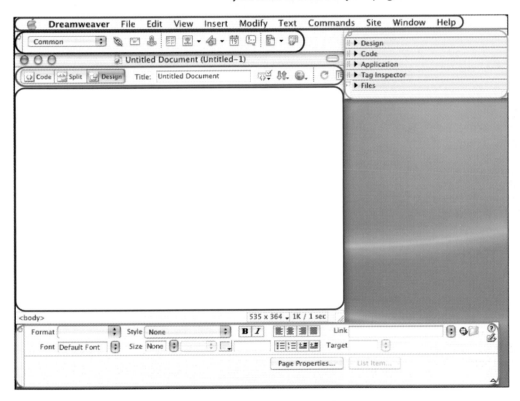

Menus

Contains the commands for using Dreamweaver. Many of these commands are duplicated within the windows, panels, and inspectors of Dreamweaver.

Panels

Provide access to the Design, Code, Application, Tag Inspector, and Files panels.

Properties Inspector

This window is used to edit attributes. It changes to feature the attributes of any element selected in the Document window.

Note: Most of the screen shots you see in this book were taken on a PC. Except for minor differences, the icons, menus, and commands are the same on a Macintosh. When PC and Macintosh commands are different, the Macintosh commands are in parentheses. For example: Press Enter *(* Return *).*

SHOW OR HIDE A WINDOW

You can show or hide accessory windows, also called panels and inspectors, by using commands in the Window menu.

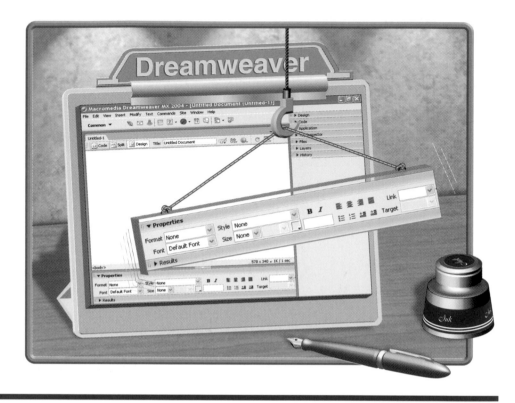

SHOW OR HIDE A WINDOW

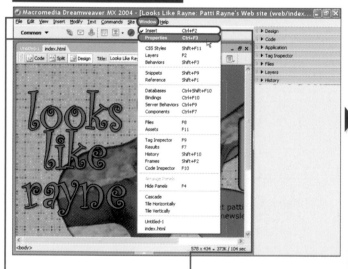

1 Click **Window**.

2 Click the window you want to open.

■ A checkmark (✔) next to a window name denotes an open window.

■ Dreamweaver shows the window.

■ To hide a window, click **Window** and then the checked window name.

■ You can click **Window** and then **Hide Panels** to hide everything except the Document window and toolbar.

14

You can exit Dreamweaver
to close the program.

EXIT DREAMWEAVER

1 Click **File**.

2 Click **Exit (Quit)**.

■ Before closing,
Dreamweaver alerts you to
save any open documents
that have unsaved changes.

■ Dreamweaver closes.

GET HELP

You can use the help tools that are built into Dreamweaver to get answers to your questions on techniques that you do not understand.

GET HELP

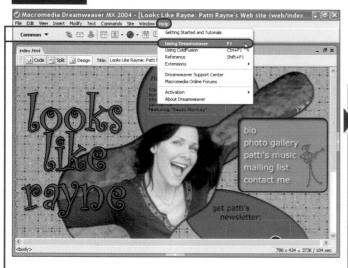

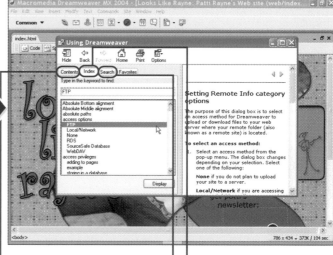

1 Click **Help**.

2 Click **Using Dreamweaver**.

■ You can also click the Help icon (?) in the Properties inspector.

■ The Using Dreamweaver help page opens.

■ You can click the **Contents** tab to scroll and select available Help topics.

■ You can click the **Index** tab for access to an index of topics.

3 Click the **Search** tab to search for a specific topic.

Are there different ways of accessing the Help tools in Dreamweaver?

Very often, yes. For example, you may be able to access a command one way through a Dreamweaver menu, another way through the Insert panel or Properties inspector, and yet another way by right-clicking (Control +clicking) an object with the mouse.

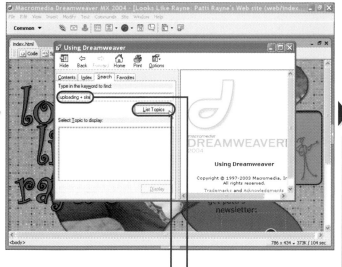

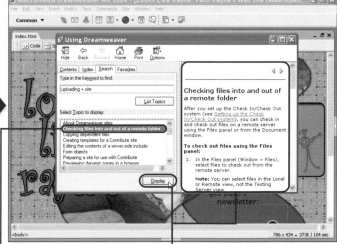

■ The Search window appears.

4 Type one or more keywords, separating multiple keywords with a plus sign (+) for your search.

5 Click **List Topics**.

■ A list of topics appears.

6 Click a topic from the search result list.

7 Click **Display**.

■ Information on your topic appears.

Our

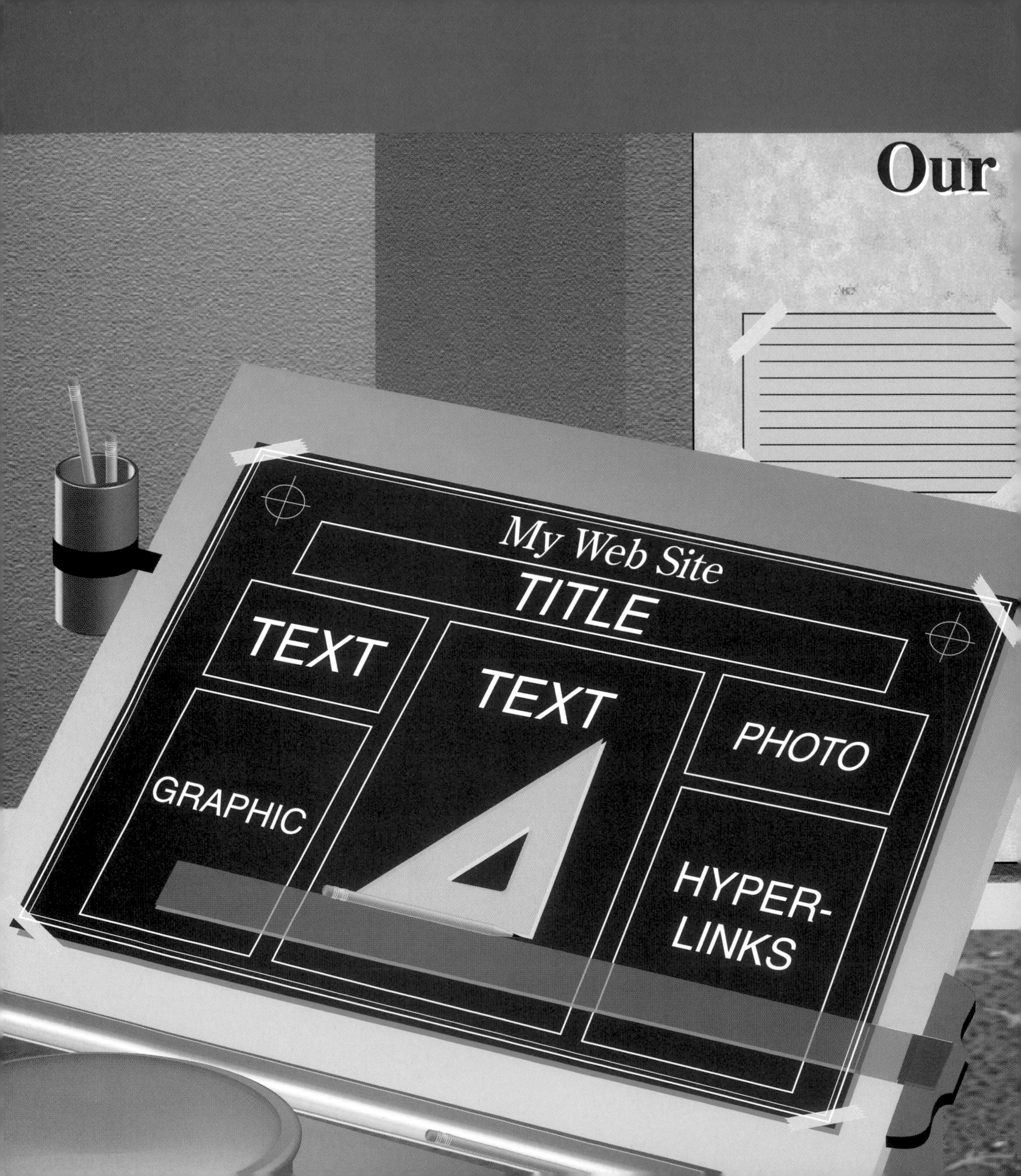

mily Vacation

ummer 2003

Setting Up Your Web Site

You start a project in Dreamweaver by setting up a local site on your computer and then creating the first Web page of the site. This chapter shows you how.

Set Up a New Web Site 20

Create a New Web Page 22

Add a Title to a Web Page 23

Save a Web Page 24

Preview a Web Page in a Browser 26

Graphics

Photos

Text

SET UP A NEW WEB SITE

Before creating your Web pages, you need to define a local site for storing the information in your site, such as your HTML documents and image files. Defining a local site allows you to manage your Web-page files in the Site window. For more on the Site window, see Chapter 14.

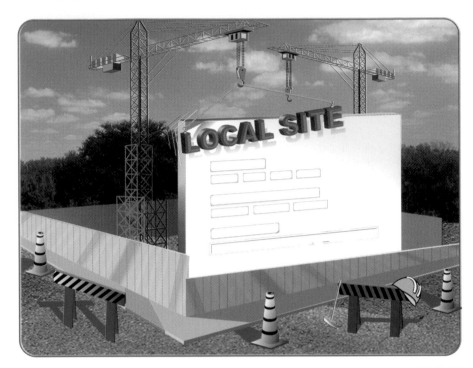

SET UP A NEW WEB SITE

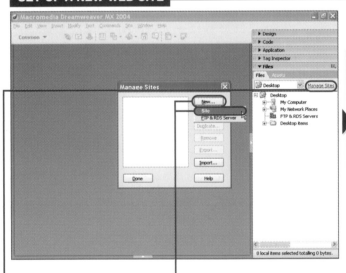

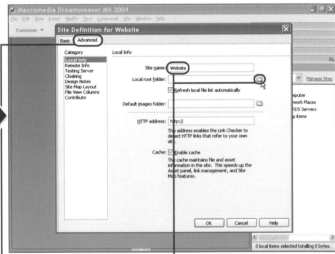

1 Click **Manage Sites** in the Files panel to open the Manage Sites dialog box.

2 Click **New**.

3 Click **Site** from the menu that appears.

■ The Site Definition dialog box appears.

4 Click the **Advanced** tab.

5 Type a name for your site.

6 Click 📁 and select the local folder for your site.

Why is it important to keep all my Web site files in a main folder on my computer?

Keeping everything in the same folder enables you to easily transfer your site files to a Web server without changing the organization of the files. If you do not organize your site files on the Web server the same as they are organized on your local computer, hyperlinks may not work, and images may not display properly. For more on working with Web site files, see Chapter 14.

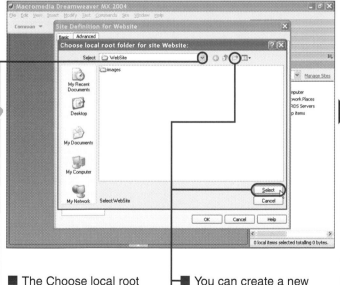

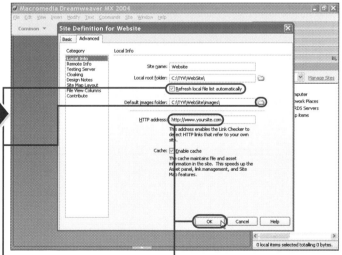

■ The Choose local root folder dialog box appears.

7 Click ⌄ and select the folder where you want to store your Web pages.

■ You can create a new folder by clicking 📄.

8 Click **Select**.

9 Click this option to refresh your local file list every time you download files (☐ changes to ☑).

10 Click 📁 and select the folder where you want to store the images for your Web site.

11 Type the URL (online address) of your Web site.

12 Click **OK**.

13 Click **Done** on the Manage Sites Window.

CREATE A NEW WEB PAGE

A new feature in Dreamweaver MX 2004 is the initial Start Page. There are many useful shortcuts on this screen, including some for creating a new Web page.

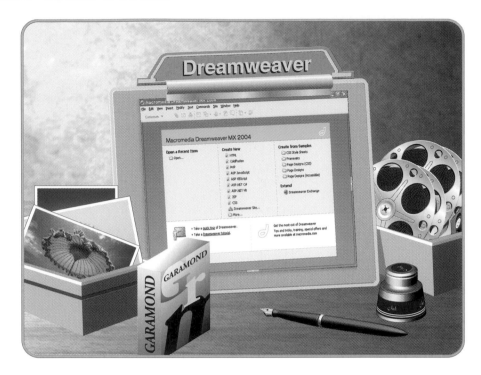

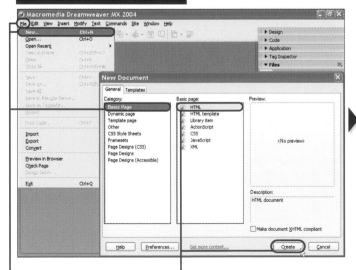

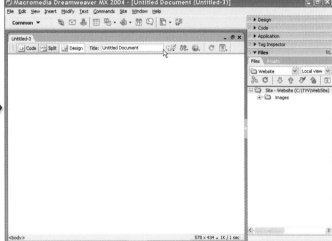

1 Click **File**.

2 Click **New**.

3 In the New Document dialog box, click **Basic Page**.

4 Click **HTML**.

5 Click **Create**.

■ An untitled Document window appears.

Note: The page name and filename are untitled until you save them.

■ You can also create preformatted pages by choosing any of the **Page Designs** categories in the New Document dialog box.

ADD A TITLE TO A WEB PAGE

Adding a title to a Web page tells viewers what page they are on and what they will find on the page, plus it helps search engines index pages with more accuracy. A Web-page title appears in the title bar when the page opens in a Web browser.

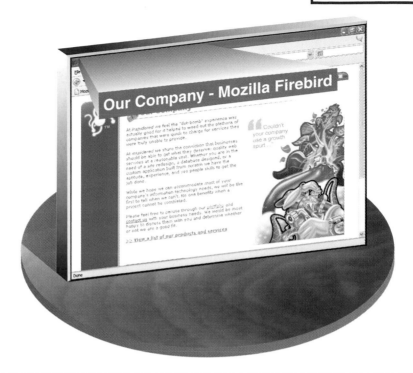

ADD A TITLE TO A WEB PAGE

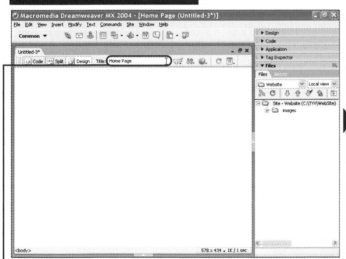

1 Type a name for your Web page in the Title text box.

2 Press Enter (Return).

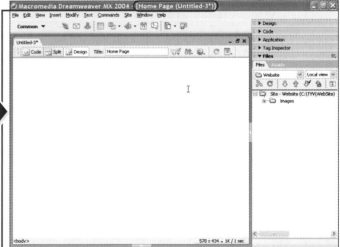

■ The title appears in the title bar of the Document window.

SAVE A WEB PAGE

You should save your Web page before closing the program or transferring the page to a remote site. It is also a good idea to save all your files frequently to prevent work from being lost due to power outages or system failures. For more information on connecting to remote sites, see Chapter 14.

SAVE A WEB PAGE

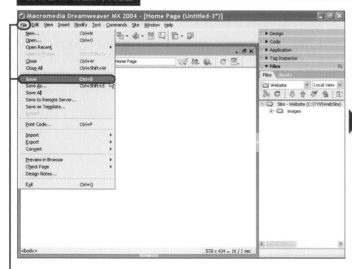

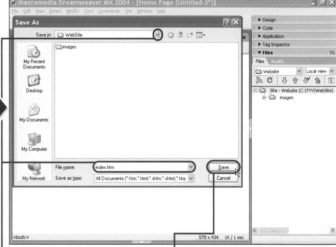

SAVE YOUR DOCUMENT

1 Click **File**.

2 Click **Save**.

■ You can click **Save As** to save an existing file with a new filename.

■ If you are saving a new file for the first time, the Save As dialog box appears.

3 Click ⌄ and select your local site folder.

4 Type a name for your Web page.

■ Your local site folder is where you want to save the pages and other files for your Web site.

5 Click **Save**.

Where should I store the files for my Web site on my computer?

You should save all the files for your Web site in the folder that you defined as the local root folder. To set up a local site, see page 20. Keeping all the files of the site in this folder, or in subfolders inside this folder, makes it easier to hyperlink between local files, and to transfer files to a remote Web server.

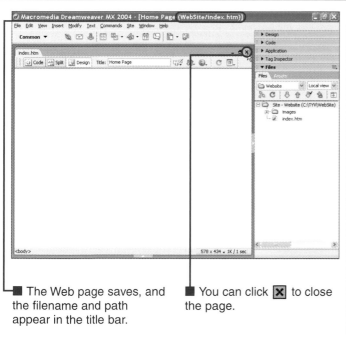

■ The Web page saves, and the filename and path appear in the title bar.

■ You can click ☒ to close the page.

REVERT A PAGE

1 Click **File**.

2 Click **Revert**.

■ The page reverts to the previously saved version. All the changes made since last saving are lost.

Note: If you exit Dreamweaver after a document is saved, Dreamweaver cannot revert to the previous version.

PREVIEW A WEB PAGE IN A BROWSER

You can see how your page will appear online by previewing it in a Web browser. The Preview in Browser command works with the Web browsers installed on your computer. Keep in mind that Dreamweaver does not come with browser software.

PREVIEW A WEB PAGE IN A BROWSER

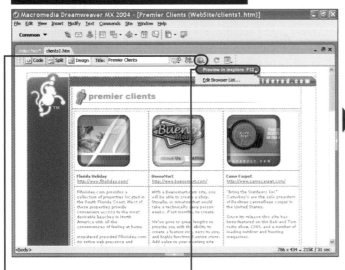

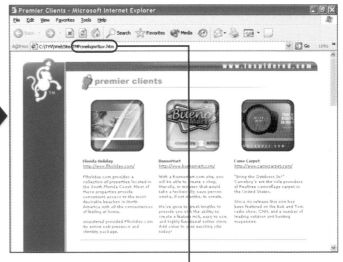

1 Click the Preview in Browser button ( ).

2 Click a Web Browser from the drop-down menu that appears.

■ You can also preview the page in your primary browser by pressing **F12**.

■ Your Web browser launches and opens the current page.

■ The file has a temporary filename for viewing in the browser.

Why does Dreamweaver create a temporary file when I preview my page?

Dreamweaver creates a temporary file when you preview your page so you do not have to save the document to see what it would look like in the browser. If you do not want Dreamweaver to create temporary files, you can disable it by clicking **Edit**, **Preferences**, **Preview in Browser**, and then unchecking **Preview Using Temporary File**.

Why can I use more than one browser for previews?

Dreamweaver lets you add more than one browser because not all Web browsers display Web pages the same way; for example, Lynx is a text-based browser. With this list, testing your Web page in a different browser is just a few mouse-clicks away.

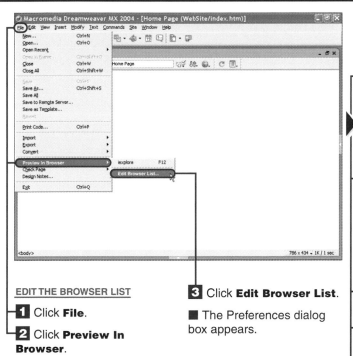

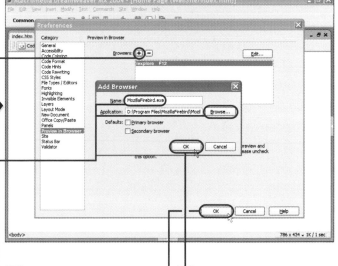

EDIT THE BROWSER LIST

■1 Click **File**.

■2 Click **Preview In Browser**.

■3 Click **Edit Browser List**.

■ The Preferences dialog box appears.

■4 Click ⊞ to open the Add Browser dialog box.

■5 Type a name for your browser.

■6 Click **Browse** and select a browser for your computer.

■7 Click **OK** to close the Add Browser dialog box.

■8 Click **OK** to close the Preferences dialog box.

■ The newly added browser appears in the browser list.

CHAPTER 3

Exploring the Dreamweaver Interface

Take a tour of the panels and windows that make up Dreamweaver's interface, and discover all the handy tools and features that make this an award-winning Web design program.

Save Web Page

RETURN TO: Apply Font ◁

Apply Bold

Set Alignment

Font Color

Apply Italic

History Panel

Leisure Vacations, Inc.

Custom Command

Format Heading
Change Font
Change Size
Make Text Red
Center Text

Place Graphics
Resize Image
Place Image
Add Border
Save for Web

Custom Command

Customize the Document Window 30

Format Content with the Properties
Inspector 32

Add an E-Mail Link from the
Insert Panel 34

Correct Errors with the History
Panel 35

Open a Panel 36

Create and Apply a Custom
Command 38

Set Preferences.................................40

CUSTOMIZE THE DOCUMENT WINDOW

The Document window is the main workspace in Dreamweaver, where you create Web pages, and enter and format text, images, and other elements. Customizable panels now lock into position to keep the workspace clear and make it more intuitive to use.

CUSTOMIZE THE DOCUMENT WINDOW

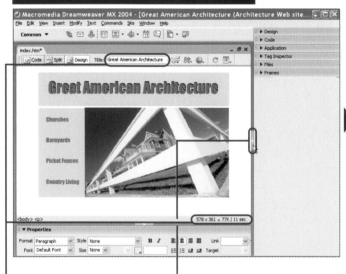

1 Type a title for your document in the Title text box.

■ The status bar displays the file size and estimated download time for the page.

2 If you want more design space, click the small tab (▯) to close these panels.

■ The panels close.

■ You can click ▯ again to bring the panels back.

3 Click the Properties inspector arrow (▽) to expand the panel.

How can I keep my favorite features handy?

You can make many adjustments to the interface in Dreamweaver by opening and closing the various panels. Most of the panels and options are available from the Window menu. For example, to open the History panel, click **Window** and then **History**. As you work, you may choose to have different panels opened or closed to give you greater workspace or provide easier access to features you are using.

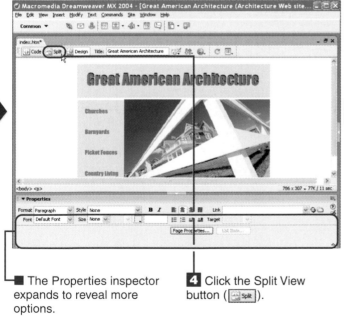

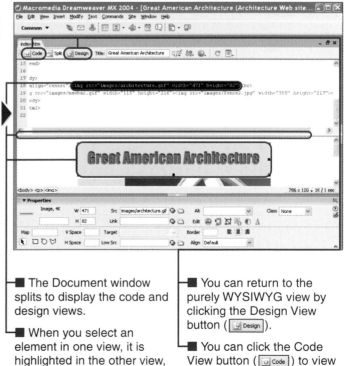

■ The Properties inspector expands to reveal more options.

4 Click the Split View button (Split).

■ The Document window splits to display the code and design views.

■ When you select an element in one view, it is highlighted in the other view, making it easy to find formatting tags.

■ You can return to the purely WYSIWYG view by clicking the Design View button (Design).

■ You can click the Code View button (Code) to view just the code.

FORMAT CONTENT WITH THE PROPERTIES INSPECTOR

The Properties inspector enables you to view the properties associated with the object or text currently selected in the Document window. Text fields, drop-down menus, buttons, and other form elements in the Properties inspector allow you to modify these properties.

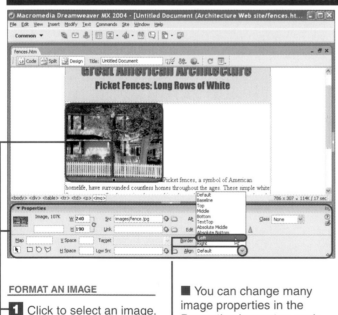

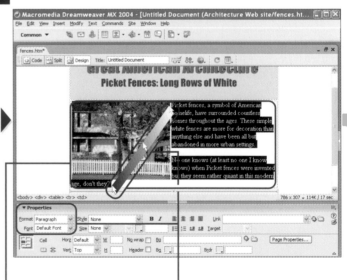

FORMAT AN IMAGE

1 Click to select an image.

■ The image properties appear.

■ You can change many image properties in the Properties inspector, such as dimensions, filename, and alignment.

2 Click the Align ▼.

3 Click an alignment to wrap the text around the image.

■ The text automatically wraps around the image when Left alignment is applied.

4 Click and drag to select some text.

■ Your text properties appear.

When would I use more than one font on a Web page?

When you choose a font face in Dreamweaver, you will find that the program offers fonts in groups of three. For example, one option is Arial, Helvetica, and sans-serif, and another option is Times New Roman, Times, and serif. Dreamweaver provides these collections because the fonts that display on a Web page are determined by the fonts available on the visitor's computer, and you cannot guarantee what fonts a user will have. Therefore, browsers use the first font that matches in a list of fonts. Thus, with the first example, the font will display in Arial if it is on the visitor's computer, in Helvetica if Arial is not available, and in any sans-serif font available if neither of the two fonts named is available.

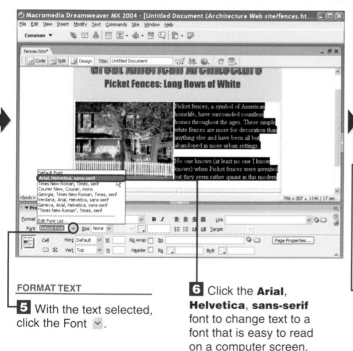

FORMAT TEXT

5 With the text selected, click the Font ✓.

6 Click the **Arial**, **Helvetica**, **sans-serif** font to change text to a font that is easy to read on a computer screen.

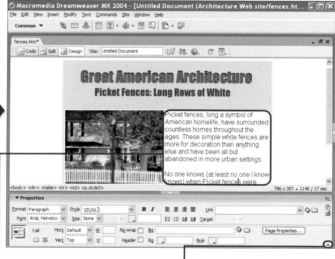

■ Your text automatically changes to reflect formatting choices made in the Properties inspector.

■ You can change many text properties in the Properties inspector, such as format, size, and alignment.

■ You can click the Properties inspector arrow (▽) to switch between standard and expanded modes of the inspector.

ADD AN E-MAIL LINK FROM THE INSERT PANEL

You can insert elements, such as images, tables, and layers, into your pages with the Insert panel. The panel, located at the top of the window, features a drop-down menu that reveals options for Common elements, Forms, Text, and more.

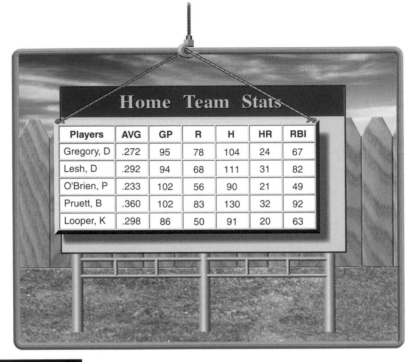

Home Team Stats

Players	AVG	GP	R	H	HR	RBI
Gregory, D	.272	95	78	104	24	67
Lesh, D	.292	94	68	111	31	82
O'Brien, P	.233	102	56	90	21	49
Pruett, B	.360	102	83	130	32	92
Looper, K	.298	86	50	91	20	63

ADD AN E-MAIL LINK FROM THE INSERT PANEL

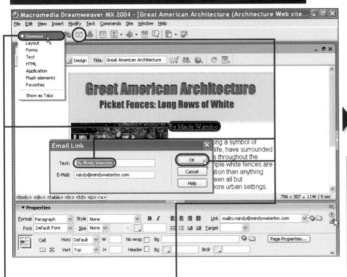

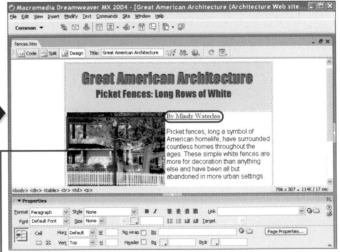

1 Click ⌄ and select the **Common** Insert panel.

2 Click and drag to select some text.

3 Click the Email Link button (⌨) in the Common Insert panel.

■ The Email Link dialog box appears.

4 Type an e-mail address.

5 Click **OK**.

■ In the example shown, the text changes into an e-mail hyperlink.

■ You can click any button in the Insert panel to add that element to your document.

The History panel keeps
track of the commands you
perform in Dreamweaver.
You can return your page
to a previous state by
backtracking through
those commands. This
is a convenient way to
correct errors.

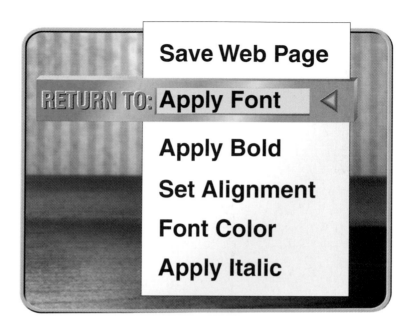

Save Web Page

RETURN TO: **Apply Font**

Apply Bold

Set Alignment

Font Color

Apply Italic

CORRECT ERRORS WITH THE HISTORY PANEL

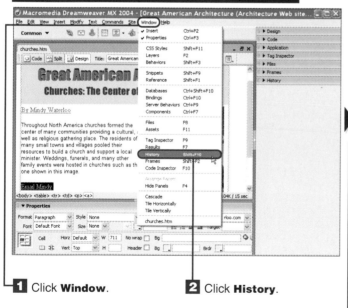

1 Click **Window**.

2 Click **History**.

■ The History panel
appears.

■ To undo one or more
commands, click and drag
the slider (▷) upward.

■ To redo the commands,
click and drag the slider (▷)
downward.

*Note: If you scroll backward, the later
changes are deleted. You can only
add steps to the end of the
sequence.*

OPEN A PANEL

Dreamweaver MX 2004 features an uncluttered workspace with windows that lock into place and can expand or collapse. You can also rearrange panels and move them around the screen to create the best interface for you.

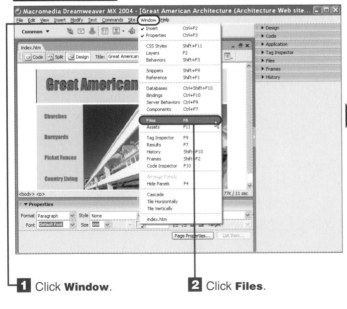

1 Click **Window**.

2 Click **Files**.

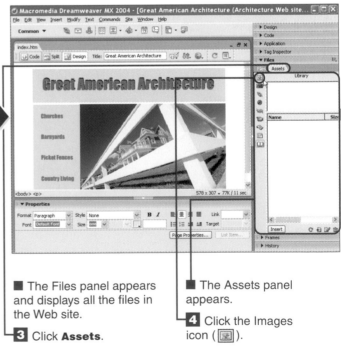

■ The Files panel appears and displays all the files in the Web site.

3 Click **Assets**.

■ The Assets panel appears.

4 Click the Images icon ( ).

How can I keep track of my assets?

The Assets panel provides access to many handy features, such as the Colors assets, which list all the colors used on a site. For example, this is useful if you are using a text color and you want to use the same color consistently on every page. Similarly, the Links assets make it easy to access links used elsewhere in your site so you can set frequently used links quickly and easily.

■ All the images available in the site appear in the Assets panel.

5 Click any image filename to preview the image in the display area at the top of the Assets panel.

6 Click the **Files** tab to collapse the panel.

■ The Assets panel collapses.

Note: When you collapse a panel, such as the Files panel, others become more visible.

■ You can click ▶ to expand any panel.

CREATE AND APPLY A CUSTOM COMMAND

You can select a sequence of commands that has been recorded in the History panel and save the sequence as a custom command. The new command will appear under the Commands menu. You can apply it to other elements on the page to automate repetitive tasks.

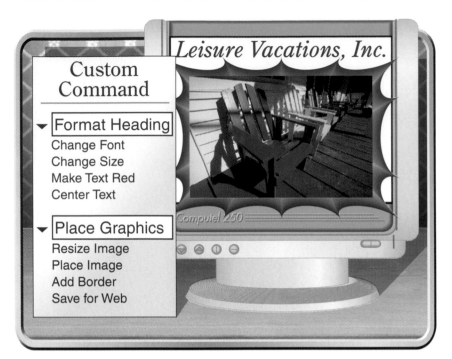

CREATE AND APPLY A CUSTOM COMMAND

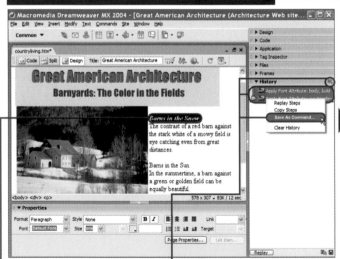

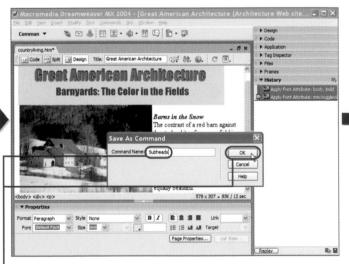

CREATE A COMMAND

1 Select an element and perform a sequence of commands.

2 To select the steps you want to save as a single command, Ctrl +click (Shift +click) each selection.

3 Click 🔠 to open the menu.

4 Click **Save As Command**.

■ The Save As Command dialog box appears.

5 Type a name for the command.

6 Click **OK** to save the command.

■ Dreamweaver saves the command.

Note: You cannot use this feature with all commands. For example, clicking and dragging an element cannot be included in a command.

How do I change the name of a custom command?

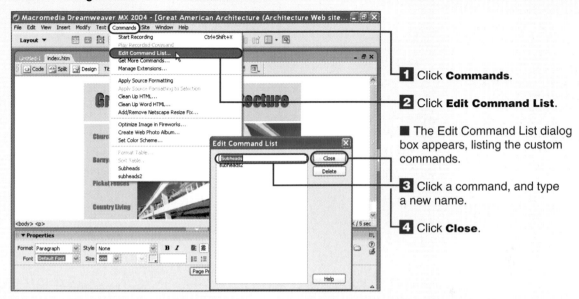

1 Click **Commands**.

2 Click **Edit Command List**.

■ The Edit Command List dialog box appears, listing the custom commands.

3 Click a command, and type a new name.

4 Click **Close**.

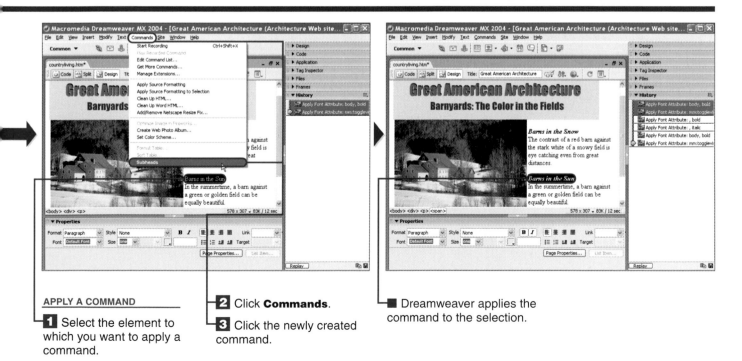

APPLY A COMMAND

1 Select the element to which you want to apply a command.

2 Click **Commands**.

3 Click the newly created command.

■ Dreamweaver applies the command to the selection.

SET PREFERENCES

You can easily change the default appearance and behavior of Dreamweaver by specifying settings in the Preferences dialog box. You can modify the user interface of Dreamweaver to better suit how you like to work.

SET PREFERENCES

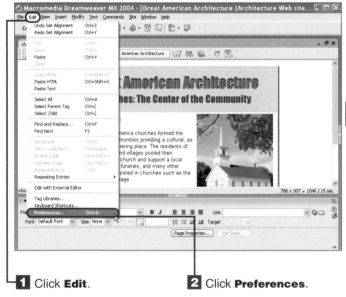

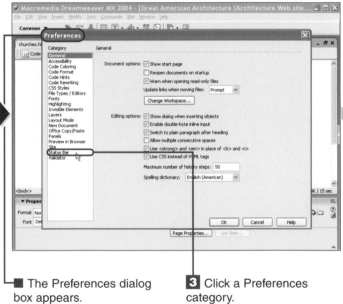

1 Click **Edit**.

2 Click **Preferences**.

■ The Preferences dialog box appears.

3 Click a Preferences category.

**How do I ensure that
Dreamweaver does not
change my HTML or other
code?**

You can select options under
the Code Rewriting category
in the Preferences dialog box
to ensure that Dreamweaver
does not automatically correct
or modify your code. You can
turn off its error-correcting
functions, specify files that it
should not rewrite based on
file extension, or disable its
character encoding features.

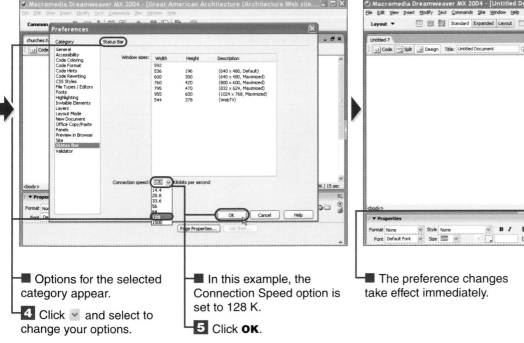

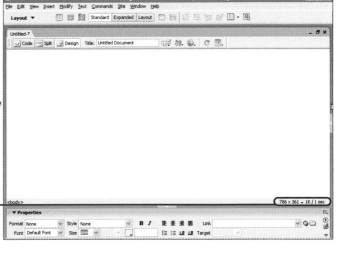

■ Options for the selected
category appear.

4 Click ∨ and select to
change your options.

■ In this example, the
Connection Speed option is
set to 128 K.

5 Click **OK**.

■ The preference changes
take effect immediately.

■ In this example, the status
bar now displays download
times that assume a 128 K
connection speed.

Realty - Re

tent="castle, be
)each, ocean, driv
)artment, studio, se
s, south, castillo, de
al, vacation, paradis
nference, conventio
dults, specials">

Style Shee

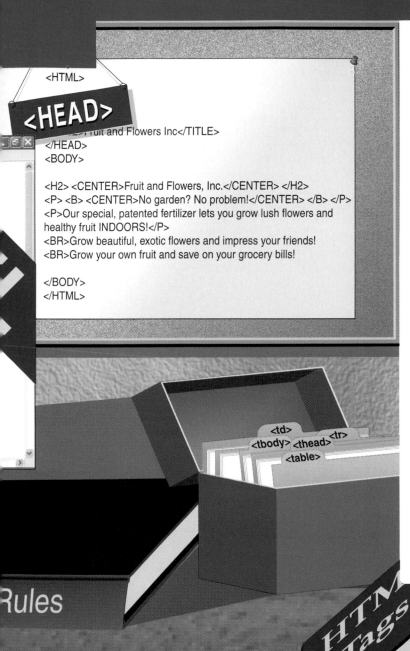

CHAPTER 4

Working with HTML

Dreamweaver helps you build your Web pages by writing HTML. This chapter introduces the important features of this language and the tools in Dreamweaver that enable you to edit HTML.

Introduction to HTML...........................44

Work in Design View and Code
   View...46

Explore Head and Body Tags 48

Explore Block-Formatting Tags 49

Explore Text-Formatting Tags 50

Explore Image and Hyperlink Tags 51

Clean Up HTML Code.......................52

View and Edit Head Content 54

Access Reference Information
   about HTML Tags 56

INTRODUCTION TO HTML

Dreamweaver creates your Web pages by writing HTML. This saves you time by not having to write the code yourself.

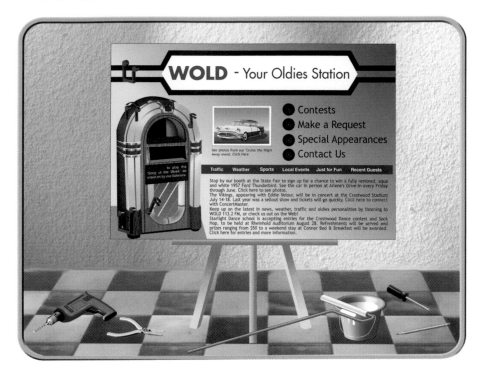

HTML

Hypertext Markup Language (HTML) is the formatting language that you use to create Web pages. When you open a Web page in a browser, it is HTML code telling the browser how to display the text, images, and other content on the page. At its most basic level, Dreamweaver is an HTML-writing application, although it can do many other things as well.

HTML Tags

The basic unit of HTML is a *tag*. You can recognize HTML tags by their angle brackets:

```
<p>Today the weather is <b>nice</b>.
<br>Tomorrow it may <i>rain</i>.</p>
```

You can format text and other elements on your page by placing it inside the HTML tags.

How Tags Work

Some HTML tags work in twos: Opening and closing tags surround content in a document and control the formatting of the content. For example: <b> tags set off bold text. Closing tags are documented by a forward slash (/). Other tags can stand alone, such as the <br> tag that adds a line break. HTML tags are not case-sensitive; you can uppercase, lowercase, or mixed case the letters.

HTML Documents

Because HTML documents are plain text files, you can open and edit them with any text editor. In fact, in the early days of the Web, most people created their pages with simple editors such as Notepad (Windows) and SimpleText (Macintosh). However, writing HTML by hand is a slow, tedious process, especially when creating advanced HTML elements such as tables, forms, and frames.

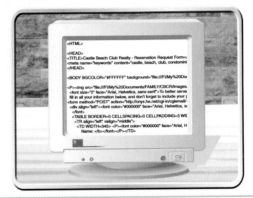

Create Web Pages without Knowing HTML

Dreamweaver streamlines the process of creating Web pages by giving you an easy-to-use, visual interface with which to generate HTML. You specify formatting with menu commands and button clicks, and Dreamweaver takes care of writing the underlying HTML code. When you build a Web page in the Document window, you see your page as it will eventually appear in a Web browser, instead of as HTML.

Direct Access to the HTML

Dreamweaver gives you direct access to the raw HTML code if you want it. This can be an advantage for people who know HTML and want to do some formatting of their page by typing tags. The Code View mode, Code Inspector, and Quick Tag Editor in Dreamweaver enable you to edit your page by adding HTML information manually. Access to the code also means you can add HTML features that Dreamweaver might not yet support.

WORK IN DESIGN VIEW AND CODE VIEW

You can switch to Code View in the Document window to inspect and edit the HTML and other code of a Web page.

You will probably do most of your work in Design View, which displays your page approximately as it will appear in a Web browser.

WORK IN DESIGN VIEW AND CODE VIEW

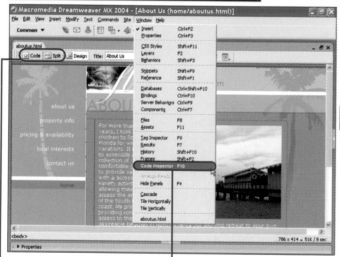

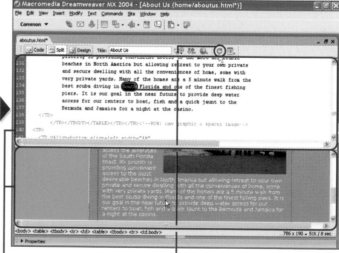

1 In the Document window, click a code-viewing option.

■ Clicking the Code View button (Code) displays the source code of your page in the Document window.

■ Clicking the Split View button (Split) splits the window and displays both your source code and the design in the Document window.

■ Clicking **Window** and then **Code Inspector** displays the code in a separate window.

■ The Code and Design Views appear in the Document window.

■ The HTML and other code appear in one pane.

■ The Design View appears in the other pane.

2 Click the code and type to edit the text, or to add or modify the HTML.

3 Click the Refresh button (C).

How do I turn on line numbers in Code View or make code wrap at the right edge of the window?

Both of these options, as well as others, are available by clicking the Options button () at the top of the Document window when you are in Code View.

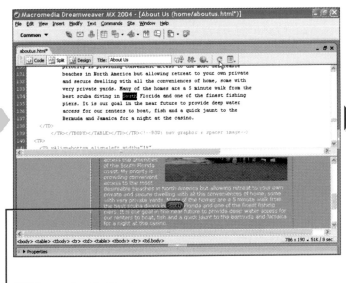

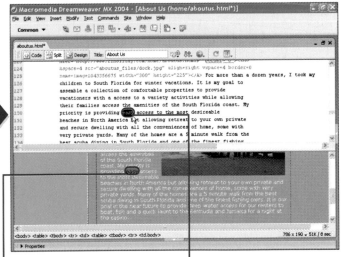

■ The content in Design View updates to reflect the code changes.

4 Click in the Design View window and type to make changes.

■ The content in the Code View updates dynamically as you make your changes.

EXPLORE HEAD AND BODY TAGS

You define the basic structure of every HTML document with several basic tags. To view the HTML of a Web page, click a Code View icon in the Document window, or click Window and then Code Inspector.

<head> Tags

Opening and closing <head> tags surround descriptive and accessory information for a page. This includes <title> and <meta> tag content.

<html> Tags

Opening and closing <html> tags begin and end every HTML document.

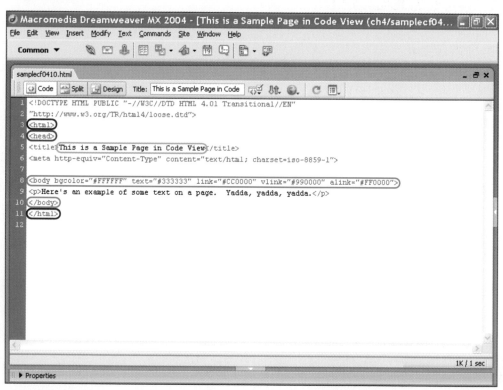

<body> Tags

Opening and closing <body> tags surround content that appears inside the Web browser window. The bgcolor attribute of the <body> tag defines the text color.

Page Title

Opening and closing <title> tags display the content in the Document window title bar.

EXPLORE BLOCK-FORMATTING TAGS

You can organize information in your Web page with block-formatting tags. A block tag tells a Web browser to start a new line with the enclosed text. To view the HTML of a Web page, click a Code View button in the Document window, or click Window and then Code Inspector.

CODE VIEW

This page features html with `<h>` heading, `<p>` paragraph, and `<ul>` unordered list tags.

DESIGN VIEW

This page features a heading, a paragraph, and an unordered list.

`<p>` Tag

The `<p>` tag organizes information into a paragraph.

`<h>` Tag

An `<h>` tag organizes information into a heading. There are six levels of headings, `<h1>` (the largest) through `<h6>` (the smallest).

Heading

An `<h>` tag creates a bold heading.

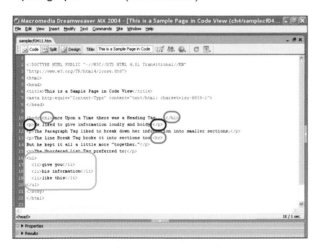

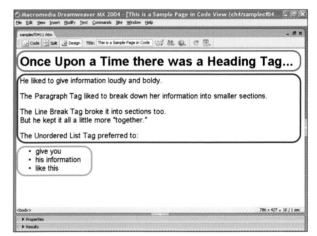

`<br>` `<ol>`, and `<pre>` Tags

Other block-formatting tags include `<br>` (line break), `<ol>` (ordered list), and `<pre>` (preformatted text).

`<ul>` and `<li>` Tags

The `<ul>` tag defines an unordered list. Each list item is defined with an `<li>` tag.

Paragraph

A `<p>` tag separates a paragraph from other text.

Unordered List

A `<ul>` tag creates an unordered, bulleted list.

EXPLORE TEXT-FORMATTING TAGS

You can format the style of sentences, words, and characters with text-formatting tags. Text-formatting tags, also known as inline tags, tell a Web browser to format text without starting a new line. To view the HTML of a Web page, click a Code View button in the Document window, or click Window and then Code Inspector.

CODE VIEW

This page demonstrates the use of <font> font tags containing size and color attributes, <b> bold tags, and <i> italic tags.

DESIGN VIEW

This page features text with a different font size, as well as bold and italic text.

<font> Tag

The <font> tag controls various characteristics of text on a Web page.

size Attribute

The size attribute goes inside the <font> tag and specifies the size of text.

Font Size

The size attribute controls the text size.

Font Color

The color attribute controls the text color.

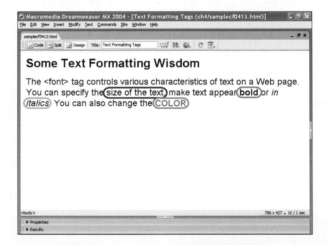

color Attribute

The color attribute also goes inside the <font> tag and specifies the color of text.

<b> Tag

The <b> tag defines text as bold.

<i> Tag

The <i> tag defines text as italic.

Italic Text

The <i> italic tag creates *italicized* text.

Bold Text

The <b> bold tag creates **bold** text.

You can add an image to your page with the `<img>` tag and then create a hyperlink with the `<a>` tag. To view the HTML of a Web page, click the Code View button in the Document window, or click Window and then Code Inspector.

CODE VIEW

This page demonstrates how to use `<img>` image and `<a>` hyperlink tags.

DESIGN VIEW

This page features a right-aligned image and a text hyperlink.

`<img>` Tag

The `<img>` tag inserts an image into a page.

src Attribute

The `src` attribute specifies an image file to insert.

align Attribute

The `align` attribute specifies the alignment of an image.

Text Hyperlink

Clicking a hyperlink takes you to the linked document.

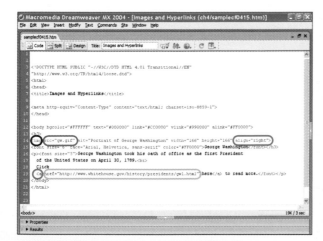

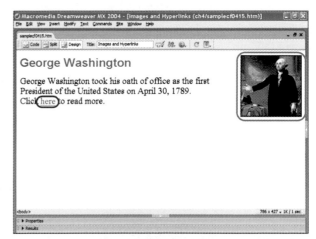

`<a>` Tag

The `<a>` tag specifies the content that will serve as a hyperlink.

href Attribute

The `href` attribute specifies the hyperlink destination.

Right-Aligned Image

The image is placed as far right as possible.

CLEAN UP HTML CODE

Dreamweaver can optimize the HTML in your Web page by deleting redundant or non-functional tags. This can decrease a page's file size and make the source code easier to read in Code View.

It is a good idea to run the Clean Up HTML command when editing documents originally created in other HTML editors, such as FrontPage.

CLEAN UP HTML CODE

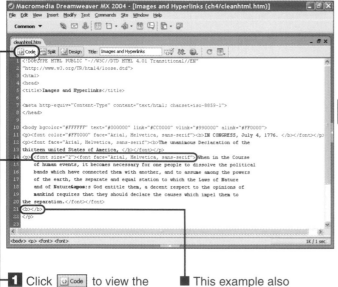

1 Click Code to view the HTML in Code View.

■ In this example, multiple `<font>` tags appear in the code, adding unnecessary bulk.

■ This example also includes an empty `<b>` tag. Because this tag serves no purpose, you can delete it.

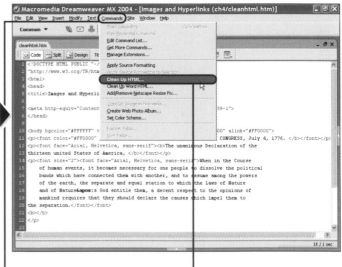

2 Click **Commands**.

3 Click **Clean Up HTML**.

How do empty tags end up appearing in Dreamweaver's HTML?

Sometimes if you heavily edit Web-page text in the Document window, such as cutting and pasting sentences, reformatting words, and so on, Dreamweaver will inadvertently remove text from inside tags without removing the tags themselves.

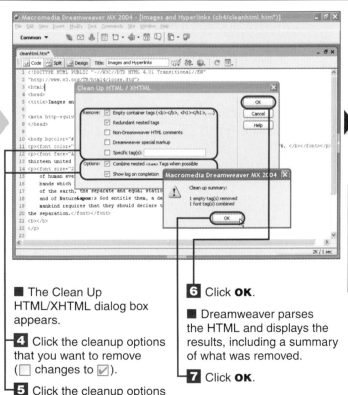

Does Dreamweaver fix invalid HTML?

By default, Dreamweaver rewrites some instances of invalid HTML. When you open an HTML document, Dreamweaver rewrites tags that are not nested properly, closes tags that are not allowed to remain open, and removes extra closing tags. If Dreamweaver does not recognize a tag, it highlights it in red and displays it in the Document window, but does not remove it. You can change or turn off the behavior by clicking **Edit**, **Preferences**, and then selecting the category **Code Rewriting**.

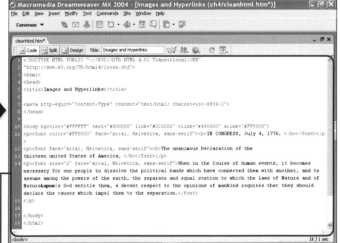

■ The Clean Up HTML/XHTML dialog box appears.

4 Click the cleanup options that you want to remove (☐ changes to ☑).

5 Click the cleanup options that you want to select (☐ changes to ☑).

6 Click **OK**.

■ Dreamweaver parses the HTML and displays the results, including a summary of what was removed.

7 Click **OK**.

■ The cleaned-up HTML appears in the Document window.

VIEW AND EDIT HEAD CONTENT

Dreamweaver gives you various ways to view, add to, and edit a Web page's head content, where special descriptive information about the page is stored.

Head Info.

Description: This travel site will help you book a vacation.

Keywords: travel, vacations, airlines, hotels.

VIEW AND EDIT HEAD CONTENT

1 Click **View**.

2 Click **Head Content**.

■ Buttons indicating head content appear.

3 Click a button in the Head Content panel.

■ Information on the head content appears in the Properties inspector.

■ In this example, clicking 🔲 gives you information on the Title.

INSERT HEAD CONTENT

1 Click the Insert panel menu.

2 Click **HTML**.

3 Click a content button from the drop-down menu.

■ In this example, the Keywords button (🔲) is selected.

How can I influence how search engines rank my pages?

Search engines work by organizing the important information found in Web pages into a searchable database. Many search engines give greater importance to the description and keyword information than you can add to the head content of HTML documents. Short of paying for a high-ranking placement, you can influence how search engines rank your pages by making sure you add concise descriptions and relevant keywords to the head content of each page you create.

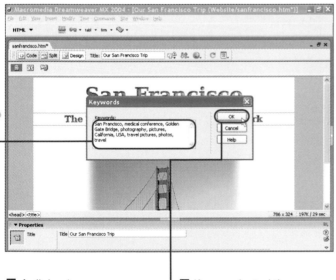

■ A dialog box appears.

4 Type the head content for the page, separating keywords with a comma.

■ If you selected the Description button ( ) in step **2**, type a sentence description for the page.

5 Click **OK**.

■ The new head content appears as a button in the head section of the Document window.

■ To view the HTML code for the new head content, click the Code View button (Code).

ACCESS REFERENCE INFORMATION ABOUT HTML TAGS

You can get quick access to reference information about HTML tags and their attributes by using the Reference tab in the Code panel. You can also insert short pieces of prewritten HTML from the Snippets panel.

USE THE REFERENCE PANEL

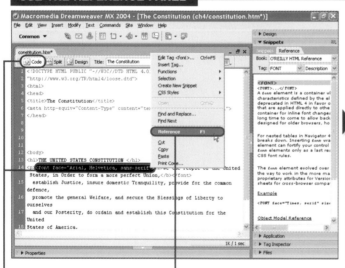

1 Click [Code] to display the HTML of the page.

2 Click and drag to select an HTML tag.

Note: It is not necessary to select the entire tag.

3 Right-click a tag in the document and select Reference from the drop-down menu.

■ The Reference panel opens, containing a description of the HTML tag.

■ Click ✓ and select a tag attribute.

■ Information appears on the attribute.

■ Click ✓ to look up a different HTML tag.

■ Click ✓ to get information about JavaScript objects or style sheet rules.

Does Dreamweaver have commands for creating all the tags listed in the Reference panel?

With Dreamweaver's commands, you create most of the tags listed in the Reference panel, in particular frequently used tags. However, there are tags listed for which Dreamweaver does not offer commands. For example, you cannot insert the `<thead>` tag with any of Dreamweaver's table commands. However, you can manually insert tags that Dreamweaver does not support with commands in Code View.

What does the text Lorem ipsum dolor mean that appears in Web pages?

The text is actually dummy text used as a placeholder when laying out pages. Although this text appears all over the Internet as placeholder text, its meaning has nothing to do with its usage. According to a 1994 issue of *Before & After* magazine, this text is based upon a modified passage from *de Finibus Bonorum et Malorum* written by Cicero in 45 B.C.E. The phrase is in reference to pain.

USE THE SNIPPETS PANEL

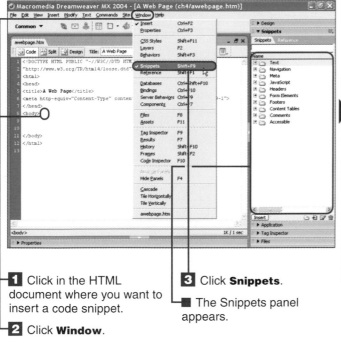

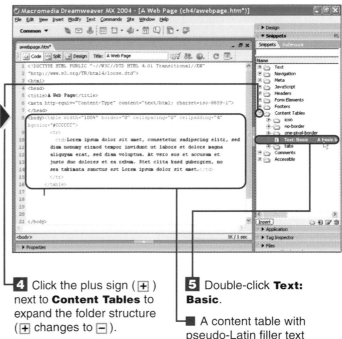

1 Click in the HTML document where you want to insert a code snippet.

2 Click **Window**.

3 Click **Snippets**.

■ The Snippets panel appears.

4 Click the plus sign (⊞) next to **Content Tables** to expand the folder structure (⊞ changes to ⊟).

5 Double-click **Text: Basic**.

■ A content table with pseudo-Latin filler text appears in the selected area of your document.

CHAPTER 5

Formatting and Styling Text

Text is the easiest type of information to add to a Web page using Dreamweaver. This chapter shows you how to create paragraphs, bulleted lists, stylized text, and more.

Create a Heading 60

Create Paragraphs 62

Create Line Breaks 64

Indent Paragraphs 65

Create Lists 66

Insert Special Characters...................68

Change the Font Face.......................70

Change the Font Size 72

Change the Font Color 73

Change the Font Size and Color
of a Page 74

Import Text from Another Document 76

CREATE A HEADING

You can add headings to structure the text on your Web page hierarchically with titles and subtitles. You can also align your heading text.

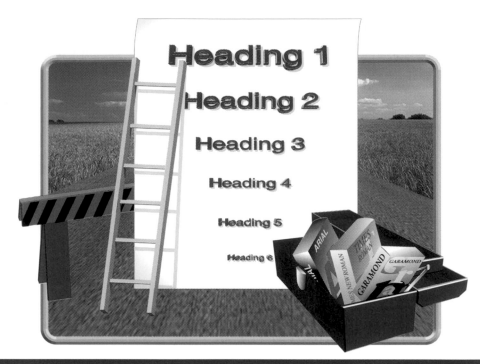

CREATE A HEADING

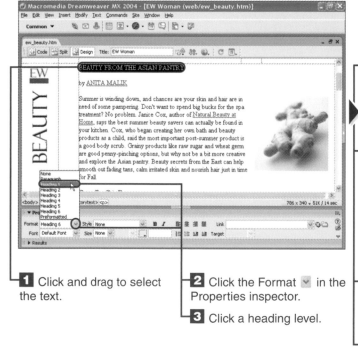

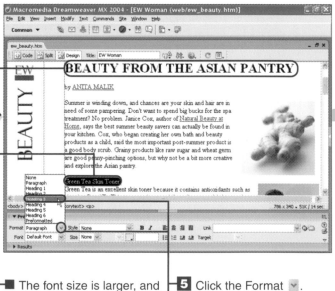

1 Click and drag to select the text.

2 Click the Format ✓ in the Properties inspector.

3 Click a heading level.

■ The font size is larger, and the text is now bold. White space separates it from other text.

4 Click and drag to select more text.

5 Click the Format ✓.

6 Click a different heading.

What heading levels should I use to format my text?

Headings 1, 2, and 3 are often used for titles and subtitles. Heading 4 is similar to a bold version of default text. Headings 5 and 6 are often used for copyright and disclaimer information in page footers.

Why does the size of the heading appear different when I view my page on another computer?

The browser uses the default text size to set the size of the heading. Heading 1 text is three times larger than the default text size. Heading 6 text is three times smaller. The size of a heading is set *relative* to the default text size.

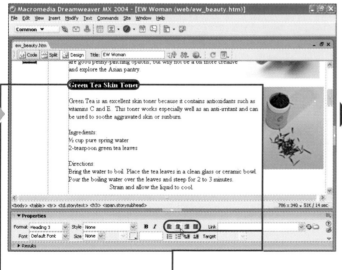

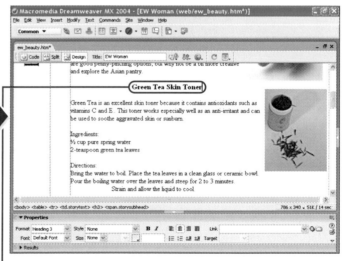

■ The second heading appears different from the first, but still bold.

Note: The greater the heading level, the smaller the text formatting.

7 Click and drag to select a heading text.

8 Click an alignment option to align your heading.

▤ Align Left

▤ Center

▤ Align Right

▤ Justify

■ The heading text is aligned on the page.

CREATE PARAGRAPHS

You can organize text on your Web page by creating and aligning paragraphs.

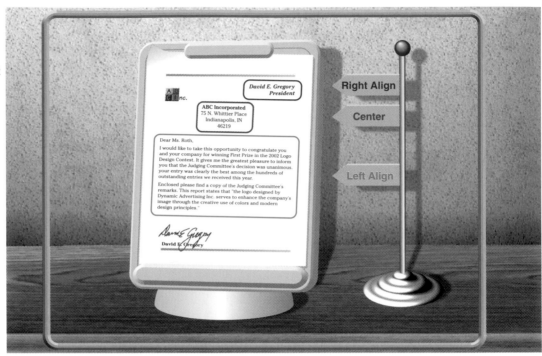

CREATE PARAGRAPHS

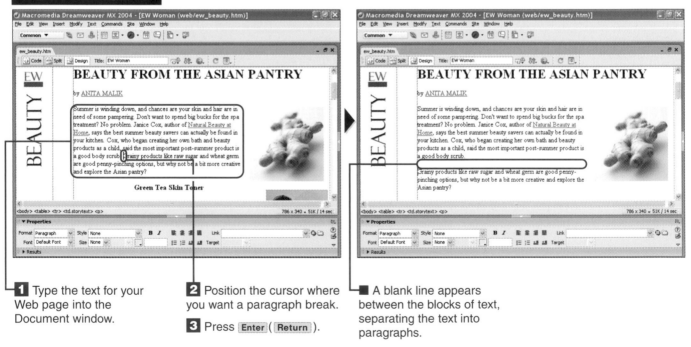

1 Type the text for your Web page into the Document window.

2 Position the cursor where you want a paragraph break.

3 Press Enter (Return).

■ A blank line appears between the blocks of text, separating the text into paragraphs.

What controls the width of the paragraphs on my Web page?

The width of your paragraphs depends on the width of the Web browser window. When a user changes the size of the browser window, the widths of the paragraphs also change. That way the user always sees all the text of the paragraph. You can also use tables to further control the width of your paragraphs. For more on tables, see Chapter 8.

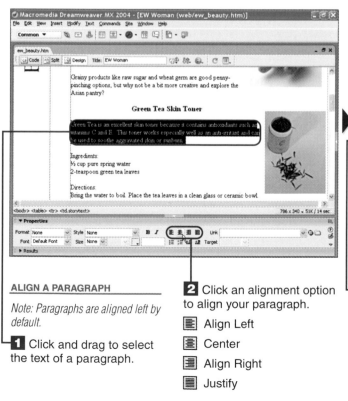

What is the HTML code for paragraphs?

In HTML, paragraphs are distinguished by opening and closing <p> tags. You can click the Code View button () to view the page's HTML. Paragraphs are also one of the few HTML tags that you can use as a closing tag, if desired.

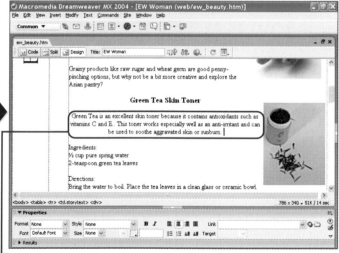

ALIGN A PARAGRAPH

Note: Paragraphs are aligned left by default.

1 Click and drag to select the text of a paragraph.

2 Click an alignment option to align your paragraph.

▤ Align Left

▤ Center

▤ Align Right

▤ Justify

■ The paragraph is aligned on the page.

CREATE LINE BREAKS

By adding line breaks to your page, you can keep adjacent lines of related text close together without creating a new paragraph.

CREATE LINE BREAKS

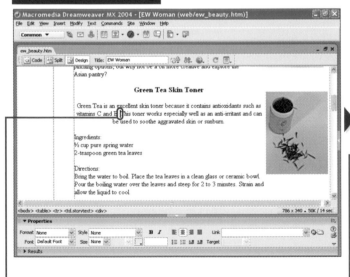

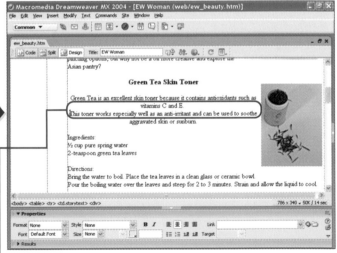

1 Click where you want the line of text to break.

2 Press `Shift` + `Enter` (`Shift` + `Return`).

 A line break is added.

Note: You can insert multiple line breaks to add more space between lines of text.

INDENT PARAGRAPHS

You can make selected paragraphs stand out from the rest of the text on your Web page by indenting them. Indents are often used for displaying quotations.

INDENT PARAGRAPHS

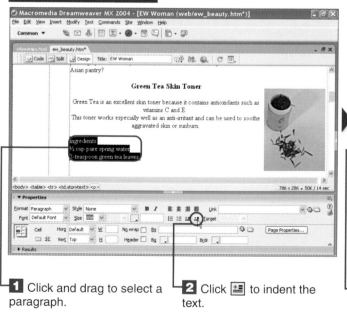

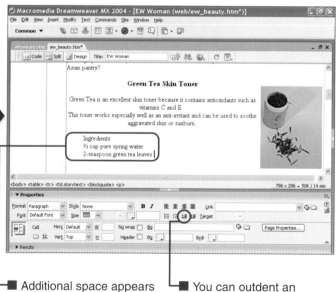

1 Click and drag to select a paragraph.

2 Click ▦ to indent the text.

■ Additional space appears in both the left and right margins of the paragraph.

■ You can repeat steps **1** and **2** to indent a paragraph further.

■ You can outdent an indented paragraph by clicking ▦.

CREATE LISTS

You can organize text items into unordered lists. Unordered lists have items that are indented and bulleted but are not listed in an order by number or letter.

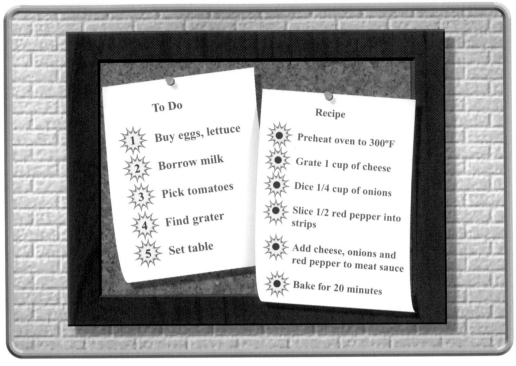

To Do

1. Buy eggs, lettuce
2. Borrow milk
3. Pick tomatoes
4. Find grater
5. Set table

Recipe

• Preheat oven to 300ºF
• Grate 1 cup of cheese
• Dice 1/4 cup of onions
• Slice 1/2 red pepper into strips
• Add cheese, onions and red pepper to meat sauce
• Bake for 20 minutes

CREATE UNORDERED LISTS

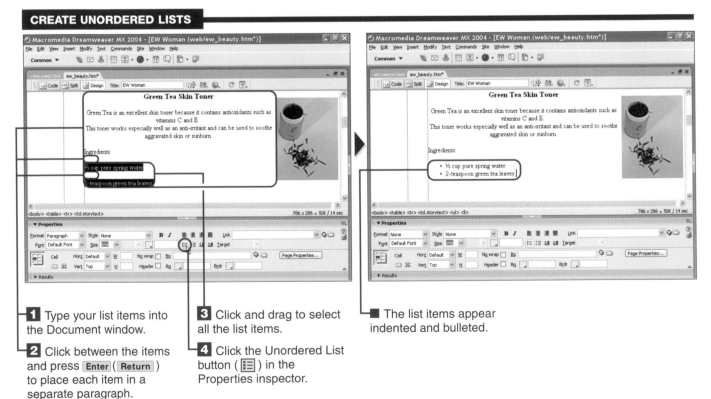

1 Type your list items into the Document window.

2 Click between the items and press `Enter` (`Return`) to place each item in a separate paragraph.

3 Click and drag to select all the list items.

4 Click the Unordered List button (☰) in the Properties inspector.

■ The list items appear indented and bulleted.

Can I modify the appearance of my unordered lists?

You can modify the style of unordered lists by highlighting an item in the list and clicking **Text**, **List**, and then **Properties**. The dialog box that appears enables you to select different bullet styles for your unordered list.

Can I modify the appearance of my ordered lists?

You can modify the style of ordered lists by highlighting an item in the list and clicking **Text**, **List**, and then **Properties**. The dialog box that appears enables you to select different numbering schemes for your ordered list.

CREATE ORDERED LISTS

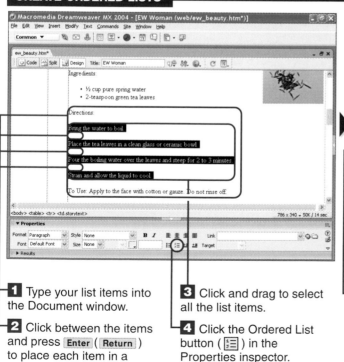

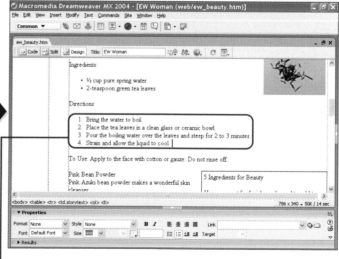

1 Type your list items into the Document window.

2 Click between the items and press **Enter** (**Return**) to place each item in a separate paragraph.

3 Click and drag to select all the list items.

4 Click the Ordered List button ( ) in the Properties inspector.

■ The list items appear indented and numbered.

INSERT SPECIAL CHARACTERS

You can insert special characters into your Web page that do not commonly appear on your keyboard.

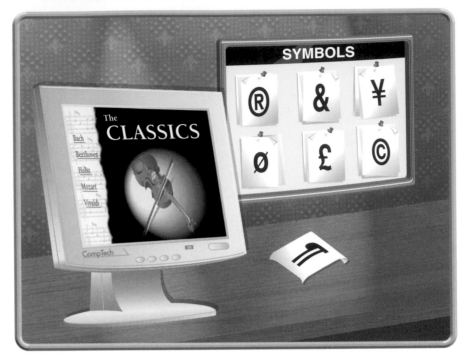

INSERT SPECIAL CHARACTERS

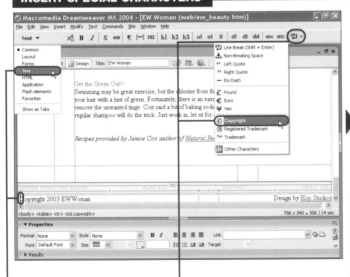

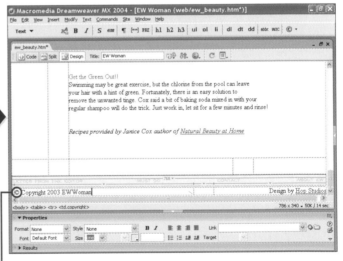

1 Click **Text** in the Insert panel.

2 Click where you want to insert the special character.

3 Click the Characters menu button (▦▾).

4 Click the special character you want to insert.

■ The special character appears in your Web page text.

How do I include non-English language text on my Web page?

Many European languages feature accented characters that do not appear on standard keyboards. You can insert many of these characters using the special characters tools described in this section.

Der Computer gefällt mir

What defines special character?

Although most browsers will display double quotation marks without problems, some standard punctuations are considered special characters. For a good reference, visit Webmonkey's Special Characters Quick Reference at http://hotwired.lycos.com/webmonkey/reference/special_characters/.

< = <
&quote; = "
& = &

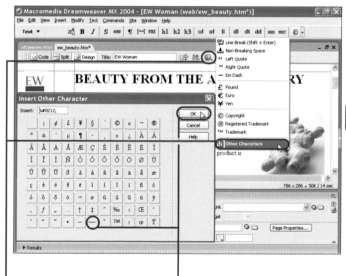

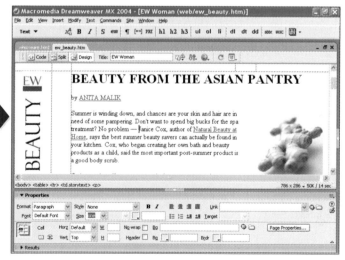

INSERT OTHER SPECIAL CHARACTERS

1 Click the Characters menu button ( ).

2 Click Other Characters ( ) from the menu to access a wider variety of special characters.

■ The Insert Other Character dialog box appears.

3 Click a special character.

■ The HTML code that defines that special character appears in the text field.

4 Click **OK**.

■ The special character appears in your Web page text.

CHANGE THE FONT FACE

For aesthetic purposes or to emphasize certain elements on your Web page, you can change the font style of your text.

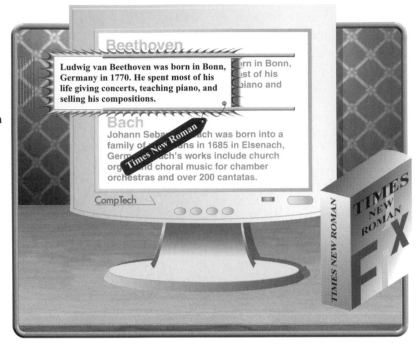

You can customize the fonts on your Web pages by using Style Sheets. Customizing by using Style Sheets is now the preferred technique to use. For more about Style Sheets, see Chapter 12.

CHANGE THE FONT FACE

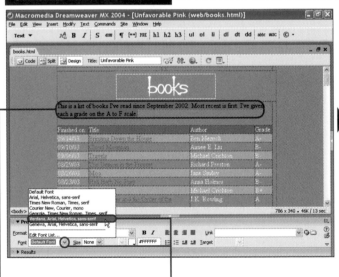

1 Click and drag to select the text.

2 Click the Font ⌄ in the Properties inspector.

3 Click a font.

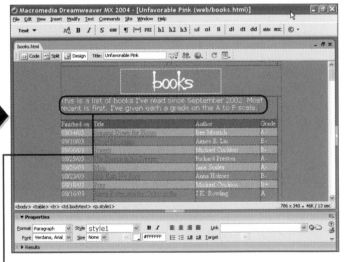

■ The text changes to the new font.

■ Dreamweaver also makes a new style for you to use elsewhere on the page.

How are fonts classified?

The two most common categories of fonts are serif and sans-serif fonts. Serif fonts are distinguished by the decorations, or serifs, on the ends of their lines. Common serif fonts include Times New Roman, Palatino, and Garamond. Sans-serif fonts lack these decorations. Common sans-serif fonts include Arial, Verdana, and Helvetica.

Why are there so few fonts available from the Font menu?

A font must be installed on the user's computer to display in the browser. Dreamweaver's default list of fonts specifies the list of common typefaces available on most computers, and alternate styles if the user does not have those fonts installed.

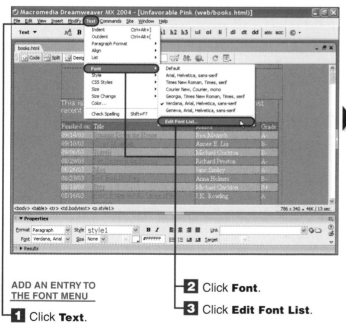

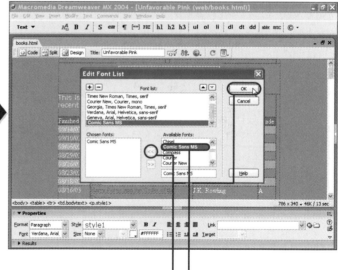

ADD AN ENTRY TO THE FONT MENU

1 Click **Text**.

2 Click **Font**.

3 Click **Edit Font List**.

■ The Edit Font List dialog box appears.

■ The fonts that appear in the Font menu are shown here.

■ The fonts installed on your computer appear in the Available Fonts list.

4 Click a font.

5 Click ⬅ to add the font.

6 Click **OK**.

■ The new font appears in the Font menu.

CHANGE THE FONT SIZE

You can emphasize or de-emphasize sections of text by changing the font size.

CHANGE THE FONT SIZE

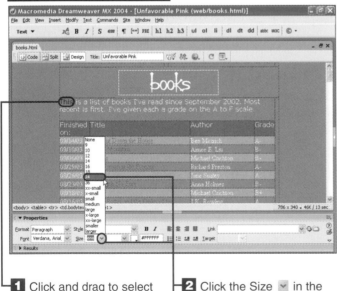

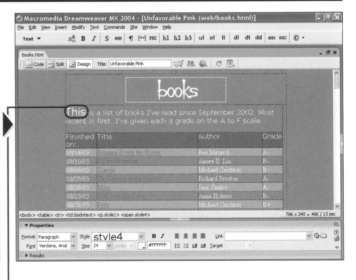

1 Click and drag to select the text.

2 Click the Size ▼ in the Properties inspector.

3 Click a font size.

■ The text size changes.

72

CHANGE THE FONT COLOR

You can change the
color of text on all
or part of your Web
page so that it
complements the
background and
other page
elements.

CHANGE THE FONT COLOR

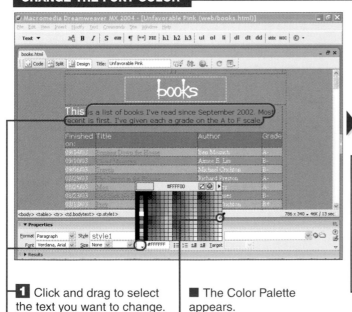

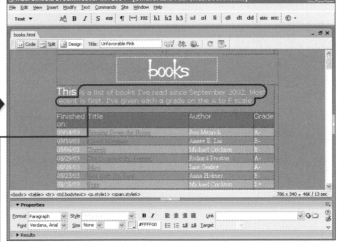

1 Click and drag to select
the text you want to change.

2 Click the Color Swatch
■ in the Properties
inspector (⇖ changes to ✐).

■ The Color Palette
appears.

3 Click a color.

■ The selected text appears
in the new color.

CHANGE THE FONT SIZE AND COLOR OF A PAGE

You can set the overall font size and color for the entire page in Page Properties. This will affect any unformatted text on the page.

CHANGE THE FONT SIZE AND COLOR OF A PAGE

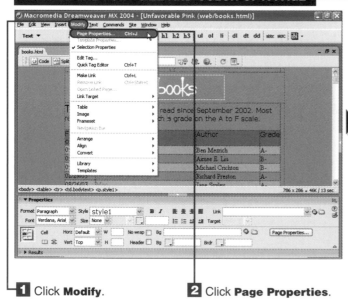

1 Click **Modify**.

2 Click **Page Properties**.

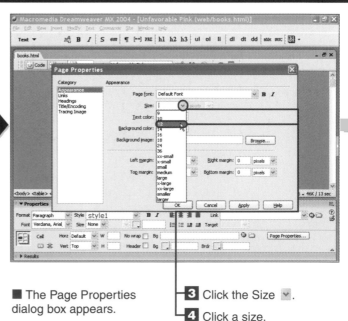

■ The Page Properties dialog box appears.

3 Click the Size ☑.

4 Click a size.

What are the letter and number combinations that appear in the color fields of Dreamweaver?

HTML represents colors using six-digit codes called *hexadecimal codes*, which represent the amount of red, green, and blue used to create a particular color. Hex codes are preceded by a pound sign (#). Instead of ranging from 0 to 9, hex-code digits range from 0 to F with A equal to 10, B equal to 11, and so on through F, which is equal to 15. The first two digits in the hex code specify the amount of red in the selected color. The next two digits specify the amount of green, and the last two digits specify the amount of blue.

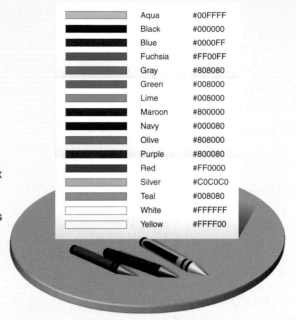

	Aqua	#00FFFF
	Black	#000000
	Blue	#0000FF
	Fuchsia	#FF00FF
	Gray	#808080
	Green	#008000
	Lime	#008000
	Maroon	#800000
	Navy	#000080
	Olive	#808000
	Purple	#800080
	Red	#FF0000
	Silver	#C0C0C0
	Teal	#008080
	White	#FFFFFF
	Yellow	#FFFF00

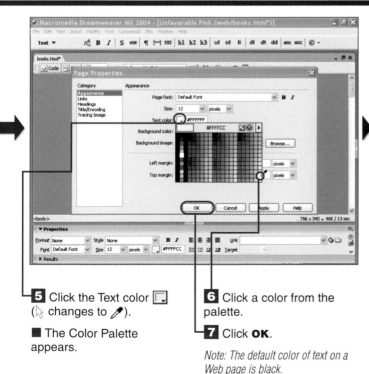

5 Click the Text color (⊡ changes to ✐).

■ The Color Palette appears.

6 Click a color from the palette.

7 Click **OK**.

Note: The default color of text on a Web page is black.

■ Your text appears in a new color and size on your Web page.

You can save time by importing text from an existing document, instead of typing it all over again. This is particularly convenient when you have tabular data that needs to appear in a table. By importing a comma- or tab-delimited text file, you do not have to re-create the entire table in HTML. Dreamweaver creates it automatically.

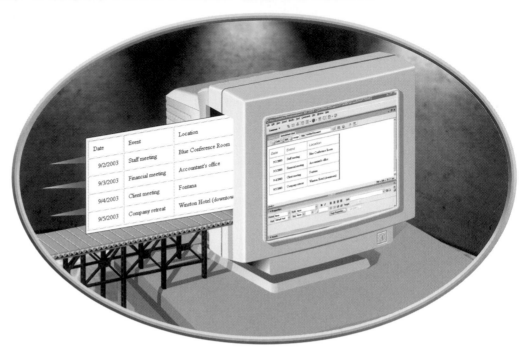

IMPORT EXCEL DOCUMENT

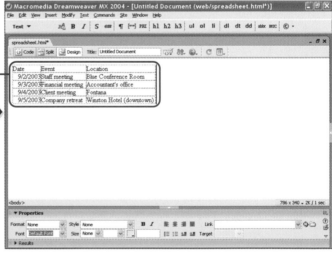

1 Click **File**.

2 Click **Import**.

3 Click **Excel Document**.

■ The Select File dialog box appears.

4 Click ▼ to find the file you want to import.

5 Click the file.

6 Click **Open**.

■ The imported Excel document appears in the Document window. The formatting from Excel is translated into HTML.

When is importing text a good idea?

Unless you type at speeds of over 100 words per minute, typing large amounts of text can be very time-consuming. If your original text file was created using a word processing program such as Microsoft Word, you can speed up the process by importing the Word document into Dreamweaver. When you import Excel documents, Dreamweaver builds tables to duplicate formatting from Excel. Once you have imported the documents, you can edit and format text, add images, tables, and multimedia normally.

IMPORT WORD DOCUMENT

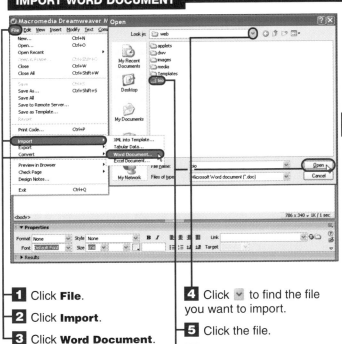

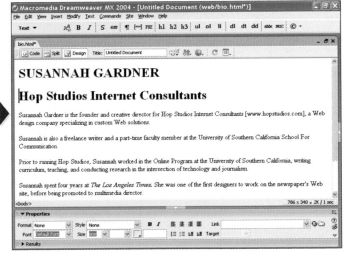

1 Click **File**.

2 Click **Import**.

3 Click **Word Document**.

■ The Select File dialog box appears.

4 Click ⬇ to find the file you want to import.

5 Click the file.

6 Click **Open**.

■ The imported Word document appears in the Document window. The formatting from Word is translated into HTML.

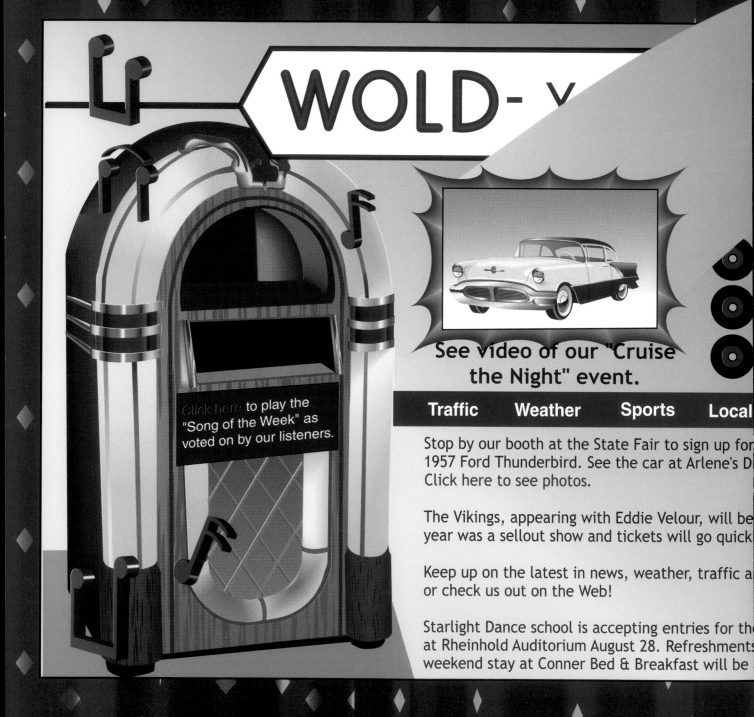

WOLD- v

See video of our "Cruise the Night" event.

Traffic   **Weather**   **Sports**   **Local**

Stop by our booth at the State Fair to sign up for
1957 Ford Thunderbird. See the car at Arlene's D
Click here to see photos.

The Vikings, appearing with Eddie Velour, will be
year was a sellout show and tickets will go quick

Keep up on the latest in news, weather, traffic a
or check us out on the Web!

Starlight Dance school is accepting entries for th
at Rheinhold Auditorium August 28. Refreshments
weekend stay at Conner Bed & Breakfast will be

Click here to play the
"Song of the Week" as
voted on by our listeners.

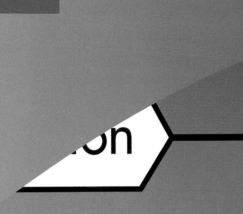

ontests

ake a Request

pecial Appearances

ontact Us

nts **Just for Fun** **Recent Guests**

ance to win a fully-restored, aqua-and-white
n every Friday through June.

ncert at the Crestwood Stadium July 14-18. Last
ck here to connect with ConcertMaster.

dies personalities by listening to WOLD 113.2 FM,

stwood Dance contest and Sock Hop, to be held
be served and prizes ranging from $50 to a
ded. Click here for entries and more information.

CHAPTER 6

Working with Images and Multimedia

You can make your Web page much more interesting by adding digital photos, scanned art, animation, and interactive visual elements. This chapter shows you how to insert and format them.

Insert an Image into a Web Page........80

Wrap Text Around an Image 82

Align an Image 84

Crop an Image 86

Resize an Image 88

Resample an Image 90

Add Space Around an Image 92

Add a Background Image 94

Change the Background Color............96

Add Alternate Text to an Image 97

Insert a Flash File 98

Insert Other Multimedia Files 100

Create a Rollover Image 102

Insert a Navigation Bar....................104

INSERT AN IMAGE INTO A WEB PAGE

You can insert different types of images into your Web page, including clip art, digital camera images, and scanned photos.

INSERT AN IMAGE INTO A WEB PAGE

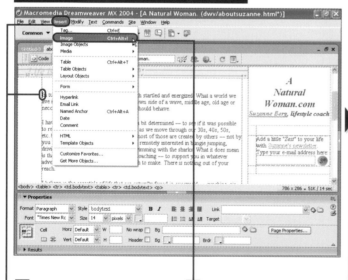

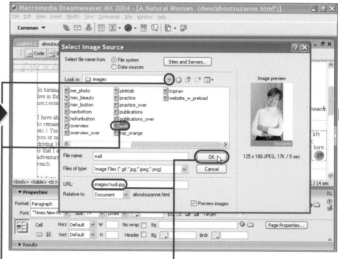

1 Click to position the mouse ⌖ where you want to insert the image.

2 Click **Insert**.

3 Click **Image**.

■ You can also click the Image button in the Common Insert bar.

■ The Select Image Source dialog box appears.

4 Click ⌄ and select the folder containing the image.

5 Click the image file that you want to insert into your Web page.

■ A preview of the image appears.

■ You can insert an image that exists at an external Web address by typing the address into the URL field.

6 Click **OK**.

What are the file formats for Web images?

The majority of the images you see on Web pages are GIF or JPEG files. Both GIF and JPEG are compressed file formats, which means they store image information in a small amount of space. GIF is best for images that use flat colors and for images that contain a limited number of colors — it only supports a maximum of 256 colors. JPEG is great for storing photographic information — it supports millions of colors. You can insert GIF and JPEG files into your Web page by using the steps described in this section.

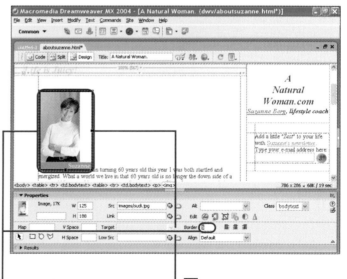

■ The image appears where you positioned your cursor in the Web page.

■ To delete an image, click the image and press Delete.

ADD A BORDER TO AN IMAGE

1 Click the image to select it.

2 Type the width, in this example in pixels, into the Border field.

3 Press Enter (Return).

■ A border appears around the image in the same color as the text.

WRAP TEXT AROUND AN IMAGE

Aligning the image to one side of a Web page allows you to wrap text around it. Wrapping text around images enables you to fit more information onto the screen and gives your Web pages a more finished, professional look. There are many align options, and you may want to try several to get the best effect for your page.

WRAP TEXT AROUND AN IMAGE

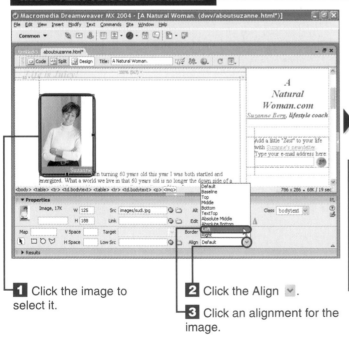

1 Click the image to select it.

2 Click the Align ⌄.

3 Click an alignment for the image.

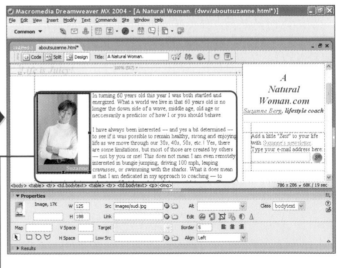

■ The text flows around the image according to the alignment you selected.

■ In this example, the text flows to the right of the left-aligned image.

Can I tell how long it will take my page to download?

The total size of your page appears in kilobytes (K) on the status bar. The total size includes the size of your HTML file, the size of your images, and the size of anything else on the page. Next to the size is the estimated download time for the page.

What is the ideal size of a Web page?

Most Web designers feel comfortable putting up a page with a total size under 40K. There are exceptions to this rule. You might break the rule for an especially important image file, for example. The 40K limit does not apply to multimedia files, although multimedia files should be kept as small as possible.

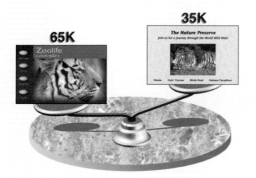

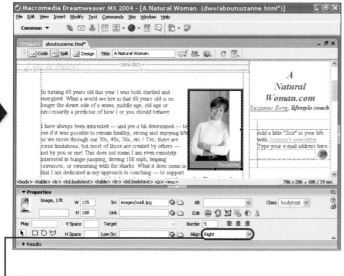

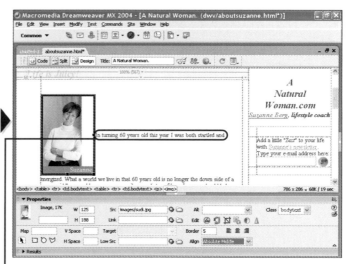

■ You can select other options from the Align ▼ for different wrapping effects, such as Right or Middle.

■ In this example, the text flows to the left of the right-aligned image.

■ In this example, the text is aligned to the middle of the image.

ALIGN AN IMAGE

The alignment of an image can give a photo or banner prominence on your page. You can center it or align it left or right, depending on the layout of your Web page.

ALIGN AN IMAGE

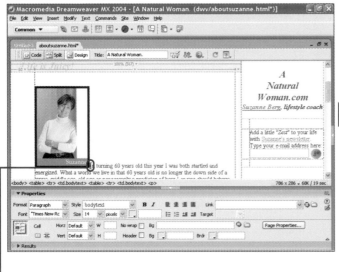

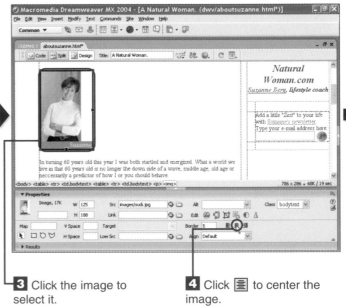

1 Click to position the mouse ⌖ to the immediate right of the image.

2 Press `Enter` (`Return`) to place the image on its own line.

3 Click the image to select it.

4 Click ▤ to center the image.

How can I use centered images to enhance my text?

You can create custom graphics or icons in a graphics-editing program and use these as visual elements on your page. Center small icons to divide main sections of text in your Web page. These icons serve the same purpose as horizontal rules, but add a more sophisticated look to your pages.

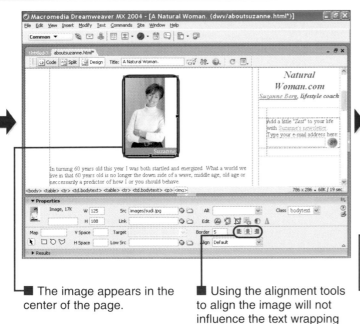

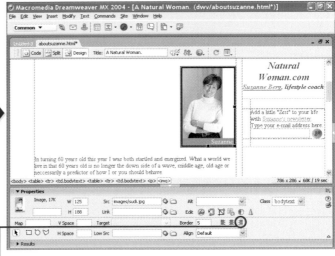

- The image appears in the center of the page.

- Using the alignment tools to align the image will not influence the text wrapping around the image.

- You can also align the image to the right side of the page by clicking 🖼.

- You can toggle the alignment selection on or off by clicking it again.

CROP AN IMAGE

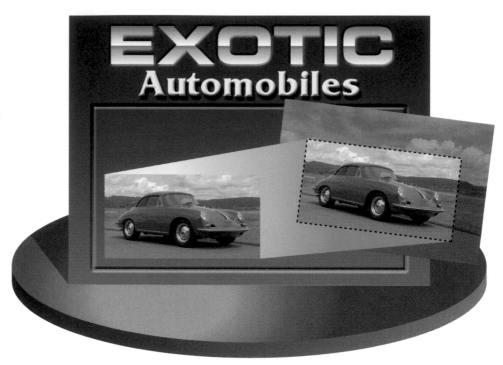

You can crop or trim an image by using the Crop tool and dragging the handles to adjust how much of the image you will show. This can be handy for quick edits without using an external graphics-editing program.

CROP AN IMAGE

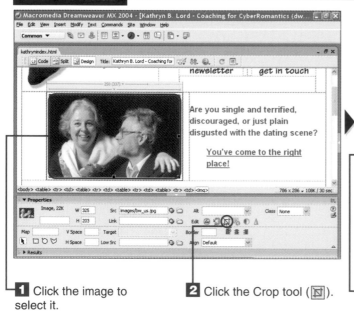

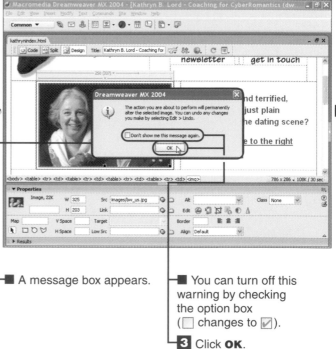

1 Click the image to select it.

2 Click the Crop tool (🔲).

■ A message box appears.

■ You can turn off this warning by checking the option box (☐ changes to ☑).

3 Click **OK**.

Should I edit images in Dreamweaver or use an external graphics program?

Macromedia has added the Crop tool to make working on a Web page faster and easier. If you need to do a simple crop, the Crop tool is faster than opening the image in a graphics-editing program like Macromedia Fireworks or Adobe Photoshop. However, you are making a permanent alteration to the image on the page. If you change your mind later, you cannot go back to an uncropped version of the image. If you think you might want to go back to the earlier version, make a copy of the image before trimming it, which leaves your original image untouched.

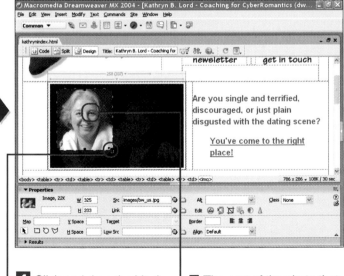

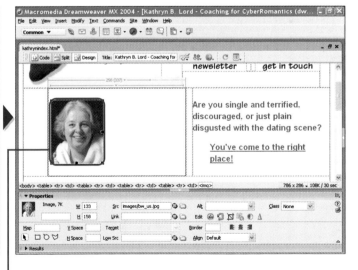

4 Click and drag the black square handles to define the area you want to crop.

■ The part of the photo that appears greyed out will delete.

5 Double-click inside the crop box.

■ The image is trimmed to the size of the crop box.

■ Your changes become permanent when you save the page.

RESIZE AN IMAGE

You can change the size of an image by changing the pixel dimensions, making the image a percentage of the browser window, or clicking and dragging the corner of the image.

Pixels, tiny, solid-color squares, make up a digital image.

RESIZE AN IMAGE

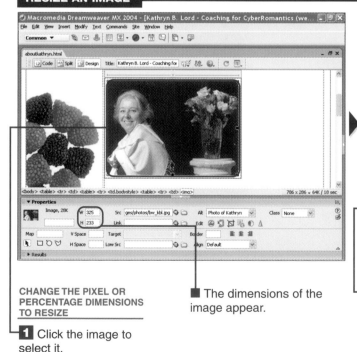

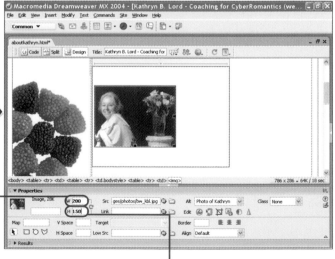

CHANGE THE PIXEL OR PERCENTAGE DIMENSIONS TO RESIZE

1 Click the image to select it.

■ The dimensions of the image appear.

2 Type the desired width of the image in pixels or as a percentage.

■ Instead of pixels, you can type a percentage of the window or table cell for the width and height. For example, type **50%** and **50%**.

3 Press Enter (Return).

4 Type the desired height of the image in pixels or as a percentage.

5 Press Enter (Return).

■ The image displays with its new dimensions.

What is the best way to change the dimensions of an image on a Web page?

Changing the pixel dimensions or clicking and dragging an image in Dreamweaver stretches or shrinks the presentation of an image on the Web page, but does not actually resize the graphic's true dimensions. Clicking and dragging an image may cause distortion or make the image lose proportion. You should use the Resampling tool to resize in Dreamweaver, or open the image in a graphics editor such as Macromedia Fireworks. This enables you to adjust the image's real height and width and save it as a new file. This maximizes the quality of the image. For more about the Resampling tool, see page 90.

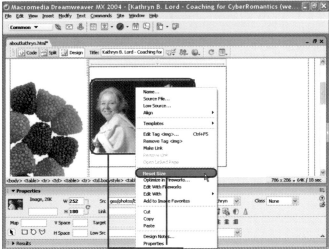

CLICK AND DRAG TO RESIZE

1 Click the image to select it.

2 Drag one of the handles at the edge of the image.

■ To resize an image proportionally, press and hold Shift as you drag a corner.

■ The image expands or contracts to its new dimensions.

RESET THE IMAGE TO ORIGINAL SIZE

■ If you change your mind after resizing an image, you can reset the image to its original size.

1 Right-click the image.

2 Click **Reset Size** from the menu that appears.

■ The image returns to its original size in pixels.

RESAMPLE AN IMAGE

You can resize images by resampling them. The Resampling tool gives you the ability to resize an image without leaving Dreamweaver or having to use an external graphics editor.

RESAMPLE AN IMAGE

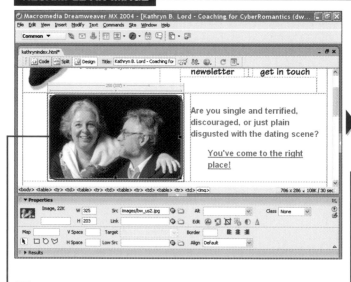

1 Click the image to select it.

2 Click and drag the square black handles to resize the image.

3 Click the Resampling tool (▦).

When should I use the Resampling tool?

Resampling is a shortcut for resizing an image without leaving Dreamweaver. The Resampling tool () is great for users who are not experienced with a graphics editor like Macromedia Fireworks. Resampling works best when you are making an image smaller. Resizing to a larger size will actually stretch pixels and your image will not look very good.

If you have Fireworks installed, you can open it to edit a graphic directly from the Dreamweaver Properties inspector by clicking the Edit/Fireworks Logo button ().

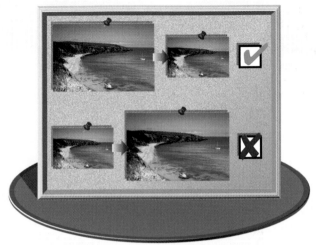

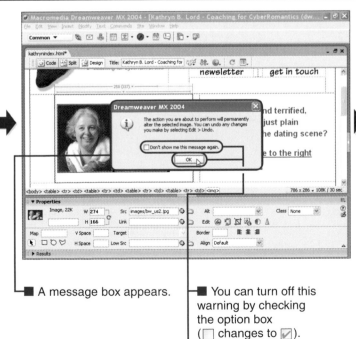

■ A message box appears.

■ You can turn off this warning by checking the option box (☐ changes to ☑).

4 Click **OK**.

■ The image is resampled, or resized, to the new dimensions.

■ Your changes become permanent when you save the page.

ADD SPACE AROUND AN IMAGE

You can add space around an image to distinguish it from the text and other images on your Web page. This creates a cleaner page layout.

ADD SPACE AROUND AN IMAGE

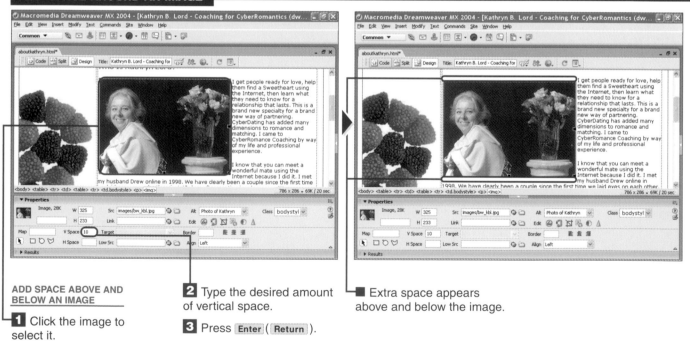

ADD SPACE ABOVE AND BELOW AN IMAGE

1 Click the image to select it.

2 Type the desired amount of vertical space.

3 Press Enter (Return).

■ Extra space appears above and below the image.

Why should I add space around my image?

In many cases, adding space around your images enhances the appearance of your Web page. The extra space makes text easier to read and keeps adjacent images from appearing as a single image.

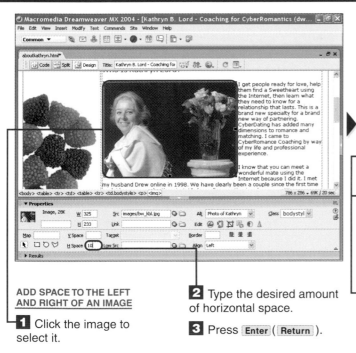

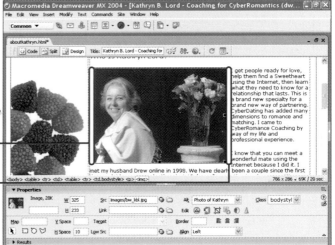

ADD SPACE TO THE LEFT AND RIGHT OF AN IMAGE

1 Click the image to select it.

2 Type the desired amount of horizontal space.

3 Press Enter (Return).

■ Extra space appears to the left and right of the image.

ADD A BACKGROUND IMAGE

You can incorporate a
background image to
add texture to your
Web page. Background
images appear beneath
any text or images on
your page.

ADD A BACKGROUND IMAGE

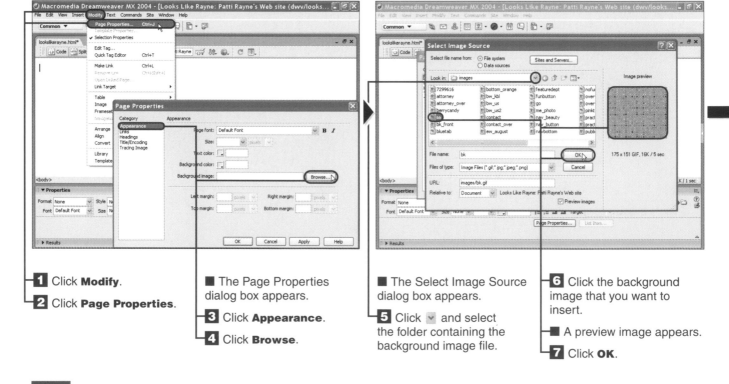

1 Click **Modify**.

2 Click **Page Properties**.

■ The Page Properties
dialog box appears.

3 Click **Appearance**.

4 Click **Browse**.

■ The Select Image Source
dialog box appears.

5 Click ⌄ and select
the folder containing the
background image file.

6 Click the background
image that you want to
insert.

■ A preview image appears.

7 Click **OK**.

What types of images make good backgrounds?

Typically, images that do not clash with the text and other content in the foreground make good backgrounds. You do not want your background images to overwhelm the rest of the page. Using an image that tiles seamlessly is also a good idea so that your background appears to be one large image that covers the entire page.

 Are backgrounds always patterns?

Although many backgrounds repeat a pattern of some kind, others can actually break your page into columns and bars. A background image can also be a tall, vertical image, or a wide, horizontal image. Since background images tile, vertical images create a stripe across the top of the page, and a horizontal image creates a left-hand bar.

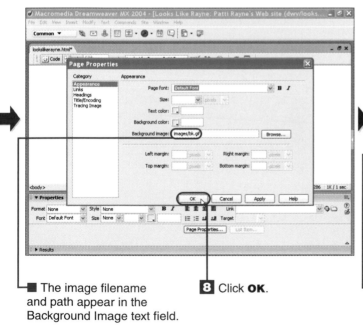

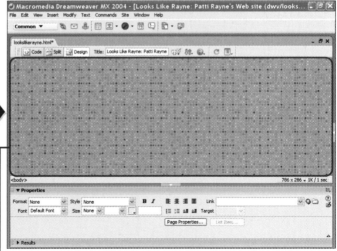

■ The image filename and path appear in the Background Image text field.

8 Click **OK**.

■ The image appears as a background on the Web page.

Note: If necessary, the image tiles horizontally and vertically to fill the entire window.

CHANGE THE BACKGROUND COLOR

For variety, you can change the background color of your Web page.

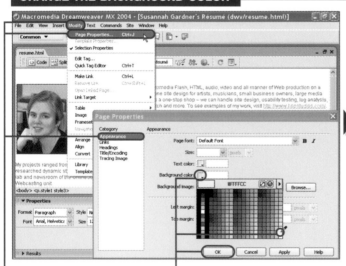

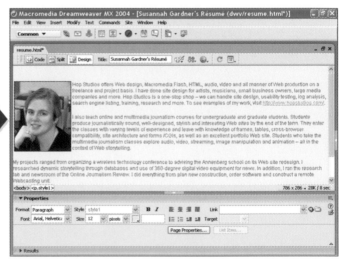

1 Click **Modify**.

2 Click **Page Properties**.

■ The Page Properties dialog box appears.

3 Click **Appearance**.

4 Click the Background color ▢ to open the color menu (⬚ changes to 🖊).

5 Click a color from the menu using the Eyedropper tool (🖊).

6 Click **OK**.

■ The background of your Web page displays in the color you selected.

Note: For additional information about Web color, see page 73.

Note: A background image will appear over any background color. To add a background image, see page 94.

ADD ALTERNATE TEXT TO AN IMAGE

You can add alternate text for users to read when they place their mouse over an image, or if an image does not appear on your page.

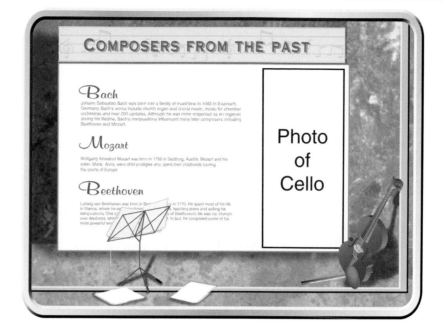

Some Web browsers cannot display images, and some users view Web pages with images turned off.

ADD ALTERNATE TEXT TO AN IMAGE

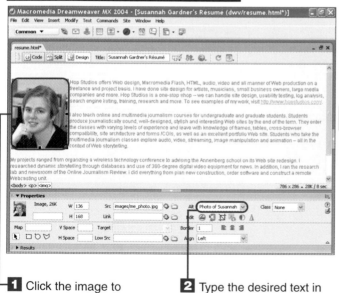

1 Click the image to select it.

2 Type the desired text in the Alt field.

3 Press Enter (Return).

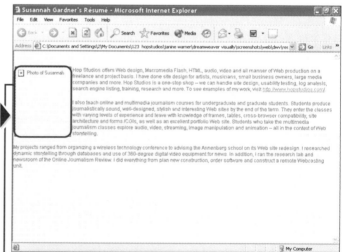

■ The alternate text appears when the image does not display in the browser window.

Note: Some browsers briefly display alternate text when you position your mouse over an image.

INSERT A FLASH FILE

You can add life to your Web page by inserting a Flash movie. A Flash movie is a multimedia file created with Macromedia Flash software. There are many uses for Flash movies, both for informational and entertainment purposes — animated banner ads, cartoons, e-learning content, interactive animations, site navigation, and so on.

INSERT A FLASH FILE

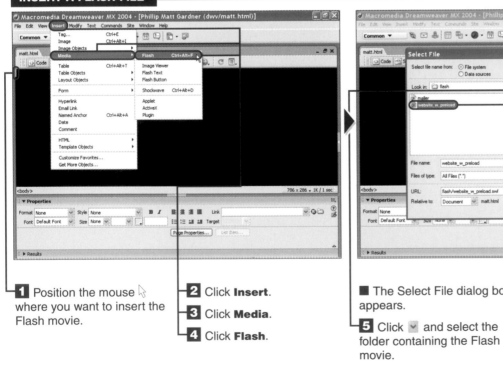

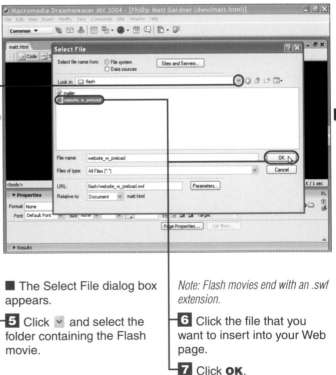

1 Position the mouse ⌖ where you want to insert the Flash movie.

2 Click **Insert**.

3 Click **Media**.

4 Click **Flash**.

■ The Select File dialog box appears.

5 Click ⌄ and select the folder containing the Flash movie.

Note: Flash movies end with an .swf extension.

6 Click the file that you want to insert into your Web page.

7 Click **OK**.

What HTML tags does Flash insert into the HTML document?

When you insert a Flash movie into a Dreamweaver document, Dreamweaver inserts the `object` tag needed for the Microsoft Internet Explorer browser and the `embed` tag needed for the Netscape Navigator browser. Dreamweaver also adds a path to the plug-in on the Macromedia site so that the Web browser can install it if it is not present. It also writes `param` tags, which instruct the Flash movie on what quality to play in (high is default), and what the name of the file is. You can create additional tags easily by clicking the Flash movie and then clicking **Parameters** in the Properties inspector.

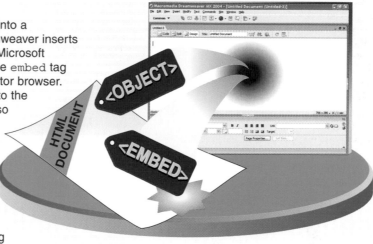

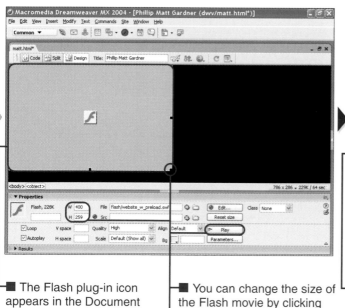

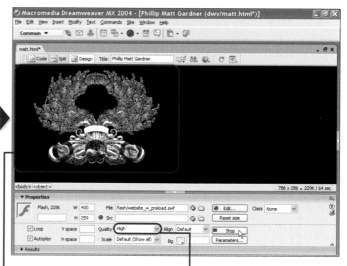

■ The Flash plug-in icon appears in the Document window.

■ You can change the size of the Flash movie by clicking and dragging its lower-left corner, or by entering a width and height in the Properties inspector.

8 Click the Play button (▷ Play) in the Properties inspector to test the Flash movie.

■ The Flash movie begins to play inside your Dreamweaver document.

■ You can click the Quality ⌄ and select the level of quality at which you want your movie to play.

INSERT OTHER MULTIMEDIA FILES

You can insert video clips and other multimedia to add variety to your Web page.

INSERT OTHER MULTIMEDIA FILES

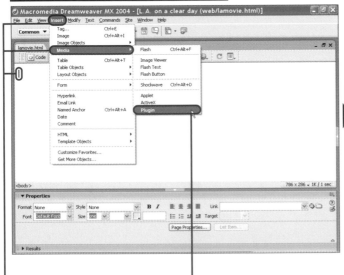

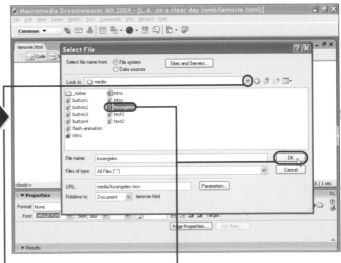

1 Position the mouse where you want to insert the multimedia file in the Document window.

2 Click **Insert**.

3 Click **Media**.

4 Click **Plugin** to add a video or sound clip.

■ Many multimedia features in Web browsers are handled by special add-ons called plug-ins.

■ The Select File dialog box appears.

5 Click and select the folder containing the multimedia file.

6 Click the multimedia file that you want to insert into your Web page.

7 Click **OK**.

**What should I know when adding
multimedia content to my site?**

You can add Flash movies, video clips,
sounds, and interactive features to jazz
up a Web site. However, remember that
some of your visitors may not be able
to view the content because their
browsers cannot support it. If your
visitors are mainly using dial-up
connections, most will not wait for the
download. In addition, some users are
unwilling to spend the time to download
and install the plug-in. From a legal
perspective, if you add music or other
copyrighted material to your multimedia
files, make sure you have the proper
permissions and are not in violation of
any copyright laws.

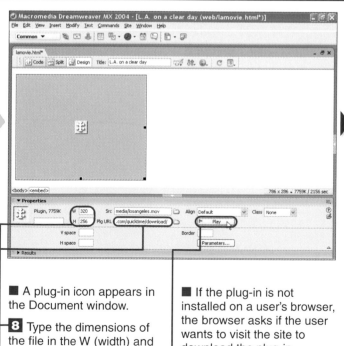

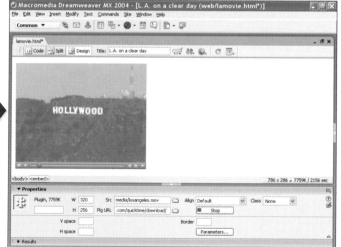

■ A plug-in icon appears in
the Document window.

8 Type the dimensions of
the file in the W (width) and
H (height) fields.

9 Type the URL of the
site where the user can
download the plug-in.

■ If the plug-in is not
installed on a user's browser,
the browser asks if the user
wants to visit the site to
download the plug-in.

10 Click [▶ Play] to test
the multimedia file.

■ You can use this feature to
test multimedia files, such as
QuickTime movies, in the
Dreamweaver Document
window.

CREATE A ROLLOVER IMAGE

Rollover images are often used to indicate interactivity on a Web page. They are especially common in navigation bars. A *rollover image* is an image that appears when you place your mouse cursor over an image on a Web page. Some rollover effects are very subtle and may not look like new images at all.

CREATE A ROLLOVER IMAGE

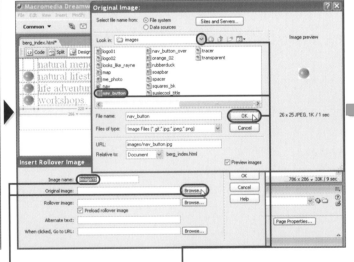

1 Position the mouse ⊹ where you want to insert the rollover image.

2 Click **Insert**.

3 Click **Image Objects**.

4 Click **Rollover Image**.

■ The Insert Rollover Image dialog box appears.

5 Type an identifying name for scripting purposes.

6 Click **Browse** to open the Original Image dialog box.

7 Click ⌄ and select the folder containing the image.

8 Click the image that you want to insert into your Web page.

9 Click **OK**.

How does the rollover image work?

Creating the interactive effect of a
rollover effect is not straight HTML.
This effect is created by using a
scripting language called JavaScript.
JavaScript is used for many kinds of
in-the-page interactivity, like
calculators, form correction, pop-up
windows, and for checking browser
versions. Unlike HTML, which is a
markup language, JavaScript is a
programming language, though it is
not as complex as languages like C,
C++, or PERL. Dreamweaver
implements JavaScript through
behaviors. To see what other kinds
of behaviors are available, use the
Window menu to select the
Behaviors panel.

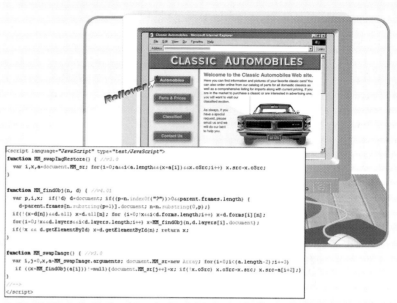

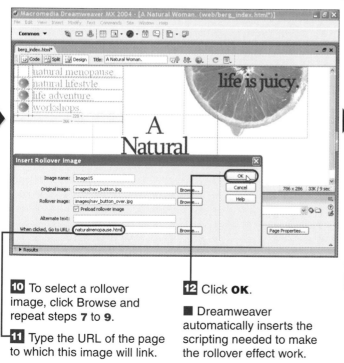

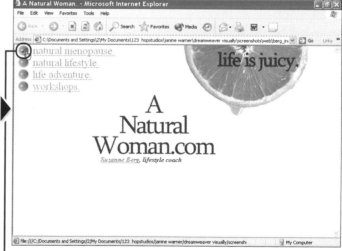

10 To select a rollover
image, click Browse and
repeat steps **7** to **9**.

11 Type the URL of the page
to which this image will link.

12 Click **OK**.

■ Dreamweaver
automatically inserts the
scripting needed to make
the rollover effect work.

■ When the mouse is
placed over the image in the
browser window, the rollover
image displays. When the
mouse is removed, the
original image reappears.

INSERT A NAVIGATION BAR

You can increase the functionality of your Web site with a navigation bar. Unless your site is only one page, your visitors will need to get around somehow, and a navigation bar is the best way to do that.

The Spice Market

Specialty Spices

Recipes

Contact Us

Welcome to *The Spice Market*, the source for spices, seasonings, and herbs.

We choose our spices from the best each country has to offer, in addition to carrying exotic and hard-to-find spices.

It doesn't stop there; we also provide storage tips from the professionals, and recipes that do justice to the quality of spices we carry. Find old favorites here, or experiment with new flavors.

INSERT A NAVIGATION BAR

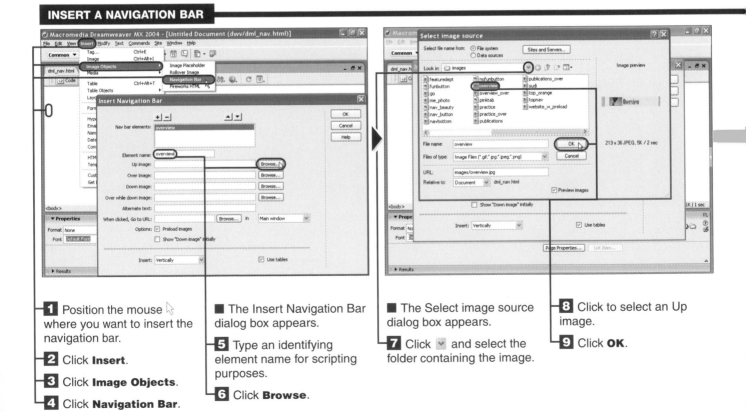

1 Position the mouse where you want to insert the navigation bar.

2 Click **Insert**.

3 Click **Image Objects**.

4 Click **Navigation Bar**.

■ The Insert Navigation Bar dialog box appears.

5 Type an identifying element name for scripting purposes.

6 Click **Browse**.

■ The Select image source dialog box appears.

7 Click ▼ and select the folder containing the image.

8 Click to select an Up image.

9 Click **OK**.

**Are all navigation bars required to appear
on the left of a Web page?**

It is common for Web pages to have left-
hand navigation bars, especially for news
Web sites or stores. Many fine Web sites
use horizontal navigation bars, or even a
right-hand navigation bar. Horizontal
navigations are somewhat limited by the
available space across the browser window,
but they are ideal for small Web sites with
only a few navigation items. Wherever you
decide to put your navigation bar, it is a
good idea for it to appear in the same place
and look the same on every page, so your
visitors will not have to search for it. You can
build a horizontal navigation bar by following
steps **1** to **4**, and then at the bottom of the
Insert Navigation Bar dialog box, click the
Insert ☑ and select **Horizontally**.

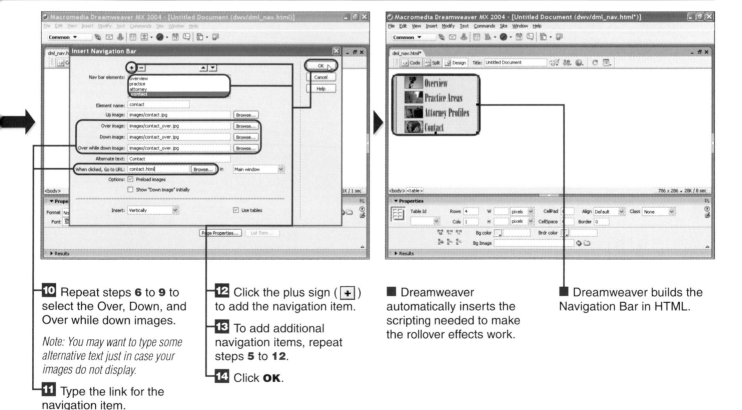

10 Repeat steps **6** to **9** to
select the Over, Down, and
Over while down images.

*Note: You may want to type some
alternative text just in case your
images do not display.*

11 Type the link for the
navigation item.

12 Click the plus sign (＋)
to add the navigation item.

13 To add additional
navigation items, repeat
steps **5** to **12**.

14 Click **OK**.

■ Dreamweaver
automatically inserts the
scripting needed to make
the rollover effects work.

■ Dreamweaver builds the
Navigation Bar in HTML.

THE BEST

Reviews of Golf Courses Here and Abroad

Discover how the professionals rate golf courses in nine countries around the world. Each course has a rating, course schematics, aerial and ground photos, along with the professionals' notes and tips for playing each hole. Historical background and course designers are listed, as well as resorts and hotels in the immediate area. Links to the courses are also included. Leave your own rating after you've played your favorite.

Contact Us
Submit A Rating

Computel 250

CHAPTER 7

Creating Hyperlinks to Connect Information

You can connect related information on different Web pages by creating hyperlinks. This chapter shows you how to turn both text and images into hyperlinks.

Link to Pages in Your Site 108

Link to Another Web Site..................110

Use an Image as a Link....................112

Create a Jump Link Within a Page 114

Create a Link to Another File Type 116

Create an Image Map 118

Create a Link Using the Files Panel....120

Open a Linked Page in a New
Browser Window 121

Create an E-Mail Link 122

Check Links 123

Change the Color of Links on a
Page..124

Submit a Rating

aren't the only ones who know their golf courses; players as well as the weekend golfers have their ns, too. To rate a golf course, fill in the informat

Phone   E-mail

e   Location

ents

LINK TO PAGES IN YOUR SITE

You can create a link
that allows readers to
move from one page of
your Web site to another.

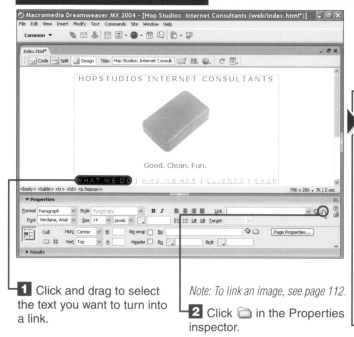

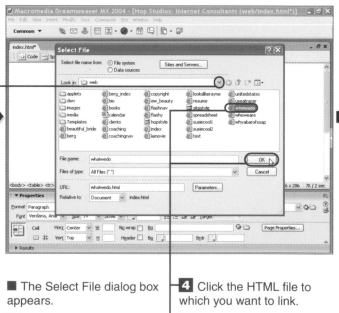

1 Click and drag to select
the text you want to turn into
a link.

Note: To link an image, see page 112.

2 Click 📁 in the Properties
inspector.

■ The Select File dialog box
appears.

3 Click ▾ and select the
folder containing the
destination page.

4 Click the HTML file to
which you want to link.

5 Click **OK**.

How should I organize the files that make up my Web site?

You should keep the files that make up your Web site in the folder that you define as your local site folder. This makes finding pages and images and creating links between your pages easier. It also ensures that all the links work correctly when you transfer the files to a live Web server. Additionally, you should store all your images in a folder called Images. If you have many pages under one section, you should further divide the file structure to include subfolders for the pages in each section of the site. For more on setting up your Web site, see Chapter 2, and for more on transferring files to a Web server, see Chapter 14.

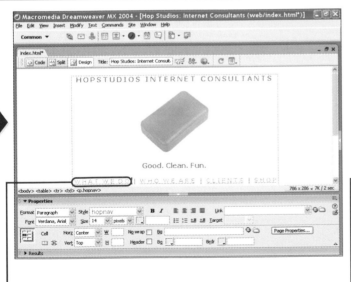

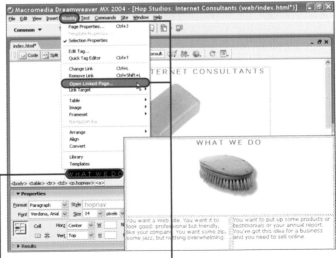

■ The new link appears in color and underlined.

■ Links are not clickable in the Document window.

■ You can test the link by previewing the file in a Web browser.

Note: To preview a Web page in a browser, see page 26.

OPEN AND EDIT A LINKED PAGE

1 Click anywhere on the text of the link whose destination you want to open.

2 Click **Modify**.

3 Click **Open Linked Page**.

■ The link destination opens in a Document window.

LINK TO ANOTHER WEB SITE

You can give viewers access to additional information about topics by linking to pages in other Web sites.

LINK TO ANOTHER WEB SITE

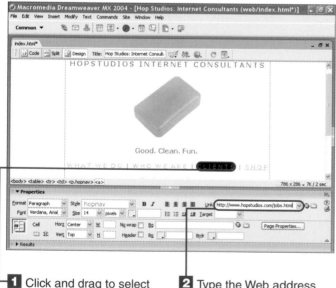

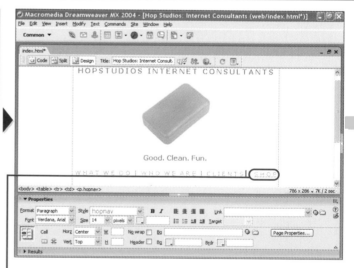

1 Click and drag to select the text you want to turn into a link.

2 Type the Web address of the destination page, including the **http://**, in the Link field in the Properties inspector.

■ The new link appears colored and underlined.

■ Links are not clickable in the Document window.

■ You can test the link by previewing the file in a Web browser.

Note: To preview a Web page in a browser, see page 26.

How do I make sure my links to other Web sites always work?

You usually have no control over the Web pages on other sites to which you have linked. If you have linked to a Web page whose file is later renamed or taken offline, your viewers will receive an error message when they click the link. Maintain your site by periodically checking your links. You can also use software or Web site tune-up services to perform this checking for you. Neither one can bring back a page that no longer exists, but both can tell you what links you need to remove or update.

■ You can click the linked text in the browser to test the link.

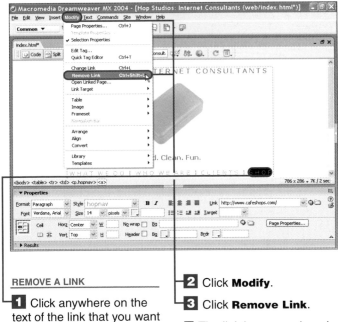

REMOVE A LINK

1 Click anywhere on the text of the link that you want to remove.

2 Click **Modify**.

3 Click **Remove Link**.

■ The link is removed, and the text no longer appears colored and underlined.

USE AN IMAGE AS A LINK

An image link allows users to click an image to go to another Web page. It is very common to build a Web site's navigation by using images as links.

USE AN IMAGE AS A LINK

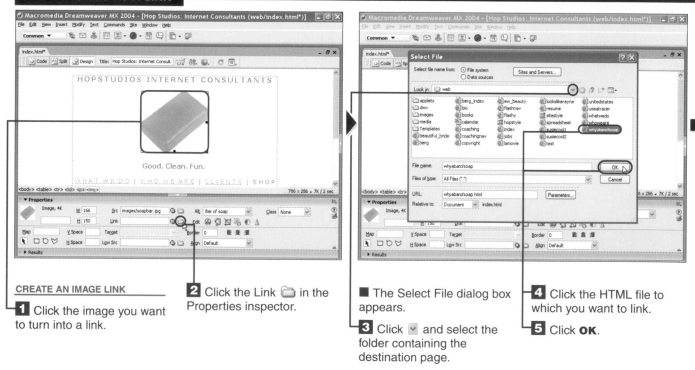

CREATE AN IMAGE LINK

1 Click the image you want to turn into a link.

2 Click the Link in the Properties inspector.

■ The Select File dialog box appears.

3 Click and select the folder containing the destination page.

4 Click the HTML file to which you want to link.

5 Click **OK**.

How do I create a navigation bar for my Web page?

Many Web sites include sets of images that act as link buttons on the top, side, or bottom of each page. These button images let viewers navigate through the pages of the Web site. You can create these button images by using an image-editing program such as Adobe Photoshop or Macromedia Fireworks.

How will visitors to my site know to click an image?

Unlike links, linked images are not a different color or underlined, so it is possible that your visitors will not know an image is a link. Use your layout and context to let visitors know that an image is clickable. When appropriate, you might want to create a text link.

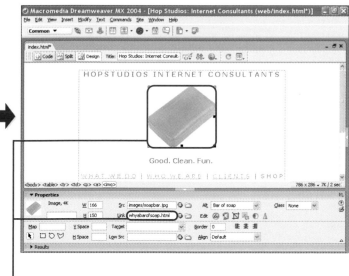

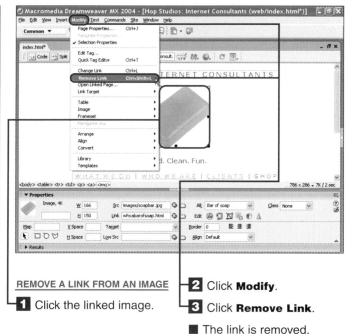

■ Your image is now a link.

■ Links are not clickable in the Document window, but you can test the link by previewing the file in a Web browser.

Note: To preview a Web page in a browser, see page 26.

REMOVE A LINK FROM AN IMAGE

1 Click the linked image.

2 Click **Modify**.

3 Click **Remove Link**.

■ The link is removed.

CREATE A JUMP LINK WITHIN A PAGE

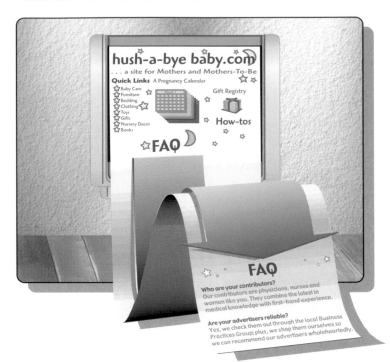

You can create a link to other content on the same page. Same-page links are useful when a page is very long. A common use for this type of link is often seen on a Web site's Frequently Asked Questions (FAQ) page.

CREATE A JUMP LINK WITHIN A PAGE

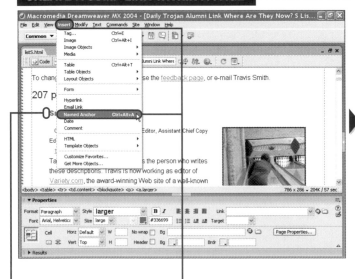

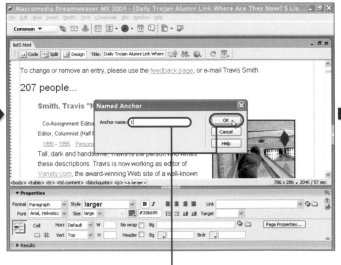

1 Position the mouse where you want to insert the named anchor.

2 Click **Insert**.

3 Click **Named Anchor**.

■ The Named Anchor dialog box appears.

4 Type a name for the anchor.

5 Click **OK**.

What is an example of a useful same-page hyperlink?

Web designers often employ same-page hyperlinks. For example, you frequently see them at the bottom of a page. The Back to Top link brings you to the beginning of the page when you click it. If you have a Web page that is a glossary, same-page links let you link to different parts of the glossary from a link menu at the top of the page. A Frequently Asked Questions (FAQ) page is also a common example of when to use same-page links. You can list all your questions at the top of the page, and link each one to a detailed answer further down on the page.

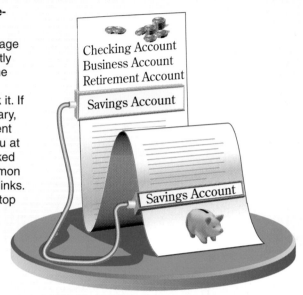

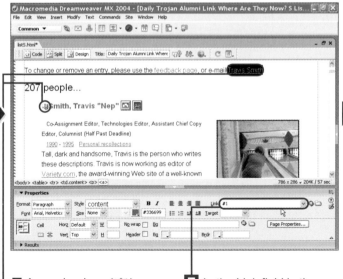

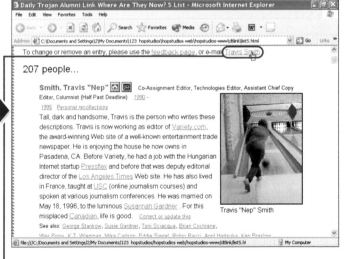

■ An anchor icon (🔖) appears in the Document window.

6 Click and drag to select the text you want to turn into a link.

7 In the Link field in the Properties inspector, type a pound sign (#), followed by the name of the anchor.

■ The selected text is now linked to the named anchor.

■ The new hyperlink is not clickable in the Document window.

■ You can test the link by previewing the file in a Web browser.

Note: To preview a Web page in a browser, see page 26.

CREATE A LINK TO ANOTHER FILE TYPE

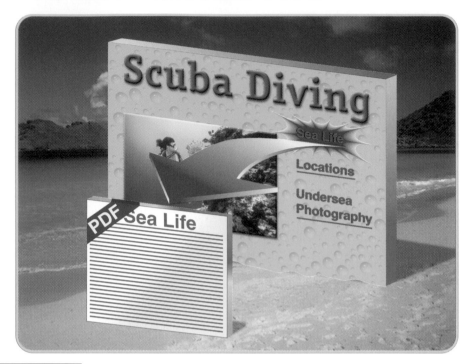

Links do not have to lead just to other Web pages. You can link to other file types, such as image files, word processing documents, PDF files, or multimedia files.

CREATE A LINK TO ANOTHER FILE TYPE

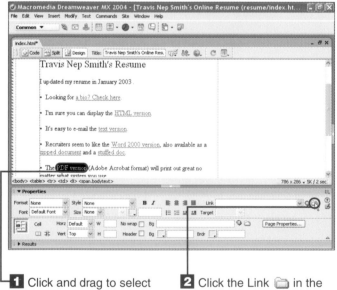

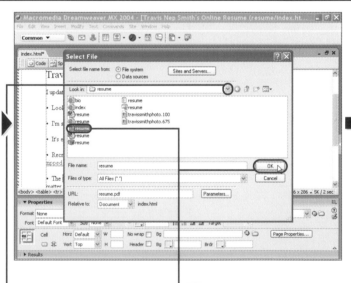

1 Click and drag to select the text you want to turn into a link.

2 Click the Link 📁 in the Properties inspector.

■ The Select File dialog box appears.

3 Click ✓ and select the folder containing the destination file.

4 Click the file to which you want to link.

5 Click **OK**.

How do users see files that are not HTML documents?

What users see when they click links to other types of files depends on how their Web browser is configured and what applications they have installed on their computer. For instance, if they link to a QuickTime movie (`.mov`), users need to have QuickTime software installed on their computer to see the movie. If a user does not have the software installed, the browser typically asks if the user wants to download the file and save it so they can view it later — after they have installed the correct software.

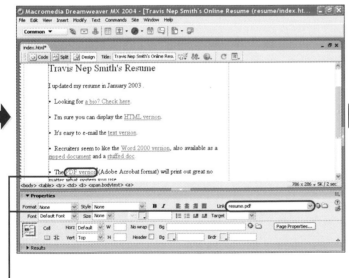

■ The new link appears in color and underlined.

■ Links are not clickable in the Document window.

■ You can test the link by previewing the file in a Web browser.

Note: To preview a Web page in a browser, see page 26.

■ When you click the link in the browser, the linked file opens.

■ In this example, the linked PDF appears in the browser window when the link is clicked.

To make a single image link to several different pages, you can assign different links called hotspots to different parts of the image by using Dreamweaver's image-mapping tools.

CREATE AN IMAGE MAP

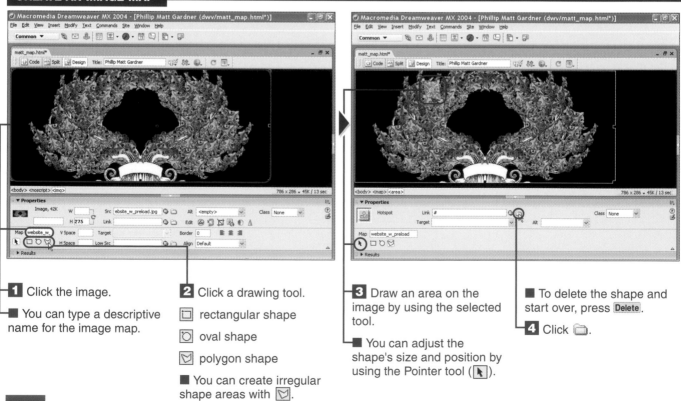

1 Click the image.

■ You can type a descriptive name for the image map.

2 Click a drawing tool.

▭ rectangular shape

◯ oval shape

▽ polygon shape

■ You can create irregular shape areas with ▽.

3 Draw an area on the image by using the selected tool.

■ You can adjust the shape's size and position by using the Pointer tool (▶).

■ To delete the shape and start over, press Delete.

4 Click ▢.

How can I create an interactive map of the United States with each state having a different link?

An interactive map is a common place to see hotspots in action. You can create one by adding a map of the U.S. to your Web page and defining a hotspot over each state. Use the Polygon tool (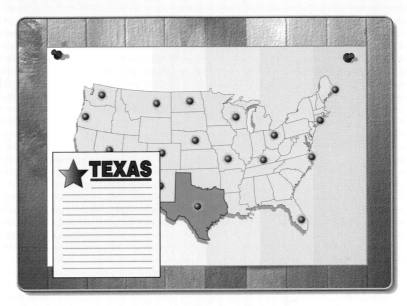) to draw around the states. Finally, assign a different link to each state. You can also use an image map to make different parts of a single navigation image link to pages on your Web site.

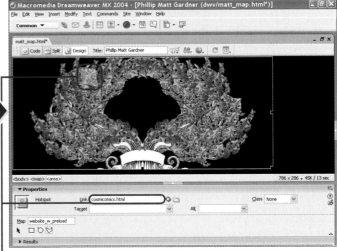

■ The Select File dialog box appears.

5 Click ⌄ and select the folder containing the destination file.

6 Click the file to which you want to link.

7 Click **OK**.

■ The area defined by the shape becomes a link to the selected file. In this example, the leaves of a tree link to a page called cosmicomics.html.

■ You can repeat steps **3** to **8** to add other linked areas to your image.

■ The image-map shapes will not appear when you open the page in a Web browser.

Note: You should avoid overlapping hotspots. The results are unpredictable across browsers.

CREATE A LINK USING THE FILES PANEL

You can create links
quickly and easily by
clicking and dragging to
the Site panel.

CREATE A LINK USING THE FILES PANEL

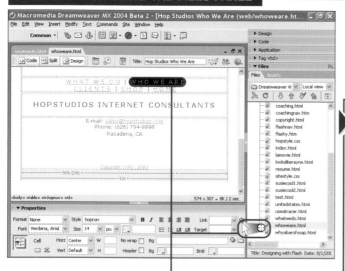

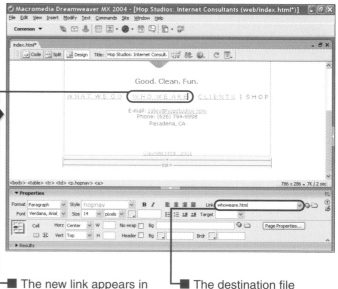

*Note: Arrange your workspace
making sure that both the Document
window and Files panel are visible
for this task.*

1 Click and drag to select
the text you want to turn into
a link.

2 Click and drag the Point
to File icon (⊕) to the
destination file in the Site
panel (◇ changes to ⊕).

■ The new link appears in
color and underlined.

■ The destination file
displays in the Link field in
the Properties inspector.

OPEN A LINKED PAGE IN A NEW BROWSER WINDOW

You can create a
link that opens a new
browser window when
clicked. The destination
page opens in the new
window.

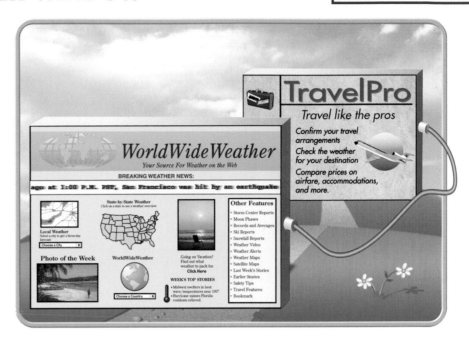

Opening a new window lets
you keep a previous Web
page open on a viewer's
computer.

OPEN A LINKED PAGE IN A NEW BROWSER WINDOW

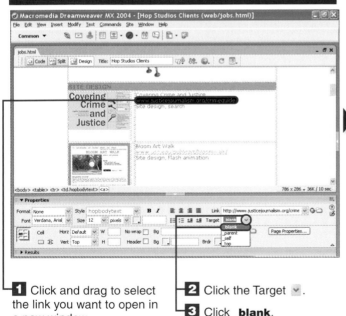

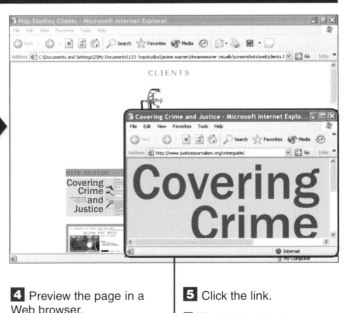

1 Click and drag to select
the link you want to open in
a new window.

2 Click the Target ▾.

3 Click **_blank**.

4 Preview the page in a
Web browser.

*Note: To preview a Web page in a
browser, see page 26.*

5 Click the link.

■ The link destination
appears in a new window.

CREATE AN E-MAIL LINK

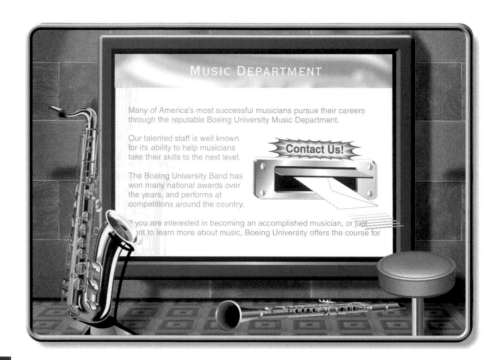

You can create a link that launches an e-mail composition window.

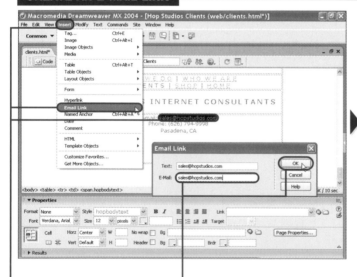

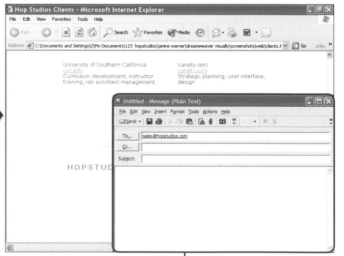

1 Click to select the text or image you what to turn into an e-mail link.

2 Click **Insert**.

3 Click **Email Link**.

■ The selected text appears in the Text field of the Insert Email Link dialog box.

4 Type the e-mail address to which you want to link.

5 Click **OK**.

■ You can also insert an e-mail link by clicking in the Link field in the Properties inspector and typing **mailto:** followed by the e-mail address.

6 To test the link, preview the page in a Web browser.

■ In Web browsers that support e-mail, clicking the link launches your default e-mail program.

■ If the browser does not have e-mail capability setup, the browser will let the user set up an e-mail client.

CHECK LINKS

You can automatically verify a Web page's links and get a report that lists any that are broken.

Deleting or renaming a link breaks the connection between Web page files.

CHECK LINKS

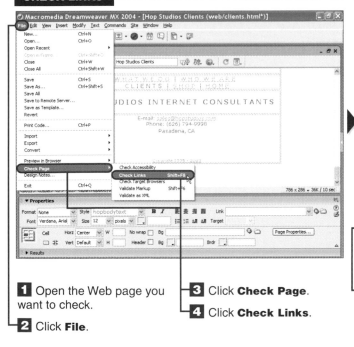

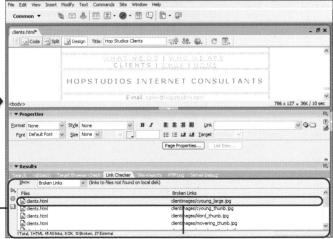

1 Open the Web page you want to check.

2 Click **File**.

3 Click **Check Page**.

4 Click **Check Links**.

■ Dreamweaver checks the local links and lists any broken links it finds.

Note: Dreamweaver is unable to verify links to Web pages on external sites.

■ You can edit a broken destination or image file by selecting it and editing the Broken Links field.

■ You can also double-click the page to open it and jump to the broken link.

CHANGE THE COLOR OF LINKS ON A PAGE

You can change the color of the links on your Web page to make them match the visual style of the text and images on your page.

Web Sites You Can Visit!

1. Suit the lure to the catch
2. Fishing Vacations
3. Fishing Shops in Your Area
4. Seasonal Calendar
5. Breed of the Month

Link
Visited link
Active link

CHANGE THE COLOR OF LINKS ON A PAGE

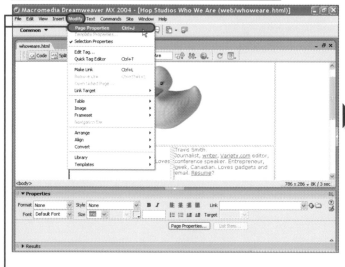

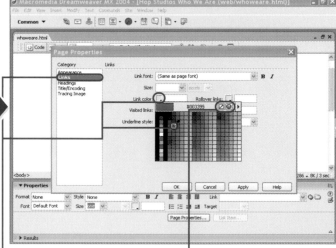

1 Click **Modify**.

2 Click **Page Properties**.

■ The Page Properties dialog box appears.

3 Click **Links**.

4 Click the Link color (▨) (☐ changes to ✐).

5 Click a color from the menu using the Eyedropper tool (✐).

■ You can click the System Color Picker button (⬤) to select a custom color, or the Default Color button (▨) to specify no color.

■ The color menu closes.

What color will my links be if I do not choose colors for them?

Blue is the default link color in the Dreamweaver Document window. What viewers see when the page opens in a browser depends on the browser settings. By default, most browsers display unvisited links as blue, visited links as purple, and active links as red.

How can I override the link colors I set?

Sometimes you may need to change the color of a linked word to something other than the set link color of a page — perhaps in a sub-navigation item. Select the text and use the Font to select a color. Once changed, the text will always appear in that color, even after it is visited.

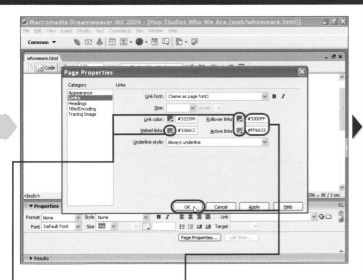

6 Click and select the colors for Visited Links, Rollover Links, and Active Links.

■ This example defines the links with a hex number, but you can specify common colors on your Web page with their names, for example red or blue, instead of choosing the colors from the color menu.

Note: To change the color of links, see page 73.

7 Click **OK**.

8 Preview the page in a Web browser.

Note: To preview a Web page in a browser, see page 26.

■ The links display in the specified colors.

DESSERTS

Chocolate chip cookies, made fresh daily in our kitchen. Served warm alone or with ice cream.		3 for $2.00 A dozen for $6.00
Chocolate mousse in three varieties – dark chocolate, cafe au lait, and creamy chocolate.		$3.65
Homemade ice cream in French Vanilla, Fresh Strawberry, Dark Chocolate, and Chocolate Chip.		$2.25
Fruit pies made in our kitchen. Peach, Apple, Strawberry, Raspberry, and Three Berry.		$2.75
Whole pies are available for takeout. Order in advance for warm pies made to order.		$15.00

CHAPTER 8

Using Tables to Design a Web Page

Tables enable you to arrange text, images, and other elements on your pages and create complex designs, even within the constraints of HTML. This chapter shows you how to create and format tables.

Insert a Table into a Web Page 128

Insert Content into a Table 130

Change the Background of a Table 132

Change the Cell Padding in a
    Table 134

Change the Cell Spacing in a
    Table 135

Change the Alignment of a Table 136

Change the Alignment of Cell
    Content 137

Insert or Delete a Row or Column 138

Split or Merge Table Cells 140

Change the Dimensions of a Cell 142

Change the Dimensions of a Table 143

Create a Layout Table 144

Rearrange a Table 146

Adjust the Width of a Table 148

INSERT A TABLE INTO A WEB PAGE

Softball Standings

Team	Games	Wins	Losses	Ties	Points
The Chargers	10	9	1	0	18
Sluggers	10	8	1	1	17
The Champs	10	7	2	1	15
The Eagles	10	5	5	0	10
Barry's Battalion	10	3	7	0	6
The Professionals	10	2	8	0	4
Baseball Bombers	10	1	9	0	2

You can use tables to organize and design pages with financial data, text, images, multimedia, and more. Use Dreamweaver's layout features to create simple tables or complex designs.

INSERT A TABLE INTO A WEB PAGE

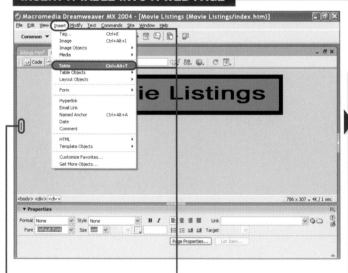

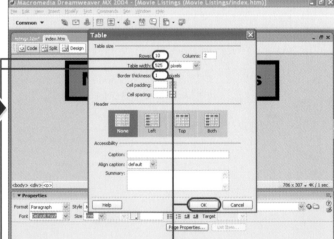

1 Position the mouse where you want to insert the table.

Note: The cursor will snap to the left margin by default, but you can insert tables between existing elements on a page, such as between two images or after a block of text.

2 Click **Insert**.

3 Click **Table**.

■ The Insert Table dialog box appears.

4 Type the number of rows and columns in your table.

5 Type the width of your table.

■ You can set the width in pixels or as a percentage of the page by clicking ⌄ and selecting your choice of measurements.

6 Type a border size in pixels.

7 Click **OK**.

How do I change the appearance of the content inside my table?

You can specify the size, style, and color of text inside a table the same way you format text in a Web page. Likewise, you control the appearance of an image inside a table the same way you control it outside a table. For more on formatting text, see Chapter 5, and for more on images, see Chapter 6.

Why would I turn off table borders?

Table borders can help define the edges of a table and organize columnar data, such as a financial report. But, if you want to use a table to arrange photos and text within the design of your table, you should usually set the border to zero so it becomes invisible. Dreamweaver assumes that is what you will want to do, so when you create a table the border is set to zero unless you specify a number. Set it to one pixel for a slim border, or try five or ten if you want a thick border.

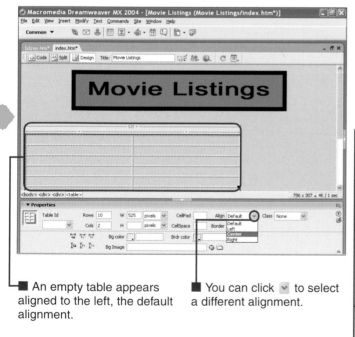

■ An empty table appears aligned to the left, the default alignment.

■ You can click 🔽 to select a different alignment.

TURN OFF TABLE BORDERS

1 Click the upper-left corner of the table to select the entire table border.

2 Type the number **0** in the Border field.

3 Press [Enter] ([Return]).

■ When you view the page in a Web browser, the dashed table border disappears.

INSERT CONTENT INTO A TABLE

You can fill the cells of
your table with anything
that you can insert on a
Web page, including text,
images, multimedia files,
form elements, and other
tables.

INSERT CONTENT INTO A TABLE

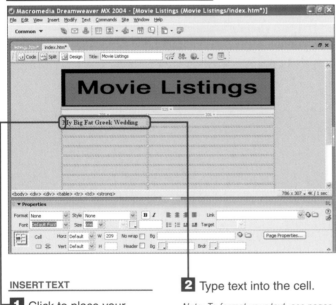

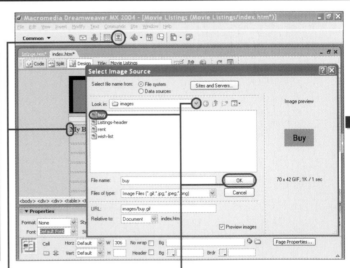

INSERT TEXT

1 Click to place your
mouse inside a table cell.

2 Type text into the cell.

*Note: To format your text, see pages
70 to 75.*

INSERT AN IMAGE

1 Click inside a table cell.

2 Click the Image button
( ) to open the Select
Image Source dialog box.

3 Click and select the
folder containing your image.

4 Click an image file.

5 Click **OK**.

How can I add captions to images on my Web page?

The best way to add a caption to the top, bottom, or side of an image is by creating a two-celled table. Place the image in one cell and the caption in the other cell. You can then adjust the table's size and alignment to position the captioned image with the rest of your page's content.

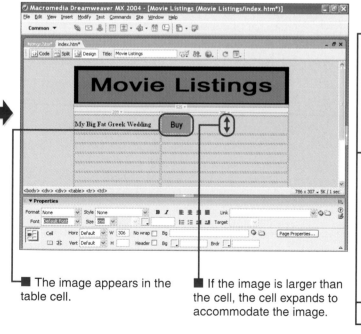

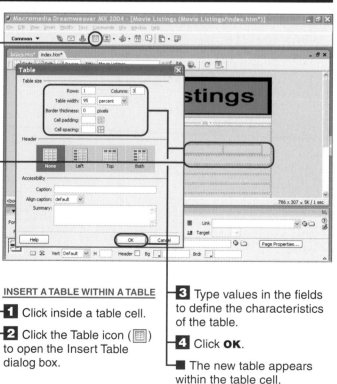

■ The image appears in the table cell.

■ If the image is larger than the cell, the cell expands to accommodate the image.

INSERT A TABLE WITHIN A TABLE

1 Click inside a table cell.

2 Click the Table icon (▦) to open the Insert Table dialog box.

3 Type values in the fields to define the characteristics of the table.

4 Click **OK**.

■ The new table appears within the table cell.

CHANGE THE BACKGROUND OF A TABLE

You can change the background of a table, cell, row, or column to add a design element or call attention to a section of a table. Just like a Web page's background, you can change a table's background color or fill the table's background with an image. For more on Web page backgrounds, see page 73.

CHANGE THE BACKGROUND OF A TABLE

1 Click to select a table or individual cell, or click and drag to select a row of cells.

2 Click the Bg Color to open the color swatch (changes to).

3 Click a color.

■ You can click the System Color Picker button ( ) to select a custom color.

■ You can click the Default Color button ( ) to specify no color.

■ The color fills the background of the table.

■ You can also type a color name or a color code directly.

Note: To change the font color of a Web page, see page 73.

How can I change the background of a table cell?

Click inside a cell and then specify the background color using the Bg Color ☐ or a background image by clicking ☐. You can give each cell a different background or format to create an appearance of a solid area with elements floating over the cell.

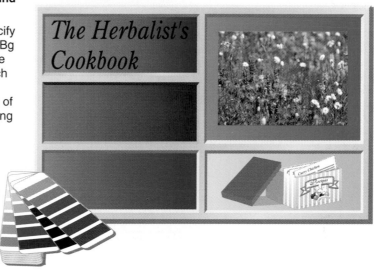

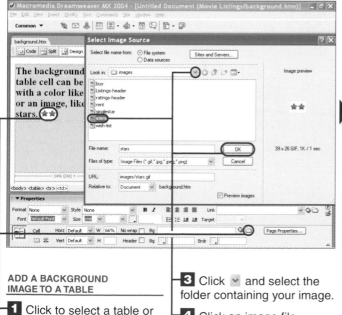

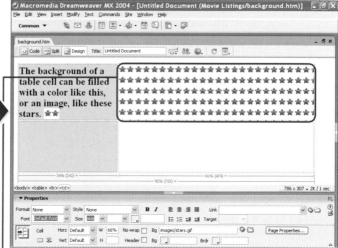

ADD A BACKGROUND IMAGE TO A TABLE

1 Click to select a table or individual cell, or click and drag to select a row of cells.

2 Click ☐ in the Properties inspector to open the Select Image Source dialog box.

3 Click ☑ and select the folder containing your image.

4 Click an image file.

5 Click **OK**.

■ The table or cell background fills with the image.

■ If space in the cell allows, the image tiles to fill the available area.

CHANGE THE CELL PADDING IN A TABLE

You can change the cell padding to add space between a table's content and its borders.

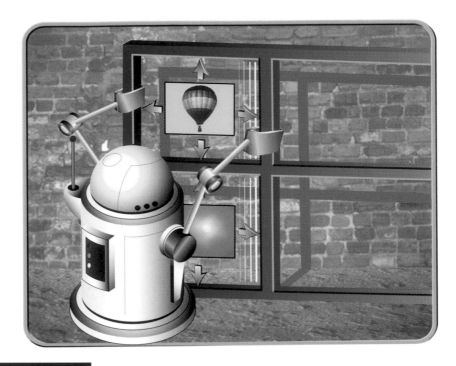

CHANGE THE CELL PADDING IN A TABLE

1 Click the upper-left corner of the table to select it.

2 In the CellPad field, type the amount of padding in pixels.

3 Press `Enter` (`Return`).

■ The space between the table content and the table borders adjusts.

Note: Adjusting the cell padding affects all the cells in a table. You cannot adjust the padding of individual cells by using the CellPad field.

You can change the cell spacing to adjust the thickness of your table borders.

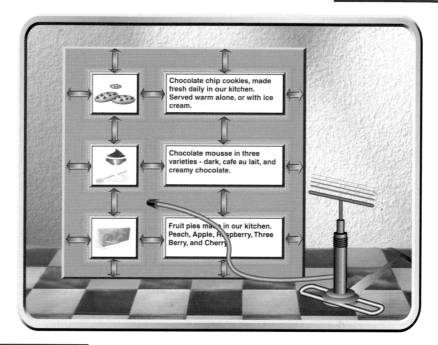

CHANGE THE CELL SPACING IN A TABLE

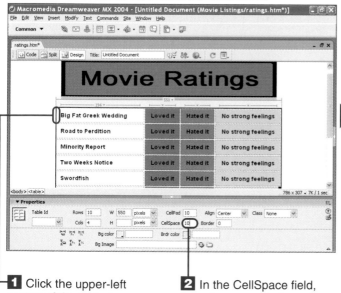

1 Click the upper-left corner of the table to select it.

2 In the CellSpace field, type the amount of spacing in pixels.

■ The width of the table's cell borders adjusts.

Note: Adjusting the cell spacing affects all the cell borders in the table. You cannot adjust the spacing of individual cell borders by using the CellSpace field.

CHANGE THE ALIGNMENT OF A TABLE

You can change the
alignment of a table
and wrap text and
other content
around it.

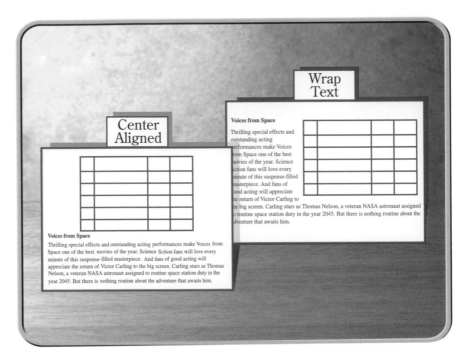

CHANGE THE ALIGNMENT OF A TABLE

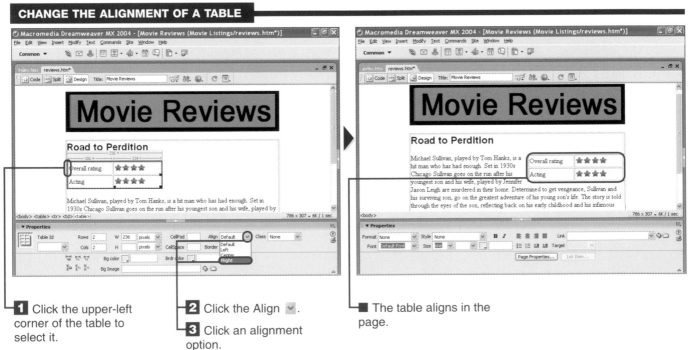

1 Click the upper-left
corner of the table to
select it.

2 Click the Align.

3 Click an alignment
option.

■ The table aligns in the
page.

You can align the
content in your table
cells horizontally and
vertically.

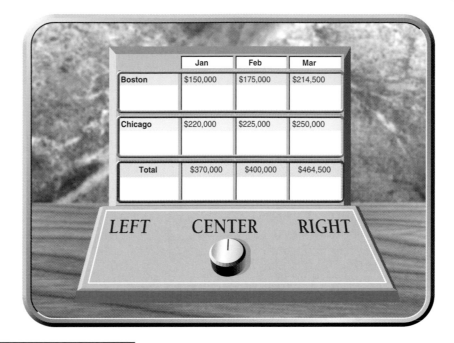

CHANGE THE ALIGNMENT OF CELL CONTENT

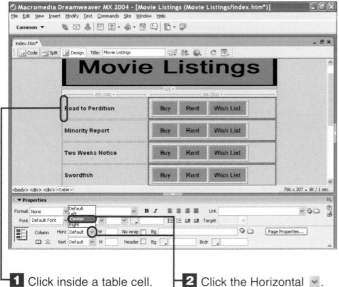

1 Click inside a table cell.

■ You can press Shift +click, or click and drag, to select multiple cells.

2 Click the Horizontal ⌄.

3 Click a horizontal alignment.

■ The content aligns.

Note: In this example, horizontal alignment was set to center for four cells simultaneously.

INSERT OR DELETE A ROW OR COLUMN

You can insert cells into your table to add content or create space between elements, and delete rows or columns to remove them.

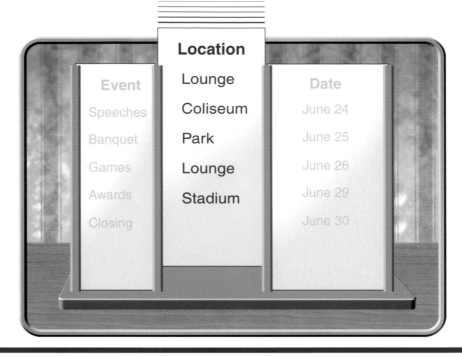

Event	Location Lounge	Date
Speeches	Coliseum	June 24
Banquet	Park	June 25
Games	Lounge	June 26
Awards	Stadium	June 29
Closing		June 30

INSERT A ROW OR COLUMN

1 Click the upper-left corner of the table to select it.

2 Type the number of rows and columns you want in the Properties inspector.

3 Press **Enter** (**Return**).

■ Empty rows or columns appear in the table.

■ To add a row or column in the middle of a table, right-click inside an existing cell and click **Table** and then **Insert Row or Column** from the menu that appears. You can also click **Modify**, **Table**, and then **Insert Row or Column**.

What happens to the content of a deleted cell?

Dreamweaver does not warn you if the cells you are deleting in a table contain content. It assumes you want to delete it, so it deletes it as well. If you accidentally remove content when deleting rows or columns, you can click **Edit** and then **Undo** to undo your last action.

How do I move content around a table?

You can move the contents of a table cell by clicking to select any image, text, or element in the cell and then dragging it out of the table or into another cell. You can also use copy and paste to move content from one cell to another or to another part of a page.

DELETE A ROW OR COLUMN

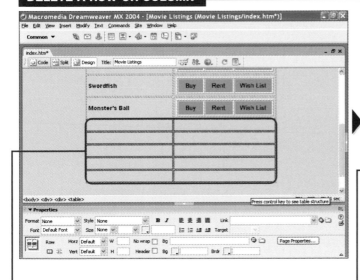

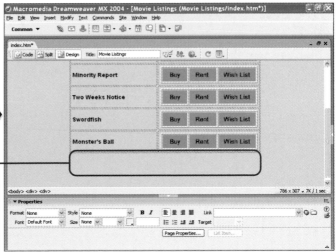

1 Press Shift +click, or click and drag, to select the cells you want to delete.

2 Press Delete.

■ The deleted table cells disappear.

Note: The content of a cell is erased when a cell is deleted.

■ You can also delete cells by right-clicking inside the cell, and click **Table** and then **Delete Row** or **Delete Column** from the menu that appears. You can also click **Modify**, **Table**, and then **Delete Row** or **Delete Column**.

SPLIT OR MERGE TABLE CELLS

You can create a more
elaborate arrangement
of cells in a table by
splitting or merging
its cells.

SPLIT A TABLE CELL

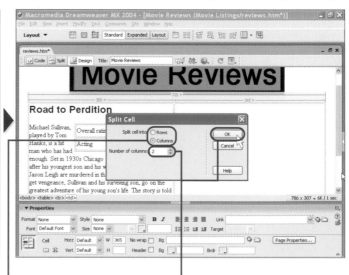

1 Click and drag to select
the cells that you want to
split.

2 Click **Modify**.

3 Click **Table**.

4 Click **Split Cell**.

■ You can also split a cell by
clicking the Split Cell button
(⊞) in the Properties
inspector.

■ The Split Cell dialog box
appears.

5 Click **Rows** or **Columns**
(○ changes to ◉) to split
the cell.

6 Type the number of rows
or columns.

7 Click **OK**.

■ The table cell splits.

Can I merge any combination of table cells?

No. The cells must have a rectangular arrangement. For example, you can merge all the cells in a two-row-by-two-column table. However, you cannot select three cells that form an *L* shape and merge them into one.

MERGE TABLE CELLS

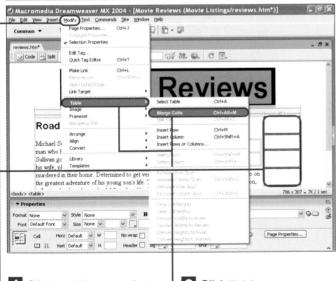

1 Click and drag to select the cells you want to merge.

2 Click **Modify**.

3 Click **Table**.

4 Click **Merge Cells**.

■ You can also merge cells by clicking the Merge Cells button (▫) in the Properties inspector.

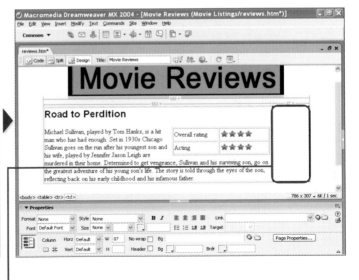

■ The table cells merge.

CHANGE THE DIMENSIONS OF A CELL

You can change the dimensions of individual table cells to organize the content in your table.

CHANGE THE DIMENSIONS OF A CELL

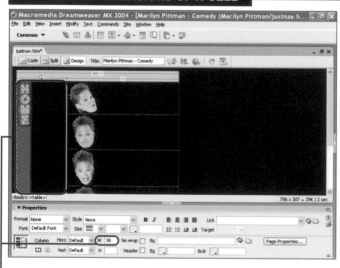

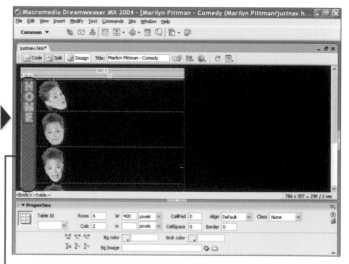

1 Click to select the cell, or click and drag to select the cells, you want to change.

2 Type the new width in pixels.

■ You can also specify a percentage of the table size instead of specifying pixels. For example, type **38** percent in the width or height box.

3 Press `Enter` (`Return`).

■ The cell readjusts to its new dimensions as well as to the cells next to the selection.

Note: Cell dimensions may be constrained by content. Dreamweaver cannot shrink a cell smaller than the size of the content it contains.

You can change the
dimensions of your
table to fit into your
Web page.

CHANGE THE DIMENSIONS OF A TABLE

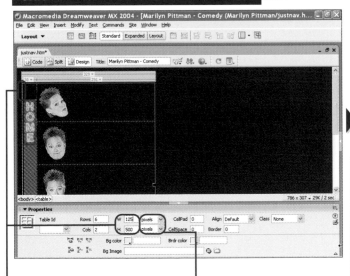

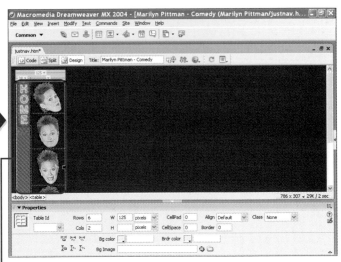

1 Click the upper-left
corner of a table to select it.

2 Type a width and height.

3 Click ⌄ and select the
width setting in pixels or a
percentage of the screen.

4 Press **Enter** (**Return**).

■ The table readjusts to its
new dimensions.

*Note: Table dimensions may
be constrained by content.
Dreamweaver cannot shrink a
table smaller than the size of the
content it contains.*

*Note: If a height or width is not
specified, the table automatically
adjusts to fit the space available on
the user's screen.*

CREATE A LAYOUT TABLE

You can create tables to better control the layout of a Web page. Tables used for layout are typically designed to fill the entire display area, and the borders are turned off so that the table itself is not visible.

CREATE A LAYOUT TABLE

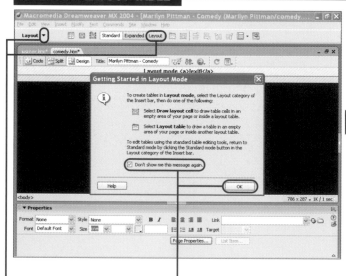

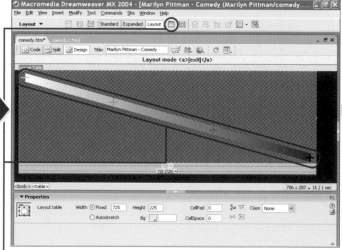

1 Click ▼ and select **Layout** from the Insert bar.

■ The Layout options appear in the Insert bar.

2 Click the **Layout** button.

■ The Getting Started in Layout View help dialog box appears.

■ You can click this option to prevent this help dialog box from appearing again (☐ changes to ☑).

3 Click **OK**.

4 Click the Layout Table button (▣) (↖ changes to ✛).

5 Click and drag the mouse ✛ to create a table.

■ The outline of a table appears.

■ You can adjust the exact size in the Properties inspector.

What can I do to help me draw my layout table cells precisely?

Click the **Layout** button on the Insert Layout bar. In Layout View, you can draw table cells anywhere on the page by clicking and dragging. Dreamweaver creates a complex table in the background with spacers to control the exact positioning of elements in your page design.

Click Drag

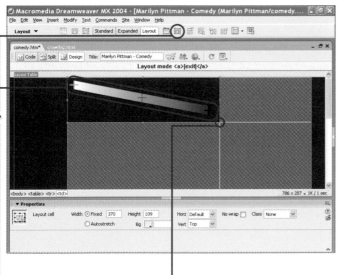

6 Click the Layout Cell button (▣) (◌ changes to +).

7 Click and drag inside the table to create a Layout Cell.

■ The attributes of the cell appear in the Properties inspector.

■ You can adjust the size and position of a cell by clicking and dragging its edge or by clicking the center of the border where the dots appear.

8 Click to position your mouse ◌ in the cell where you want to add content.

Note: To insert content, see page 130.

■ You can select the **Common** option in the Insert bar to access the Insert Image (▣) and other buttons.

Note: You can insert content in Layout View the same way as you do in Standard View, but it is easier to tab around a table in Standard View.

145

REARRANGE A TABLE

You can easily change
the size of a table's cells
in Layout or Standard
View, but for moving
cells around, Standard
View is a better option.

REARRANGE A TABLE

**CHANGE THE SIZE OF
A TABLE OR A CELL**

1 Click the edge of the
table or an individual cell
(changes to ↗).

2 Click and drag a side or
corner handle to the desired
size.

■ The table or cell resizes.

■ You cannot overlap other
cells in a table.

How do I delete a table or cell in Layout View?

Click the edge of the cell and then press `Delete`. Dreamweaver will replace the space with gray, non-editable cells. Similarly, you can delete a layout table by clicking the table's top tab and pressing `Delete`.

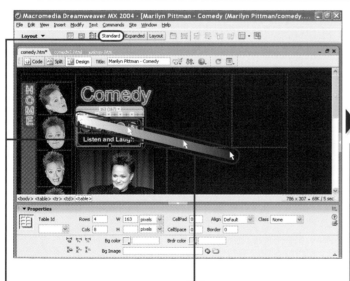

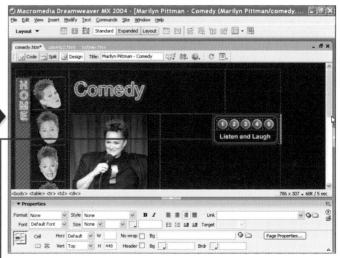

MOVE A CELL OR TABLE

1 Click the Standard button in the Layout bar to change to Standard layout view.

2 Click to select a cell or table.

3 Click and drag the cell or table to the desired location.

Note: Do not click and drag a handle.

■ The cursor changes to ⊘ when you drag over other layout cells, because cells cannot overlap.

■ The cell or table appears in the new location.

■ Undefined cells in the table adjust their sizes to make room for the cell's new position.

ADJUST THE WIDTH OF A TABLE

By using fixed and default settings, you can create a table that adjusts to fit a viewer's browser size automatically.

‹100 pixels›   ‹Autostretch›

You can define the table columns as fixed-width or as autostretch, which fills the remaining space available.

ADJUST THE WIDTH OF A TABLE

CREATE A FIXED-WIDTH COLUMN

1 Click the Layout button in the Layout bar to change to Layout view.

2 Click the small arrow above a column heading.

3 Click **Add Spacer Image** from the menu that appears.

■ If your site lacks a spacer image file that it can reference, a dialog box will appear asking if you want to create one. Click **OK**.

■ The spacer image is added to hold a fixed space in the table cell.

■ The filename of the spacer image displays in the Properties inspector. You can adjust the height and width of the spacer image to adjust spacing.

What is a spacer image?

A *spacer image* is a transparent GIF image file that is used as a *filler* to invisibly control spacing on a Web page. Essentially, you insert a spacer image into a table cell and then use the height and width attributes to control the size. The effect is that the invisible image ensures that blank spaces on your page remain consistent. This is important because browsers will sometimes display elements closer together if there is no text or image to prevent tightening up the design.

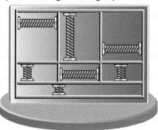

How do I make a spacer image?

You can create a *spacer image* in an image-editing program, such as Photoshop. Create a new image and set the background color to transparent. Save it as a GIF file in your Web site folder. An ideal size for a spacer image is 10 x 10 pixels; however, it can be any size. Remember you can resize it in Dreamweaver to fit the space you want to fill.

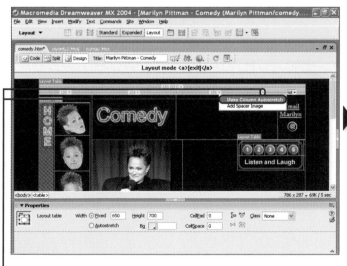

CREATE AN AUTOSTRETCH COLUMN

1 Click a column heading.

2 Click **Make Column Autostretch** from the menu that appears.

■ Dreamweaver automatically specifies a size that takes up any available space in the cell.

3 Preview the page in a Web browser.

Note: To preview a Web page in a browser, see page 26.

■ To see the autostretch effects, resize the browser window.

■ You can also resize a browser by clicking and dragging a corner of the window.

Calligraphica

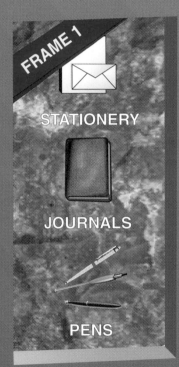

STATIONERY

JOURNALS

PENS

Italian Leather-Bound Journals

Shagreen Explorer's Journal

Maybe you'll use it to record that once-in-a-lifetime adventure . . . a honeymoon cruise . . . an anniversary trip to exotic places.

Whatever you decide to place within its rich, green covers, this journal will preserve your memories for generations to come. What adventures will *you* leave them?

Handcrafted journal of shagreen, filled with 180 pages of cream, 60 lb. cotton paper. Marbled end papers.
PRICE $129.00

Qty	Gift Wrap	Personalization

Add to Shopping Cart

CHAPTER 9

Creating Frames

You can divide the site window into multiple panes by creating frames. This chapter shows you how to organize information on your pages and create links to Frames.

Introduction to Frames......................152

Insert a Predefined Frameset 153

Save a Frameset............................154

Divide a Page into Frames 156

Create a Nested Frame....................157

Change the Attributes of a Frame......158

Add Content to a Frame 160

Delete a Frame 162

Name a Frame 163

Create a Link to a Frame.................164

Format Frame Borders.....................166

Control Scroll Bars in Frames............168

Control Resizing in Frames 169

INTRODUCTION TO FRAMES

Frames enable you to divide your Web page into multiple windows and display different content in each frame.

You can place a list of navigation links in one frame of your site, and have the links open their destination pages in a larger content frame.

Set Up a Frame

You can create a framed Web site in Dreamweaver by dividing the Document window horizontally or vertically one or more times. Each window is composed of an independent Web page that you can link independently. All pages in a frameset are described in a *frameset page* and must be saved separately.

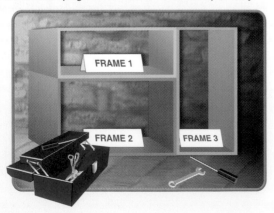

How Frames Work

Frames on a page operate independently of one another. As you scroll through the content of one frame, the content of the other frames remains fixed. You can create links in one frame that open in another frame.

You can easily
create popular
frame styles using
the predefined
framesets available
from the Frames
tab in the Insert
panel.

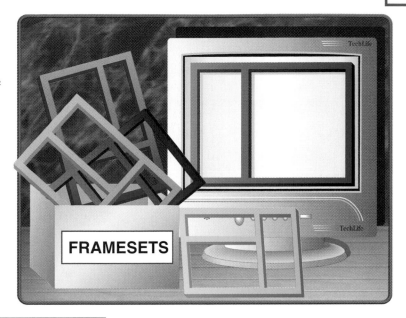

If you do not want to use
one of Dreamweaver's
framesets, you can divide
the window manually. To
divide a page into frames,
see page 156.

INSERT A PREDEFINED FRAMESET

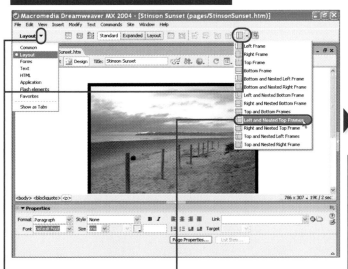

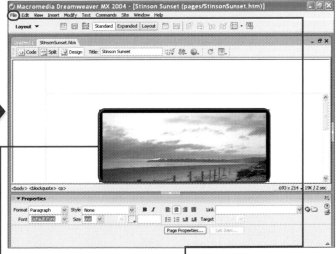

1 Click ▼ and select the
Layout bar.

■ The Insert bar changes to
reveal the Layout options.

2 Click ▼ and select a
Frame option.

3 Click the frame design
that best suits your project.

■ In this example, ▤ is
chosen.

■ Dreamweaver applies the
frames to your page.

■ If content existed in the
original page, it shifts to one
of the new frames.

■ Scroll bars appear if the
content extends outside the
frame borders.

■ You can also create a
frameset by clicking **File**
and then **New**. In the New
Document dialog box, click
the category **Frameset**,
click a predefined frameset,
and then click **Create**.

*Note: To add text, images, or other
elements to a frame, see page 160.*

SAVE A FRAMESET

Saving your Frameset requires you to save the individual pages that appear in the frames as well as the frameset that defines how each frame will appear.

You need to save all the individual documents before you can preview your work in a browser or upload your site.

SAVE A FRAMED SITE

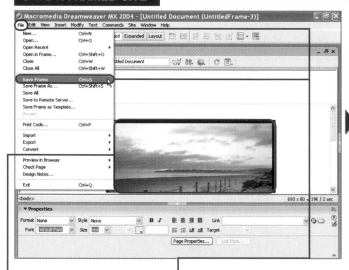

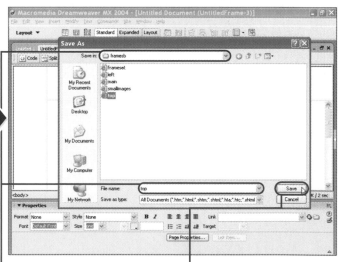

SAVE YOUR FRAMED PAGES

1 Click inside the frame you want to save.

2 Click **File**.

3 Click **Save Frame**.

Note: The Save Frame appears gray if the current frame is already saved.

■ The Save As dialog box appears.

4 Click ⌄ and select the folder where you want to save the framed page.

5 Type a name for the page.

6 Click **Save**.

■ Dreamweaver saves the page.

■ Repeat steps **1** to **6** to save other framed pages.

■ Save each page with a different filename.

Is there a shortcut for saving all the pages of my framed site?

Yes. You can click **File** and then **Save Frameset**. This will save all the framed pages and framesets that make up your site. This is definitely a time saver, but note what you have named each frame. Otherwise, it can be tricky to identify them later.

What steps do I take if I want to change just one frame?

You can open any existing page into a frame area. Place your mouse ☐ in the frame you want to change and click **File** and then **Open** to open an existing page, or click **File** and then **New** to create a new page in the designated frame area.

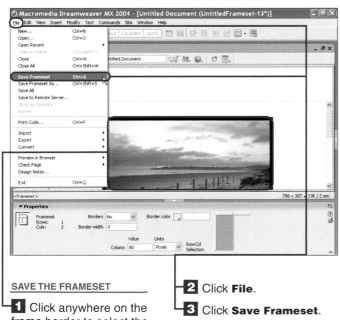

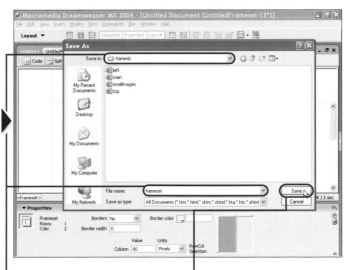

SAVE THE FRAMESET

1 Click anywhere on the frame border to select the entire frameset.

2 Click **File**.

3 Click **Save Frameset**.

■ The Save As dialog box appears.

4 Click ☐ and select the folder where you want to save the frames.

5 Type a name for the page.

6 Click **Save**.

■ Dreamweaver saves the frameset.

■ You can click **Save Frameset** or **Save All** in the File menu to save all the files in a frameset.

DIVIDE A PAGE INTO FRAMES

You can split a Document window vertically to create a frameset with left and right frames, or split it horizontally to create a frameset with top and bottom frames.

You can also choose a predefined frameset for your site. To insert a predefined frameset, see page 153.

DIVIDE A PAGE INTO FRAMES

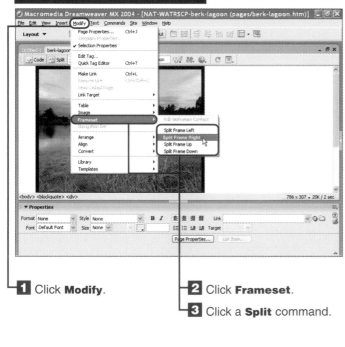

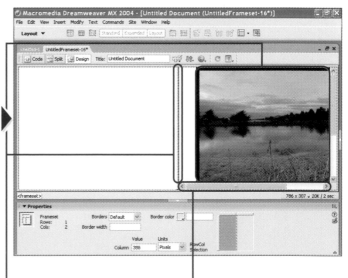

1 Click **Modify**.

2 Click **Frameset**.

3 Click a **Split** command.

■ The window splits into two frames.

■ If content existed in the original page, it shifts to one of the new frames.

■ Scroll bars appear if the content extends outside the frame borders.

Note: To add text, images, or other elements to a new frame, see page 160.

You can subdivide a frame of an existing frameset to create nested frames. With nested frames, you can organize the information in your site in a more complex way.

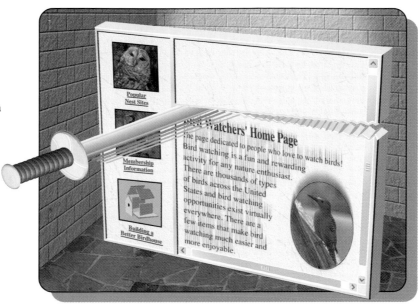

CREATE A NESTED FRAME

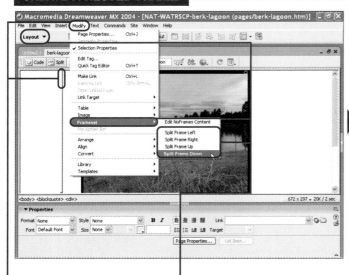

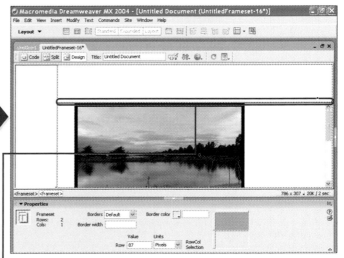

1 Click inside the frame you want to subdivide.

2 Click **Modify**.

3 Click **Frameset**.

4 Click a Split Frame command.

■ You can also select a predefined frameset design from the Layout Insert bar.

■ Dreamweaver splits the selected frame into two frames, creating a nested frame.

■ You can continue to split your frames into more frames.

Note: To add text, images, or other elements to a new frame, see page 160.

CHANGE THE ATTRIBUTES OF A FRAME

You can change the
dimensions of a frame
to attractively and
efficiently display the
information inside it.

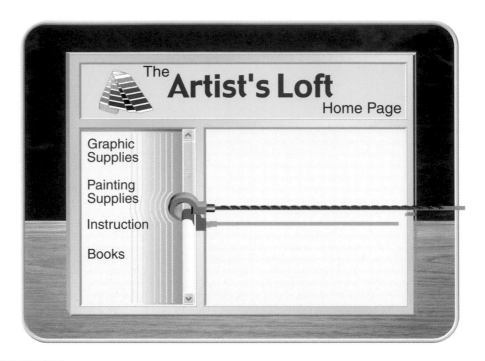

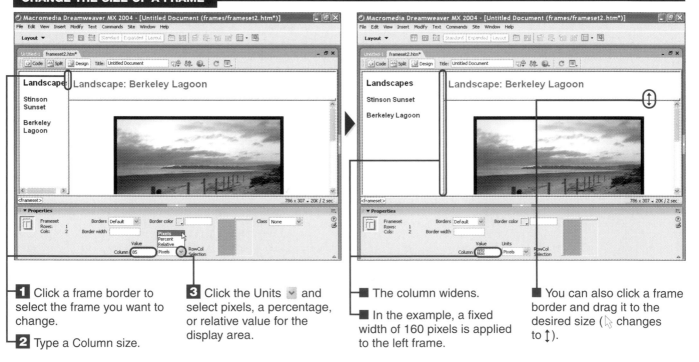

1 Click a frame border to
select the frame you want to
change.

2 Type a Column size.

3 Click the Units and
select pixels, a percentage,
or relative value for the
display area.

■ The column widens.

■ In the example, a fixed
width of 160 pixels is applied
to the left frame.

■ You can also click a frame
border and drag it to the
desired size (changes
to).

Is there a shortcut for changing the dimensions of frames?

Yes. You can click and drag a frame border to adjust the dimensions of a frame quickly. The values in the Properties inspector will change as you drag the frame border.

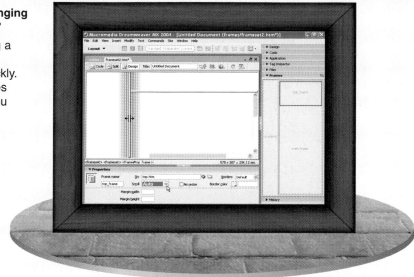

CHANGE THE ATTRIBUTES OF A FRAME

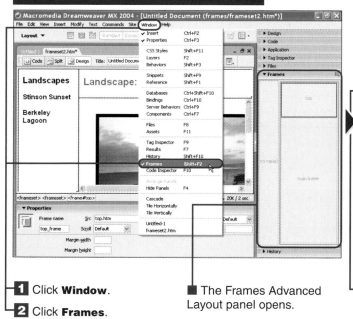

1 Click **Window**.

2 Click **Frames**.

■ The Frames Advanced Layout panel opens.

3 Click a frame in the Frames panel to select it.

4 Click ☑ or type to adjust attributes, borders, and scrolling in the Properties inspector.

■ The frame adjusts.

ADD CONTENT TO A FRAME

You can add content to a frame by inserting an existing HTML document into the frame. You can also create a new page in a frame by typing text or inserting elements such as images and tables, just as you would in an unframed page.

ADD CONTENT TO A FRAME

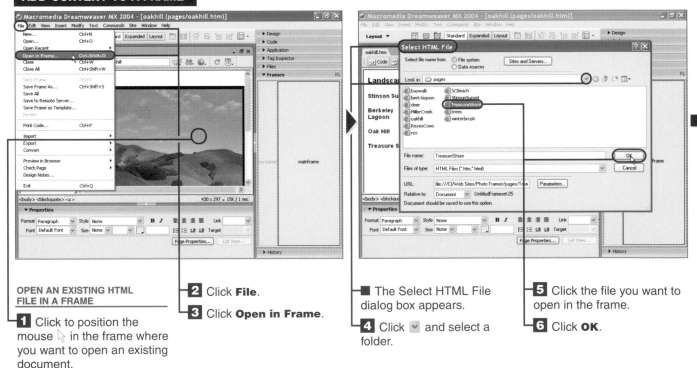

OPEN AN EXISTING HTML FILE IN A FRAME

1 Click to position the mouse in the frame where you want to open an existing document.

2 Click **File**.

3 Click **Open in Frame**.

■ The Select HTML File dialog box appears.

4 Click and select a folder.

5 Click the file you want to open in the frame.

6 Click **OK**.

Can I link a frame to a page somewhere else on the Web?

Yes. You can link to an external Web-page address by using the URL field in the Properties inspector, as with any other page, except you must specify the target. To create a link, see page 164. Because Dreamweaver cannot display external files, the Web page will not appear in the Document window. However, it will appear if you preview your site in a Web browser. To preview a Web page in your browser, see page 26.

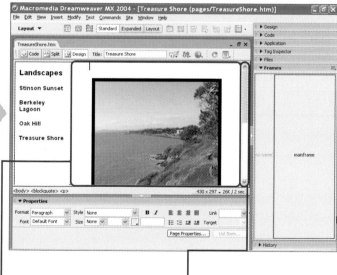

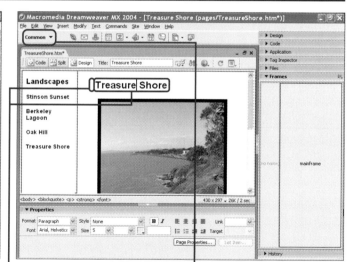

■ The selected page appears in the frame area.

■ If the content extends beyond the frame, scroll bars appear automatically. To turn off the scroll bar, see page 168.

ADD NEW CONTENT TO A FRAME

1 Click inside the frame where you want to add text.

2 Type the text you want to display.

■ You can also add images, tables, or other elements by selecting the **Common** tab and then clicking 🖾 or 🖽 from the Insert panel.

DELETE A FRAME

You can delete
existing frames or
create new frames in
a frameset to change
or expand a design.

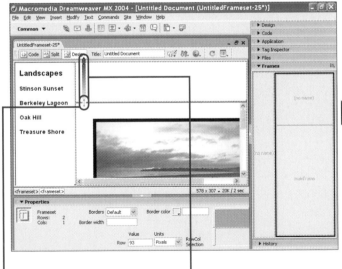

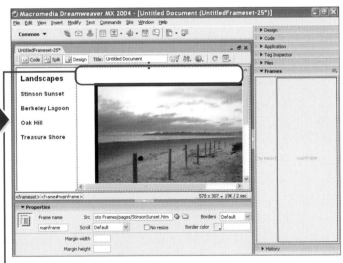

1 Position the mouse
on the border of the frame
you want to delete
(changes to ↕).

2 Click and drag the border
to the edge of the window.

■ Dreamweaver deletes the
frame.

162

To create links in one
frame that open in
another, you need to
give your frames
names. The name
targets the link
destination, indicating
where the linked page
should open in the
frameset.

NAME A FRAME

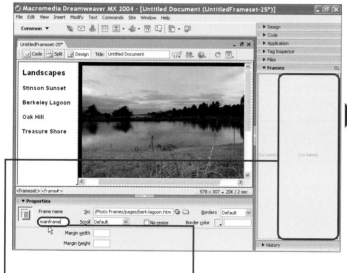

1 Click to select the frame
you want to name in the
Advanced Layout Frames
panel.

2 Type a name for the
frame.

3 Press Enter (Return).

■ The name of the frame
appears in the Frames
panel.

■ If the panel is not open,
click **Window** and then
Frames to display it.

CREATE A LINK TO A FRAME

You can create a link that opens a page in a different frame. You will want to do this for frames that contain navigation hyperlinks. For more information about links, see Chapter 7.

CREATE A LINK TO A FRAME

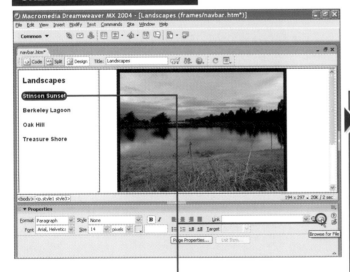

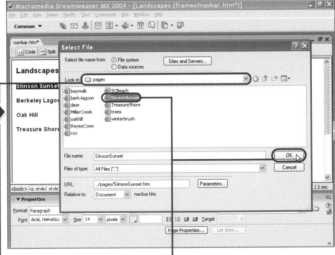

Note: This task requires the naming of your frames. To name a frame, see page 163.

1 Click to select the text or image that you want to turn into a link.

2 Click 📁 in the Properties inspector.

■ The Select File dialog box opens.

3 Click ☑ and select the folder containing the page to which you want to link.

4 Click the file.

5 Click **OK**.

How do I target links in my frames?

You can target a link to open in any section of the frame by selecting the name of the frame. Selecting **_top**, instead of a frame name, opens the linked page on top of the existing frameset. This action takes the user out of the frameset as recommended when linking to another Web site.

6 Click the Target ▾.

7 Click to select a frame where the target file will open.

■ If you have named the frame, it appears in the menu.

8 Click the Preview button (🔲) to preview the page in a Web browser.

Note: To preview a Web page in a browser, see page 26.

■ When you open the framed page in a Web browser and click the link, the destination page opens inside the targeted frame.

FORMAT FRAME BORDERS

You can modify the appearance of your frame borders to make them complement your design by specifying the color and width of your borders, or you can turn them off so they are not visible.

FORMAT FRAME BORDERS

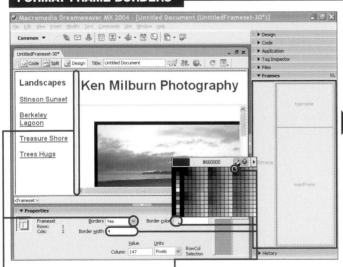

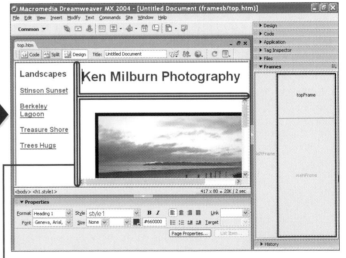

SET BORDER SHADING, COLOR, AND WIDTH

1 Click a frame border to select the frames.

2 Click the Borders ⌄ and select **Yes** or **Default** to turn on borders.

3 Type a border width in pixels.

4 Click the Border color ⬜ (⌖ changes to ⌁).

5 Click a color.

■ The frame border appears at the specified settings.

■ You can override the settings at the frameset level at the individual frame level.

■ You can also press and hold Alt (option) and click inside a frame to select it, then specify formatting in the Properties inspector.

Why would I want to make my frame borders invisible?

Turning borders off can disguise the fact that you are using frames in the first place. If you want to further disguise your frames, you can set the pages inside your frames to the same background color. To change background colors, see page 96.

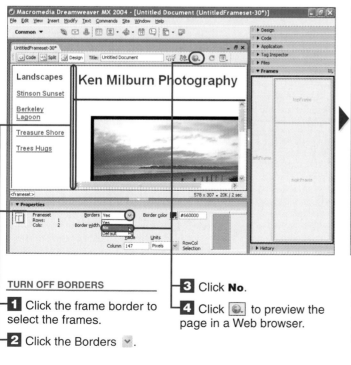

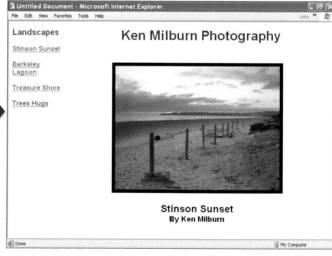

TURN OFF BORDERS

1 Click the frame border to select the frames.

2 Click the Borders ▾.

3 Click **No**.

4 Click ▣ to preview the page in a Web browser.

Note: To preview a Web page in a browser, see page 26.

■ The frame border does not display.

■ Links open in the targeted frame even with borders turned off.

CONTROL SCROLL BARS IN FRAMES

You can control whether or not scroll bars will appear in your frames. Hiding scroll bars enables you to have more control over the presentation of your site, but may also prevent some users from seeing your entire site content.

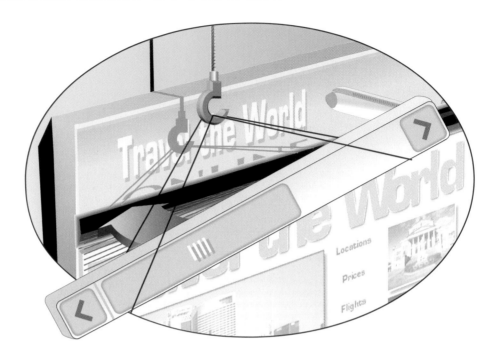

CONTROL SCROLL BARS IN FRAMES

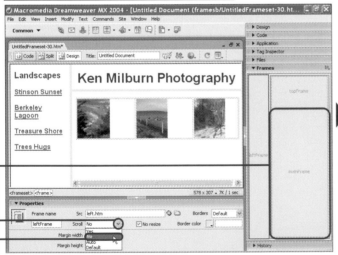

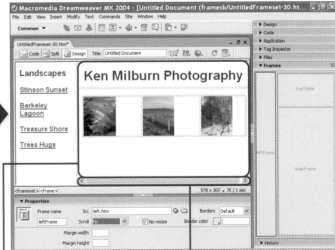

1 Click a frame in the Advanced Layout Frames panel to select it.

2 Click the Scroll ▾.

3 Click a setting from the options.

■ You may click the setting option **Yes** to keep scroll bars on; click **No** to turn scroll bars off; or click **Auto** to keep scroll bars on if necessary. In most browsers, Default and Auto have the same result.

■ The frame appears with the new setting.

■ In this example, scroll bars are turned off in the left frame where they are not necessary. They remain on in the right frame so that the viewer can access all the content in that frame.

CONTROL RESIZING IN FRAMES

The default behavior for most browsers allows users to resize frames by clicking and dragging frame borders.

You can prevent users from resizing the frames of a site. However, depending on the size of their monitor, you may make it impossible for them to view all your content.

CONTROL RESIZING IN FRAMES

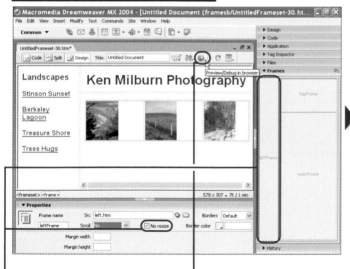

1 Click a frame in the Advanced Layout Frames panel to select it.

2 Click the **No Resize** option (☐ changes to ☑).

3 Click 🌐 to preview the page in a Web browser.

Note: To preview a Web page in a browser, see page 26.

■ The browser prevents the user from resizing the frame.

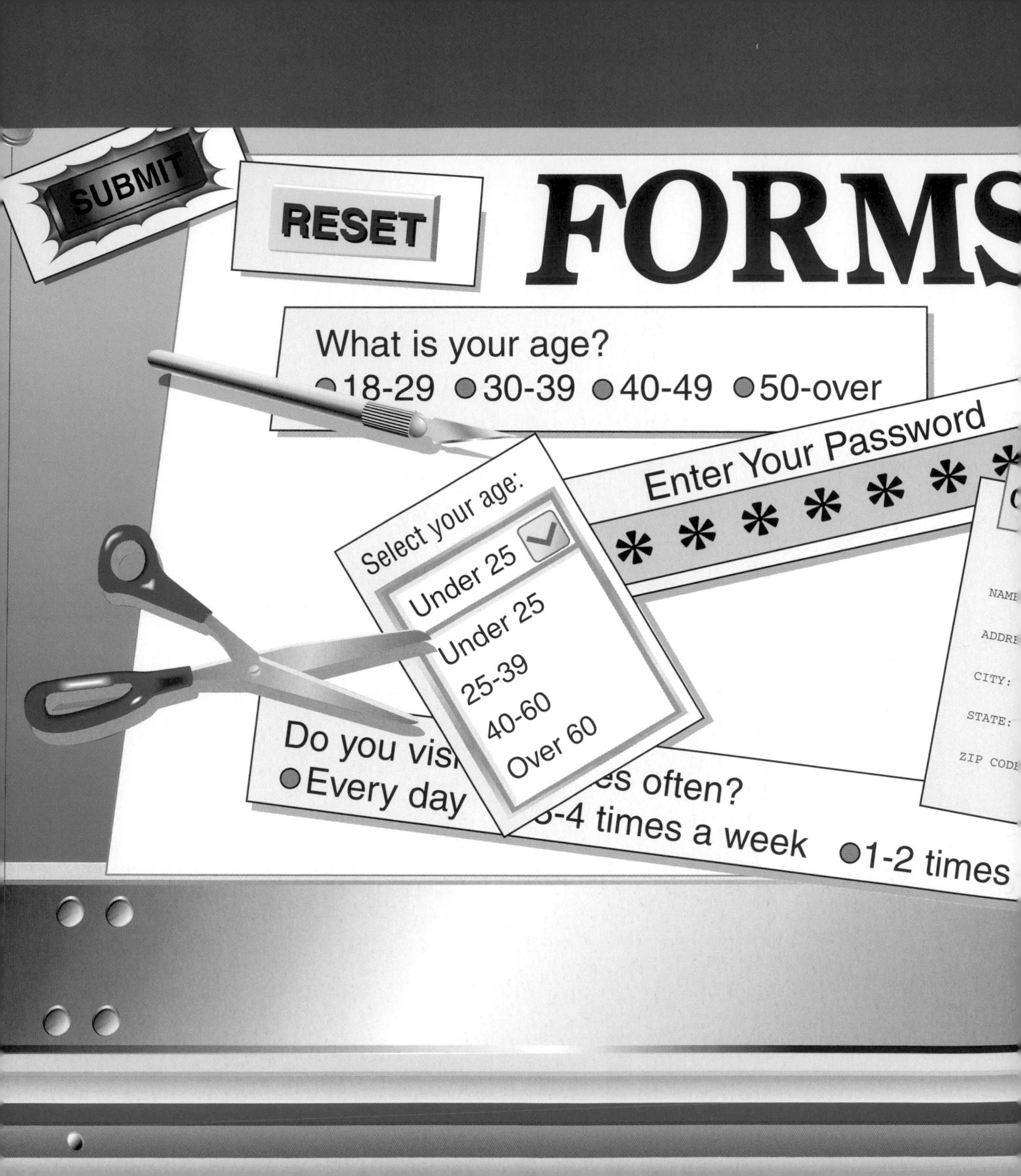

SUBMIT

RESET

FORMS

What is your age?

○ 18-29 ● 30-39 ● 40-49 ○ 50-over

Enter Your Password

✳ ✳ ✳ ✳ ✳ ✳ ✳ ✳ ✳

Select your age: ✓

Under 25

Under 25
25-39
40-60
Over 60

NAME

ADDRE

CITY:

STATE:

ZIP CODE

Do you vis...es often?

● Every day   -4 times a week   ● 1-2 times

CHAPTER 10

Creating Web-Based Forms

You can enable your site visitors to send you information by creating forms on your Web pages. This chapter shows you how to create forms with different types of fields, buttons, and menus.

Introduction to Forms 172

Define a Form 173

Add a Text Field to a Form 174

Add a Check Box to a Form 176

Add a Radio Button to a Form 178

Add a Menu or List to a Form 180

Add a Password Field to a Form 182

Add a Submit or Reset Button
    to a Form 183

INTRODUCTION TO FORMS

Adding forms to your Web site makes it more interactive, enabling viewers to enter and submit information to you through your Web pages.

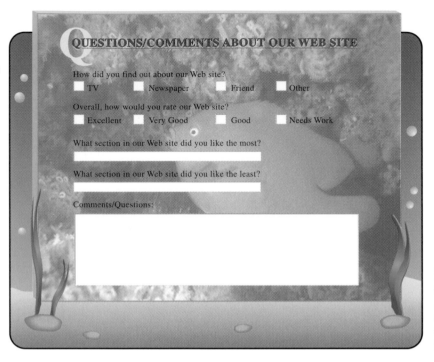

QUESTIONS/COMMENTS ABOUT OUR WEB SITE

How did you find out about our Web site?
☐ TV   ☐ Newspaper   ☐ Friend   ☐ Other

Overall, how would you rate our Web site?
☐ Excellent   ☐ Very Good   ☐ Good   ☐ Needs Work

What section in our Web site did you like the most?

What section in our Web site did you like the least?

Comments/Questions:

Every form works in conjunction with a *form handler*, a type of program or script that processes the form information.

Create a Form

You can construct a form by inserting text fields, pull-down menus, check boxes, and other interactive elements into your page. You can also assign the Web address of a form handler to the form so that the information can be processed. Visitors to your Web page fill out the form and send the information to the form handler by clicking a Submit button.

Process Form Information

The *form handler* is a program or script that processes the form information and does something useful with it, such as forwarding the information to an e-mail address or entering it into a database. Many ready-made form handlers are available free on the Web in ASP, CGI, PHP, or ColdFusion. Your Internet hosting company may also have forms available for you to use with your site.

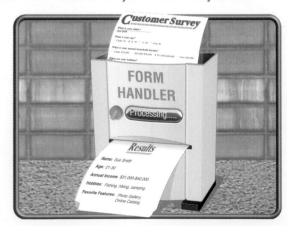

You set up a form on your Web page by first creating a container that holds the text fields, menus, and other form elements. Dreamweaver assigns the Web address of the *form handler* — the program that processes the form — to this container.

DEFINE A FORM

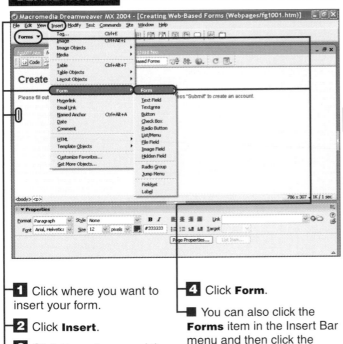

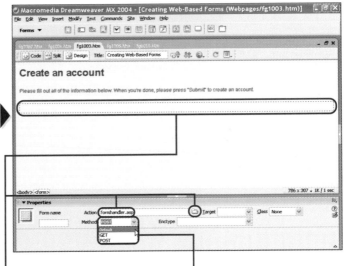

1 Click where you want to insert your form.

2 Click **Insert**.

3 Click **Form** to expand the menu.

4 Click **Form**.

■ You can also click the **Forms** item in the Insert Bar menu and then click the Form button (▢).

■ A red, dashed box appears on the page.

5 Type the address of the form handler file in the Action field.

■ You can also click 🗀 and select the form handler file.

6 Click ⌄ and select **POST** or **GET**.

■ GET is the default and most common method used by Webmasters.

■ The form container is set up. To build the form, add form elements inside the red box.

ADD A TEXT FIELD TO A FORM

You can add a text field to enable viewers to submit text through your form. Text fields are probably the most common form element, enabling users to enter names, addresses, brief answers to questions, and other short pieces of text.

ADD A TEXT FIELD TO A FORM

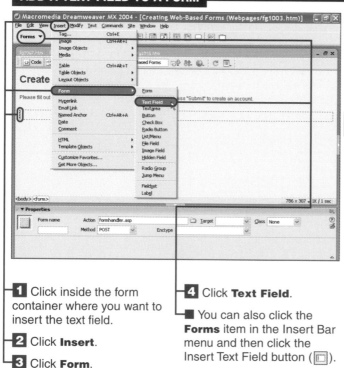

1 Click inside the form container where you want to insert the text field.

2 Click **Insert**.

3 Click **Form**.

4 Click **Text Field**.

■ You can also click the **Forms** item in the Insert Bar menu and then click the Insert Text Field button (▣).

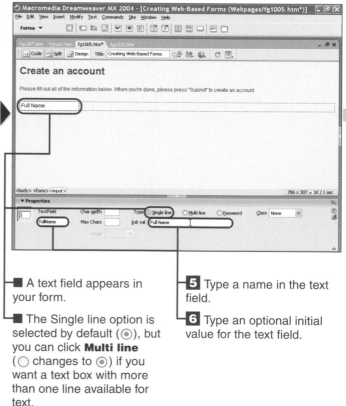

■ A text field appears in your form.

■ The Single line option is selected by default (◉), but you can click **Multi line** (◯ changes to ◉) if you want a text box with more than one line available for text.

5 Type a name in the text field.

6 Type an optional initial value for the text field.

**Can I define the style of text
that appears in the text field?**

The browser determines what
style of text appears in the
form fields by default. It is
not possible to format this
type of text with plain HTML.
Using style sheets, you can
manipulate the way the text
looks in the form fields. However,
be aware that only the newer
browsers support this feature.

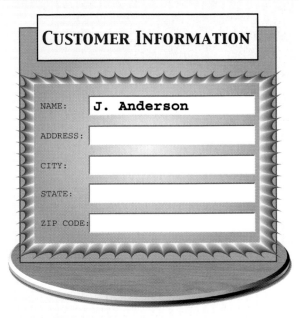

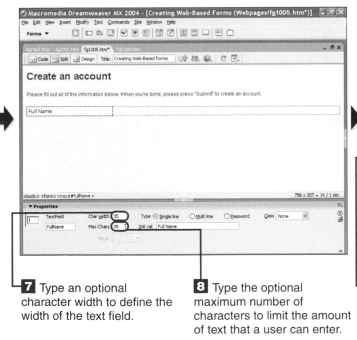

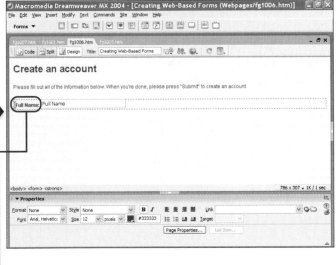

7 Type an optional
character width to define the
width of the text field.

8 Type the optional
maximum number of
characters to limit the amount
of text that a user can enter.

9 Type a label for the text
field so that users know what
to enter.

■ Dreamweaver applies
your specifications to the
text field.

ADD A CHECK BOX TO A FORM

Check boxes enable
you to present multiple
options in a form and
allow the user to select
one, several, or none
of the options.

ADD A CHECK BOX TO A FORM

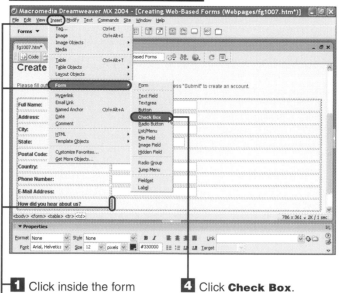

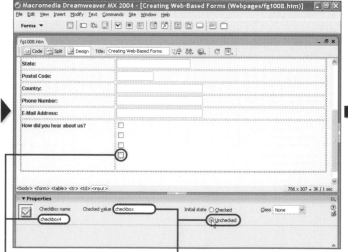

1 Click inside the form
container where you want to
insert your check boxes.

2 Click **Insert**.

3 Click **Form**.

4 Click **Check Box**.

■ You can also click the
Forms item in the Insert
Bar menu and then click
the Insert Check Box
button (▣).

5 Repeat steps **2** to **4** until
you have the desired number
of check boxes in your Web
page.

6 Click a check box.

7 Type a name for the
check box.

8 Type a checked value for
the check box.

■ This value is assigned to
the box when the user
checks it.

9 Click to select an
initial state option
(○ changes to ◉).

Can I have several different groups of check boxes in the same form?

Yes. How you organize the check boxes in a form — in one group, several groups, or each check box by itself — is up to you. If you want to provide various choices in one group, you can assign the same name to all the check boxes in that group and give each one a different Checked Value. The form handler treats those check boxes as a group.

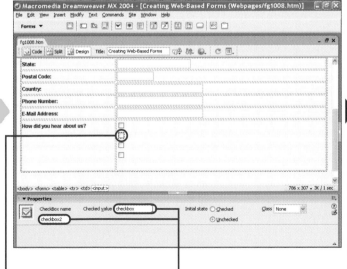

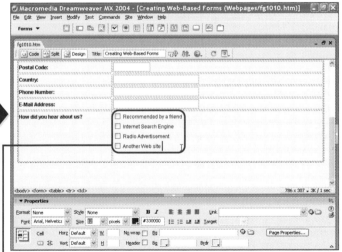

10 Click to select the other check boxes in the group, one at a time.

■ The selected textbox has a dashed box around it.

11 Type a name for each check box.

12 Type a checked value for each check box.

■ You can enter the same or different names for all the check boxes in a set.

13 Type labels for the check boxes so that users know what to check.

■ Dreamweaver applies your specifications to the check boxes.

ADD A RADIO BUTTON TO A FORM

You can let users select one option from a set of several options by adding a set of radio buttons to your form. With radio buttons, a user cannot select more than one option from a set.

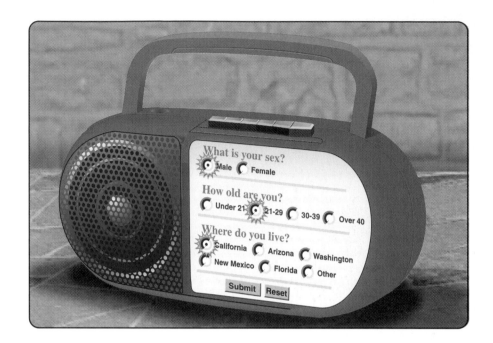

ADD A RADIO BUTTON TO A FORM

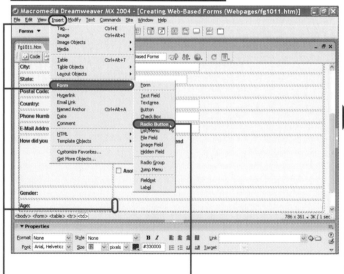

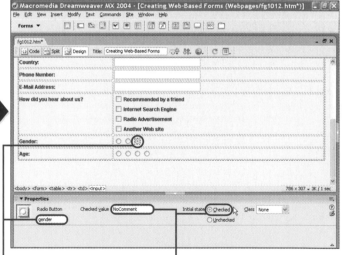

1 Click inside the form container where you want to insert your radio buttons.

2 Click **Insert**.

3 Click **Form**.

4 Click **Radio Button**.

■ You can also click the **Forms** item in the Insert Bar menu and then click the Insert Radio Button button (▣).

5 Repeat steps **2** to **4** until you have the desired number of radio buttons in your Web page.

6 Click a radio button.

7 Type a name for the radio button.

8 Type a checked value for the radio button.

9 Click to select an initial state option (○ changes to ◉).

What happens if I give each radio button in a set a different name?

A user can select more than one button in the set at a time, and after a button is selected, the user cannot deselect it. This defeats the purpose of radio buttons. If you want to enable your users to select more than one choice or to deselect a choice, use check boxes (☑) instead of radio buttons (◉).

Are there alternatives to using check boxes or radio buttons?

Yes, there are alternatives such as menus and lists. Instead of using check boxes, you can use multi-select lists, which enables users to select more than one item from a list. You can replace a radio button with a menu, which allows only one choice from a list.

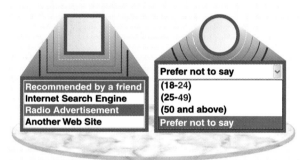

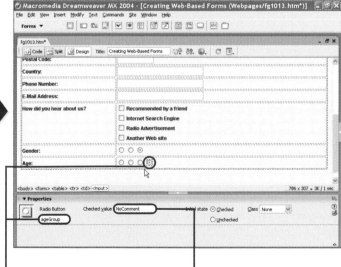

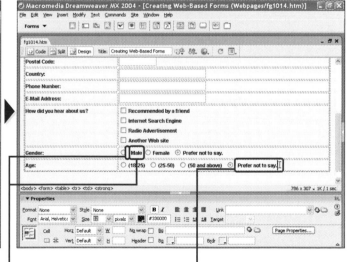

10 Click to select the other options, one at a time.

11 Type the same name for all radio buttons in the set.

■ Assigning each button the same name ensures that only one in the set is on at a time.

12 Type a unique checked value for each radio button.

■ This value is assigned to the radio button when the user checks it.

13 Click next to a radio button.

14 Type a label for the radio button.

15 Repeat steps **13** and **14** for each radio button.

■ Dreamweaver applies your specifications to the radio buttons.

ADD A MENU OR LIST TO A FORM

A menu allows users to choose one option from a list of options. It works much in the same way as a set of radio buttons. A list allows users to choose one or more options from a list of options, similar to a set of check boxes.

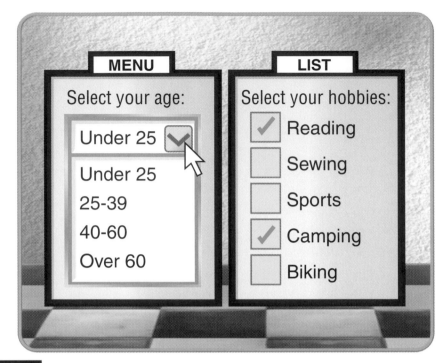

MENU

Select your age:

Under 25

Under 25
25-39
40-60
Over 60

LIST

Select your hobbies:

☑ Reading
☐ Sewing
☐ Sports
☑ Camping
☐ Biking

ADD A MENU OR LIST TO A FORM

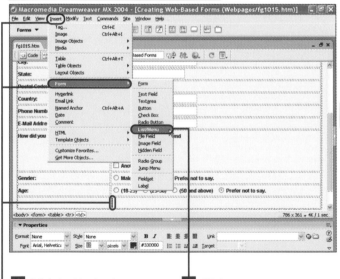

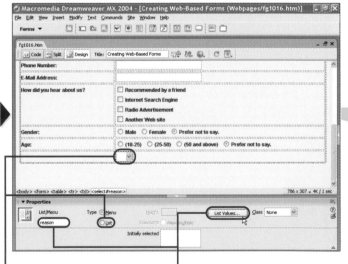

1 Click inside the form container where you want to insert your list or menu.

2 Click **Insert**.

3 Click **Form**.

4 Click **List/Menu**.

■ You can also click the **Forms** item in the Insert Bar menu and then click the Insert List/Menu button (▦).

■ A menu appears in your Web page.

5 Click the menu to select it.

■ To display a list instead of a menu, click the **List** option (○ changes to ◉).

6 Type a name for the menu.

7 Click **List Values**.

■ The List Values dialog box appears.

What determines the width of a menu or list?

The widest item determines the width of your menu or list. To change the width, you can change the width of your item descriptions.

Can I choose more than one item from a menu?

You can only select one item from a menu because of its design. If you want more than one selection, use a list and set it to allow multiple selections. You can also set the height greater than 1 so you can see your selections.

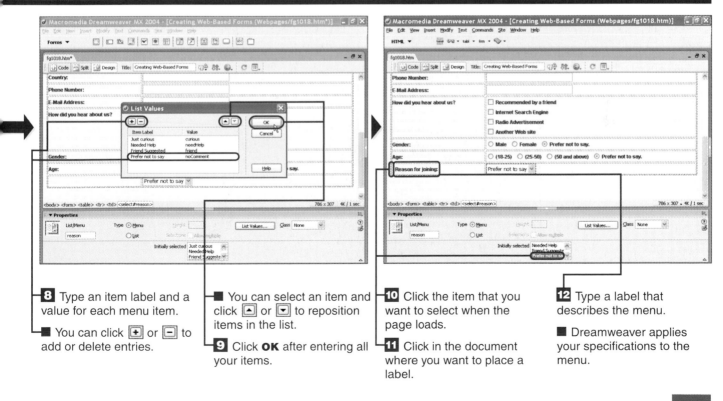

8 Type an item label and a value for each menu item.

■ You can click ⊞ or ⊟ to add or delete entries.

■ You can select an item and click ▲ or ▼ to reposition items in the list.

9 Click **OK** after entering all your items.

10 Click the item that you want to select when the page loads.

11 Click in the document where you want to place a label.

12 Type a label that describes the menu.

■ Dreamweaver applies your specifications to the menu.

ADD A PASSWORD FIELD TO A FORM

A password field is similar to a text field, except the text in the field is hidden as the user enters it. The characters display as asterisks or bullets, depending on the type of operating system used to view the page.

The password field alone *does not* prevent someone from intercepting your information as it travels between a user's computer and the form handler.

ADD A PASSWORD FIELD TO A FORM

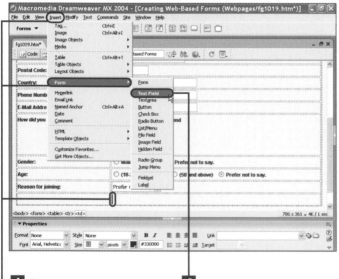

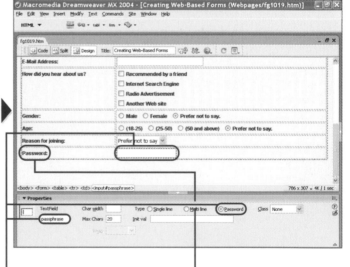

1 Click inside the form container where you want to insert the password field.

2 Click **Insert**.

3 Click **Form**.

4 Click **Text Field**.

■ You can also click the **Forms** item in the Insert Bar menu and then click the Insert Text Field button (▣).

■ A single-line text field appears in your form.

5 Click the **Password** option (○ changes to ◉).

6 Type a name for the password field.

7 Type a label for the field so that users know what to enter.

■ When you preview the page in a browser and type into the password field, asterisks or bullets appear in place of letters and numbers.

ADD A SUBMIT OR RESET BUTTON TO A FORM

You can add a button that enables users to submit information in a form, sending it to the specified form handler. Adding a Reset button allows users to erase their form entries so they can start over.

ADD A SUBMIT OR RESET BUTTON TO A FORM

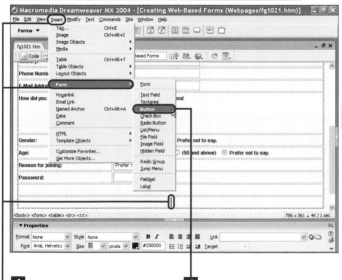

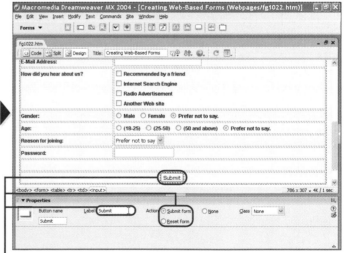

1 Click inside the form container where you want to insert the button.

2 Click **Insert**.

3 Click **Form**.

4 Click **Button**.

■ You can also click the **Forms** item in the Insert Bar menu and then click the Insert Button button (□).

■ A button appears in your Web page.

5 Click to select an action (○ changes to ◉).

6 Type a label for the button.

■ When a user clicks the Submit button, the browser sends the form information to the form handler.

■ When a user clicks the Reset button, the browser resets the form to its initial values.

183

CHAPTER 11

Using Library Items and Templates

You can save time by storing frequently used Web page elements and layouts as library items or templates. This chapter shows you how to use these features to your advantage.

Introduction to Library Items and Templates 186

View Library Items and Templates......187

Create a Library Item 188

Insert a Library Item 190

Edit and Update a Library Item to Your Web Site............................192

Detach Library Content for Editing 194

Create a Template 196

Set an Editable Region in a Template 198

Create a Page from a Template 200

Edit a Template and Update Your Web Site 202

With library items and templates, you can avoid repetitive work by storing copies of page elements and layouts that you frequently use. You can access the library items and templates that you create for your site by accessing the Assets panel.

Library Items

You can define parts of your Web pages that are repeated in your site as library items. This saves you time from creating these parts from scratch repeatedly. Each time you need a library item, you can just insert it from your library. If you ever make changes to a library item, Dreamweaver automatically updates all instances of the item across your Web site. Good candidates for library items include advertising banners, company slogans, navigation bars, and any other feature that appears many times across a site.

Templates

You can define commonly used Web pages as templates to save you time as you build your pages. Templates can also help you maintain a consistent page design throughout a site. After you make changes to a template, Dreamweaver automatically updates all the pages of your site that are based on that template. If you use just a few page layouts across all the pages in your site, consider creating templates to use.

VIEW LIBRARY ITEMS AND TEMPLATES

You can access the
library and templates
of a site by using
commands in the
Window menu. You
can also access them
via the Assets panel.

VIEW LIBRARY ITEMS AND TEMPLATES

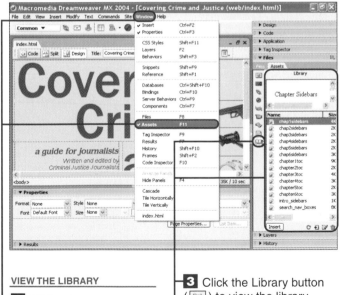

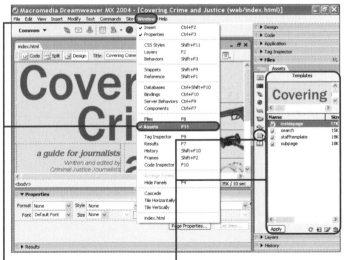

VIEW THE LIBRARY

1 Click **Window**.

2 Click **Assets**.

■ The Assets panel opens.

3 Click the Library button
() to view the library
items.

■ The Library window opens
in the Assets panel.

VIEW TEMPLATES

1 Click **Window**.

2 Click **Assets**.

■ The Assets panel opens.

3 Click the Template button
() to view the templates.

■ The Templates window
opens in the Assets panel.

CREATE A LIBRARY ITEM

You can define text, images, and other Dreamweaver objects that you want to appear frequently in your Web site as library items. Library items enable you to quickly insert such page elements without having to re-create them from scratch every time.

If you edit a library item, Dreamweaver automatically updates each instance of the item throughout your site.

CREATE A LIBRARY ITEM

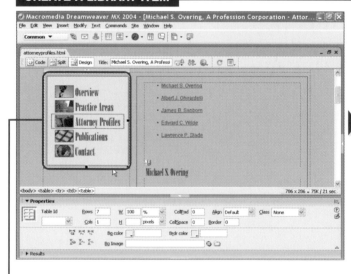

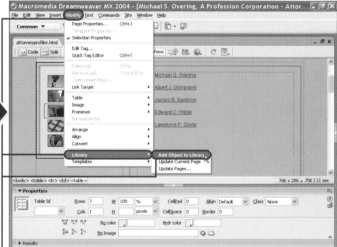

1 Click and drag to select an element or section of your page that you want to define as a library item.

Note: Before you can use the library item feature in Dreamweaver, you must first set up and define your local site. To set up a local site, see page 20.

2 Click **Modify**.

3 Click **Library**.

4 Click **Add Object to Library**.

■ A new untitled library item appears in the Library window.

188

What page elements should I make into library items?

Anything that appears multiple times in a Web site is a good candidate to become a library item. These elements include headers, footers, navigational menus, contact information, and disclaimers. Any element that appears in the body of an HTML document, such as text, images, tables, forms, layers, and multimedia, may be defined as a library item.

Can I use multiple library items on the same HTML page?

There is no limit to the number of library items you can use on a page. If your site is very standardized, there may be little on your page that is not a library item. For example, you might create a photo gallery where each page has the same layout, except for the photo.

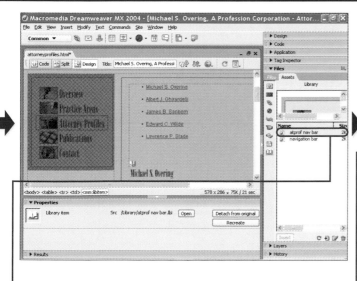

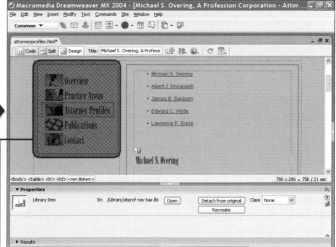

5 Type a name for the library item.

6 Press ⌈Enter⌋ (⌈Return⌋).

■ When selected, the new library item is greyed out. Areas not covered by images are highlighted in yellow.

Note: To change the highlighting color for library items in Preferences, see page 40.

■ Defining an element as a library item prevents you from editing it in the Document window.

Note: To edit and update a library item, see page 192.

INSERT A LIBRARY ITEM

Inserting an element onto your page from the library saves you from having to create it from scratch. It also ensures that the element is identical to other instances of that library item in your site.

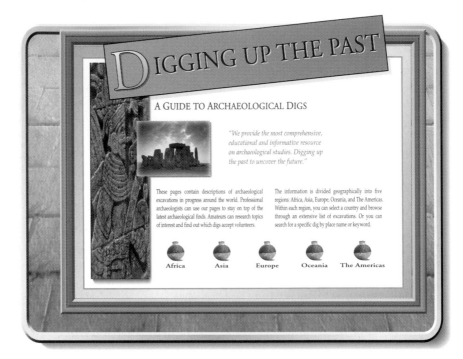

INSERT A LIBRARY ITEM

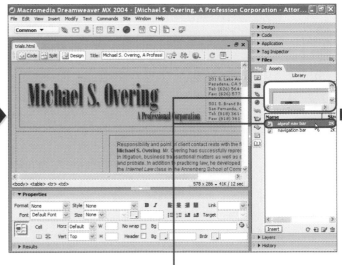

1 Position your mouse ⌖ where you want to insert the library item.

2 Click **Window**.

3 Click **Assets**.

■ The Assets panel opens.

■ If the Library is not open in the Assets panel, you can click 🕮 to view the library.

4 Click a library item.

■ The library item appears in the top of the Library window.

How do I edit a library item that has been inserted into a page?

Instances of library items in your pages are locked and cannot be edited. To edit a library item, you must edit the original version of that item from the library. Or, you can detach an instance of a library item from the library for editing, but then the instance is no longer a part of the library and will not update if the library item is changed. To edit and update a library item to your Web site, see page 192. To detach library content for editing, see page 194.

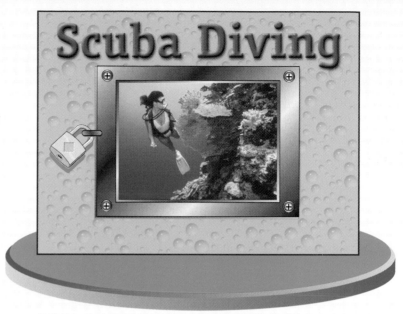

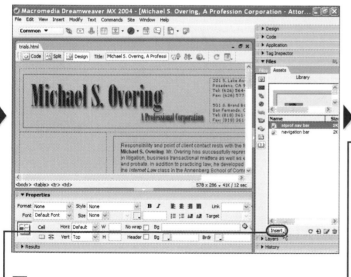

5 Click **Insert**.

■ You can also click and drag library items from the Library panel to the page to insert them.

■ Dreamweaver inserts the library item, in the Document window.

EDIT AND UPDATE A LIBRARY ITEM TO YOUR WEB SITE

You can edit a library item and then automatically update all the pages in your site that feature that item. This feature can help you save time when maintaining a Web site.

You can also edit a specific instance of a library item on a page. To edit a library item, see page 192.

EDIT AND UPDATE A LIBRARY ITEM TO YOUR WEB SITE

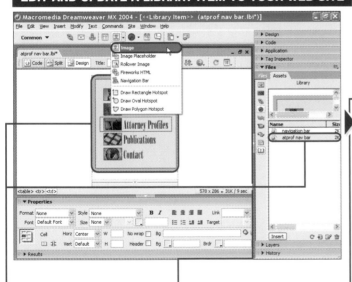

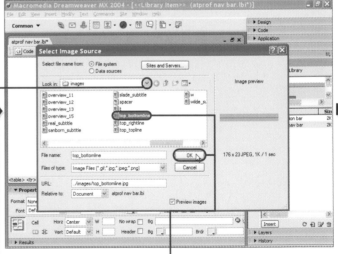

1 Double-click a library item to open it.

■ The library item opens in a new window.

2 Click the image you want to replace.

■ You can edit any element in the library item, add or delete text, or include tables.

3 On the Common bar, click the Image button (🖼) and select **Image** from the drop-down menu.

■ The Select Image Source dialog box appears.

4 Click ⌄ and locate the file you want to use.

5 Click the new image.

6 Click **OK**.

What will my pages look like after I have edited a library item and updated my site?

All the pages in your site that contain an instance of the library item will have those instances replaced with the edited version. By using the library feature, you can make a change to a single library item and have hundreds of Web pages updated automatically.

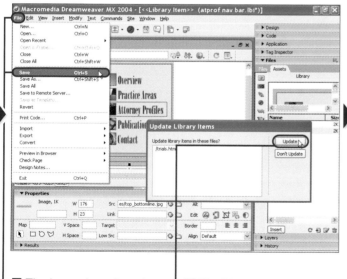

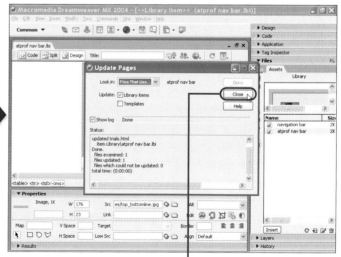

■ The image is replaced.

7 Click **File**.

8 Click **Save**.

■ The Update Library Items dialog box appears, asking if you want to update all the instances of the library item in the site.

9 Click **Update**.

■ The Update Pages dialog box appears, showing the progress of the updates.

10 After Dreamweaver updates the site, click **Close**.

■ All instances of the library item are updated.

DETACH LIBRARY CONTENT FOR EDITING

You can detach an instance of a library item from the library and then edit it just like regular content.

DETACH LIBRARY CONTENT FOR EDITING

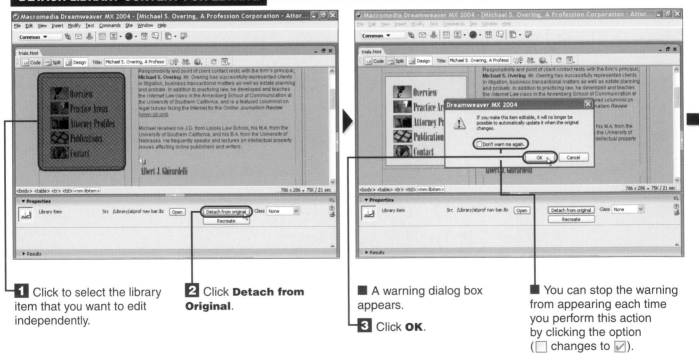

1 Click to select the library item that you want to edit independently.

2 Click **Detach from Original**.

■ A warning dialog box appears.

3 Click **OK**.

■ You can stop the warning from appearing each time you perform this action by clicking the option (☐ changes to ☑).

Why might I use the Detach from Original command on a regular basis?

You can use it if you are using library items as templates for specific design elements on your pages. For instance, if you need numerous captioned images in your Web site, you can create a library item that has a two-celled table with a generic image and caption. To place an image and caption, you insert the library item and then detach the item from the library to make it editable. You can then replace the generic image and caption with appropriate content. For more about tables, see Chapter 8.

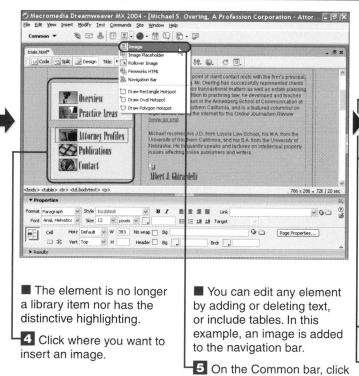

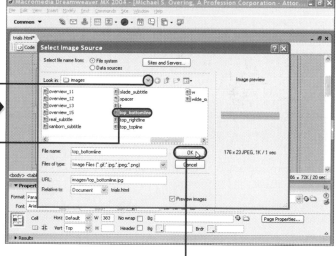

■ The element is no longer a library item nor has the distinctive highlighting.

4 Click where you want to insert an image.

■ You can edit any element by adding or deleting text, or include tables. In this example, an image is added to the navigation bar.

5 On the Common bar, click the Image button (▣) and select **Image** from the drop-down menu.

■ The Select Image Source dialog box appears.

6 Click ▾ and locate the file you want to use.

7 Click the image.

8 Click **OK**.

■ The image is inserted.

■ Editing a detached library item has no effect on the library items that are used on other pages.

CREATE A TEMPLATE

To help you save time, you can create generic template pages to use as starting points for new pages.

CREATE A TEMPLATE

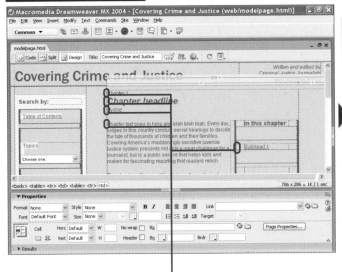

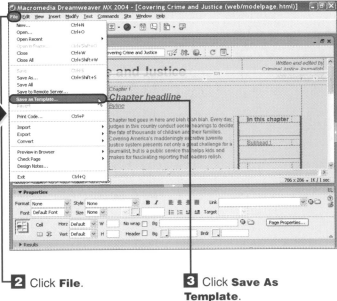

Note: To create templates for your Web pages, you must already have defined a local site. To set up a local site, see page 20.

1 Open the page that will serve as a template.

■ You can add placeholders where information will change from page to page.

2 Click **File**.

3 Click **Save As Template**.

What are the different types of content in a template?

A template contains two types of content: editable and locked. After you create a new Web page based on a template, you can only change the parts of the new page that are defined as editable. To change locked content, you must edit the original template. To set the editable region of a template, see page 198.

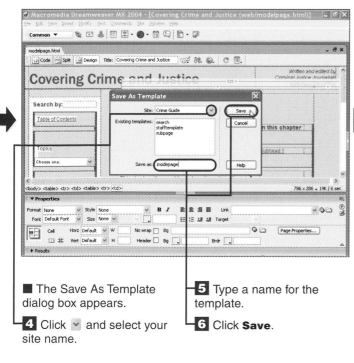

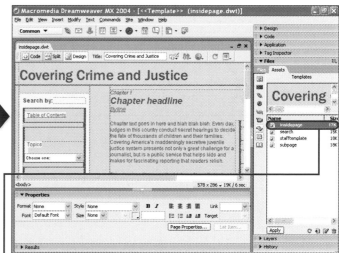

■ The Save As Template dialog box appears.

4 Click ⌄ and select your site name.

5 Type a name for the template.

6 Click **Save**.

■ The new template appears in the Templates window of the Assets panel.

■ If a template folder does not already exist, Dreamweaver automatically creates one when it saves the new template.

Note: To make the template functional, you must define the editable regions where you want to modify content. To set the editable region of a template, see page 198.

SET AN EDITABLE REGION IN A TEMPLATE

After you create a Web page template, you must define which regions of the template are editable. These regions are changeable in a page made from the template.

SET AN EDITABLE REGION IN A TEMPLATE

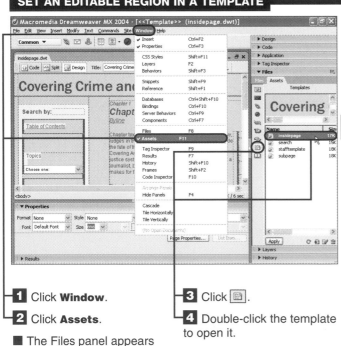

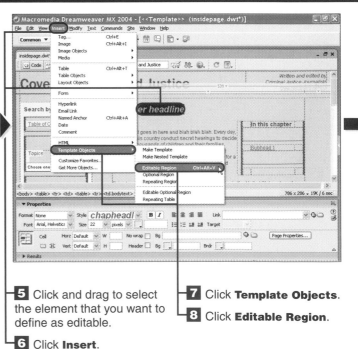

1 Click **Window**.

2 Click **Assets**.

■ The Files panel appears with the Assets tab visible.

3 Click 🗅.

4 Double-click the template to open it.

5 Click and drag to select the element that you want to define as editable.

6 Click **Insert**.

7 Click **Template Objects**.

8 Click **Editable Region**.

What parts of a template should be defined as editable?

You should define any part that will require changing from page to page as editable. Generally, variable areas in the page body are defined as editable, while site navigation, disclaimers, and copyright information are kept locked. You can even make virtually everything on the page editable except the layout.

Can I use library items in my template pages?

You can use library items in templates. When edited, the library items will update in the templates themselves, and then in all the pages created from that template. To ensure consistency, place a library item into a template if you are also using the item on pages that are not made from the template.

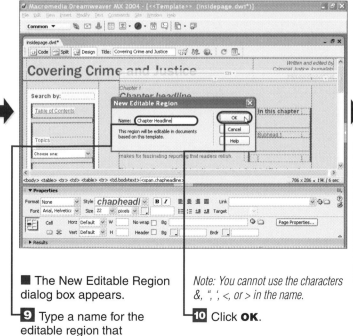

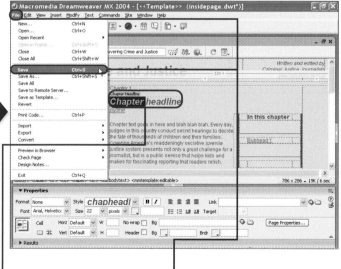

■ The New Editable Region dialog box appears.

9 Type a name for the editable region that distinguishes it from other editable regions on the page.

Note: You cannot use the characters &, ", ', <, or > in the name.

10 Click **OK**.

■ A light blue box indicates the editable region, and a tab shows the region name.

Note: To change the highlighting color for editable regions in Preferences, see page 40.

11 Repeat steps **5** to **10** for all the regions on the page that you want to be editable.

12 Click **File**.

13 Click **Save** to save the file.

CREATE A PAGE FROM A TEMPLATE

You can create a new Web page based on a template that you have already defined. This step saves you from having to build all the generic elements that appear on many of your pages from scratch.

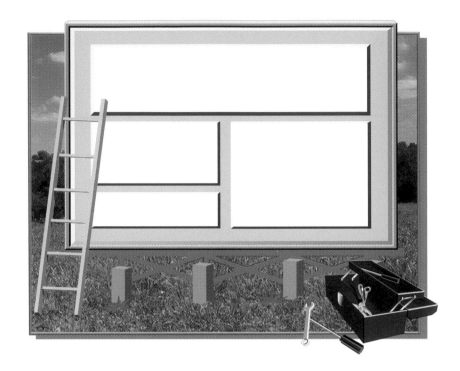

CREATE A PAGE BY USING A TEMPLATE

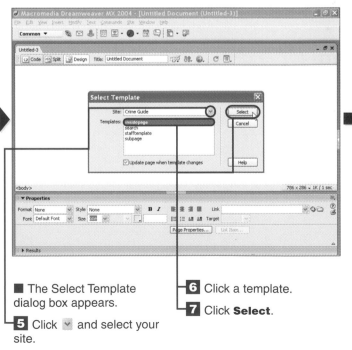

1 Create a new Web page.

Note: To create a Web page, see page 22.

2 Click **Modify**.

3 Click **Templates**.

4 Click **Apply Template to Page**.

■ The Select Template dialog box appears.

5 Click ⌄ and select your site.

6 Click a template.

7 Click **Select**.

How do I detach a page from a template?

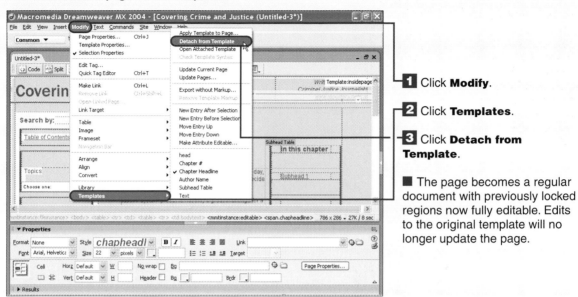

1 Click **Modify**.

2 Click **Templates**.

3 Click **Detach from Template**.

■ The page becomes a regular document with previously locked regions now fully editable. Edits to the original template will no longer update the page.

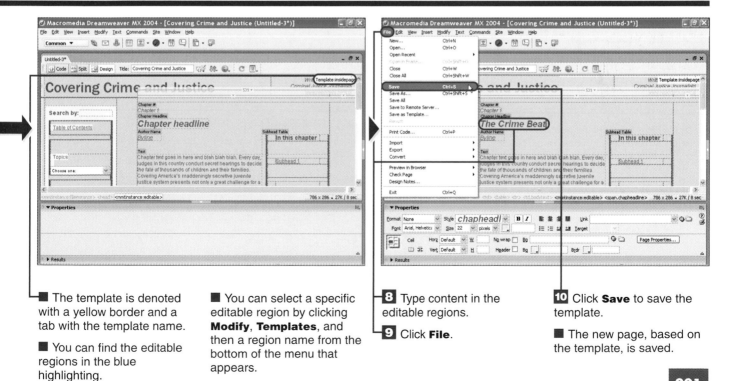

■ The template is denoted with a yellow border and a tab with the template name.

■ You can find the editable regions in the blue highlighting.

■ You can select a specific editable region by clicking **Modify**, **Templates**, and then a region name from the bottom of the menu that appears.

8 Type content in the editable regions.

9 Click **File**.

10 Click **Save** to save the template.

■ The new page, based on the template, is saved.

EDIT A TEMPLATE AND UPDATE YOUR WEB SITE

As you make updates to an original template file, Dreamweaver transmits those updates to the pages that are supported by the template. This enables you to make wholesale changes to the page design of your site in seconds.

EDIT A TEMPLATE AND UPDATE YOUR WEB SITE

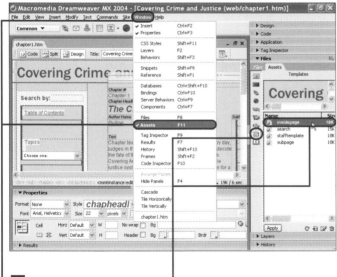

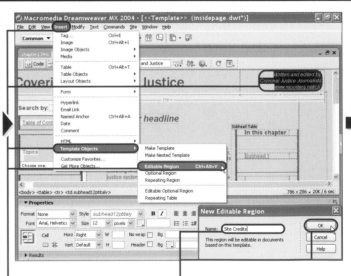

1 Click **Window**.

2 Click **Assets**.

■ The Files panel appears with the Assets tab visible. You can select 🗐 to view the available templates.

3 Click 🗐.

4 Double-click the template to open it.

5 Click and drag to select an element that you want to define as editable.

6 Click **Insert**.

7 Click **Template Objects**.

8 Click **Editable Region**.

■ The New Editable Region dialog box appears.

9 Type a name for the editable region.

10 Click **OK**.

How does Dreamweaver store page templates?

Dreamweaver stores page templates in a folder called *Templates* inside the local site folder. You can open templates by clicking **File** and then **Open**. In the Open dialog box, click ⌄ and select the **Template** folder. You can click a template file to select it. You can also open templates from inside the Assets panel.

What are editable attributes?

Editable attributes allow you to change the properties of something on a page. For example, you can make an image have editable attributes like its source, ALT text, or size. Users will need to keep the image on the page and have the option to change things about the image. To use, select an element, click **Modify**, **Templates**, and then **Make Attribute Editable**.

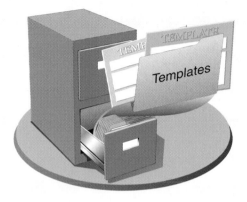

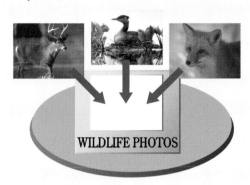

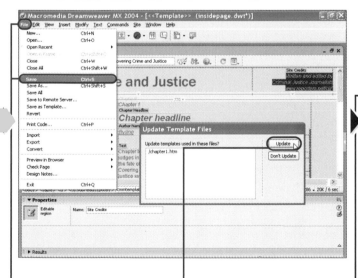

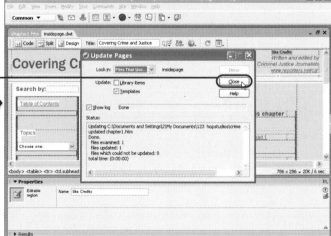

Note: To set the editable region of a template, see page 198.

■ In this example, a site credits region is added.

-11 Click **File**.

-12 Click **Save**.

■ The Update Template Files dialog box appears.

■ You can choose to update all documents in the local site that use the template.

-13 Click **Update**.

■ The Update Pages dialog box shows the update progress.

14 After Dreamweaver updates the site, click **Close**.

■ All pages that use the template are updated to reflect the changes.

SUNSHINE VACATIONS

Here at Sunshine Vacations, we are committed to making your vacation or business trip a memorable one! We provide the best rates available for flights, accommodations, and rental cars, plus important advice about what to see and do at your destination city.

Kick back, relax and enjoy the peace of mind that comes with knowing Sunshine Vacations is available 24 hours a day should you need our assistance.

STYLE SHEET

FANCY HEADLINE

BORDERED IMAGE

BOLD PARAGRAPH

BORDERED IMA

CHAPTER 12

Creating and Applying Style Sheets

This chapter shows you how to apply complex formatting to your pages using Cascading Style Sheets and HTML Styles. These features will save you lots of time, especially on large Web sites.

Introduction to Cascading
  Style Sheets 206

Customize an HTML Tag 208

Create a Custom Style 210

Apply a Style...................................212

Edit a Style 214

Create Custom Link Styles 216

Create an External Style Sheet..........218

Attach an External Style Sheet 220

Edit an External Style Sheet 222

INTRODUCTION TO CASCADING STYLE SHEETS

You can apply many different types of formatting to your Web pages with style sheets, also known as *cascading style sheets,* or *CSS.*

The Anglers' Home Page

The page dedicated to dedicated anglers.

Format Text

A separate standard from HTML, style sheets enable you to format fonts, adjust character, paragraph, and margin spacing, customize the look of hyperlinks, precisely place blocks of content, and more.

Create Global Web Page Styles

You can use style sheets to globally define your content types and formats. Use the style across your Web pages for consistent formatting; edit the style sheet to change the style globally without editing them individually.

HTML and CSS Style Sheets

You can create custom cascading style sheets, or you can redefine existing HTML tags to create HTML styles. You can use HTML styles to apply more than one formatting option at a time. You can use external CSS style sheets to apply styles across a single page, or across an entire Web site.

Embedded Style Sheets

A style sheet saved inside a particular Web page is an *embedded* style sheet. Embedded style sheet rules apply only to the page in which they are embedded.

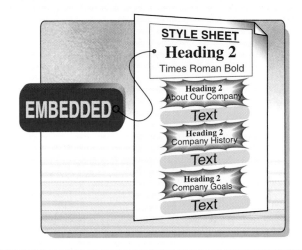

External Style Sheets

You can save style sheets as separate files; these *external* style sheets exist independently of your HTML pages. You can use external style sheets to control formatting across multiple pages and even an entire site. You can also make global changes to formatted elements when you edit style sheet definitions.

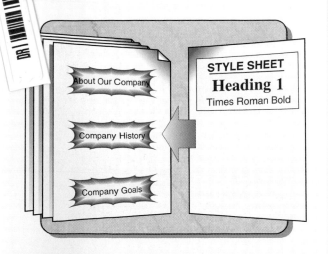

Style Sheets and Browsers

Some older browsers do not support style sheet standards, and browsers display style sheets differently. Always test pages that use style sheets on different browsers to ensure that content displays as you expect it.

Netscape Communicator

Microsoft Internet Explorer

CUSTOMIZE AN HTML TAG

You can use style sheets to customize the style that an HTML tag applies to text or other elements. Doing this enables you to apply multiple style options with one HTML tag.

CUSTOMIZE AN HTML TAG

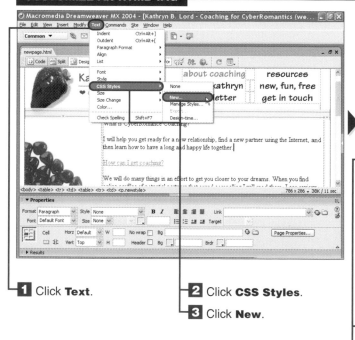

1 Click **Text**.

2 Click **CSS Styles**.

3 Click **New**.

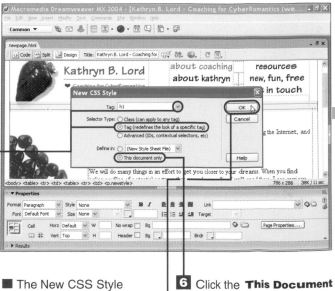

■ The New CSS Style dialog box appears.

4 Click the **Tag (to redefine the look of a specific tag)** option (○ changes to ◉).

5 Click ▾ and select a tag.

6 Click the **This Document Only** option to create an embedded style sheet for the file on which you are working (○ changes to ◉).

Note: To create style sheets for more than one document, see page 218.

7 Click **OK**.

Why should I redefine an HTML tag?

There are some good reasons for redefining existing HTML tags to create HTML styles. First, you can apply more than one style to the tag, which means you only have to use one HTML tag instead of several. Second, the style sheet options give you much finer control over how elements appear on the Web page, including point sizes for fonts. Finally, if style sheets are not supported by a user's browser, the HTML itself will still be available as a backup formatting.

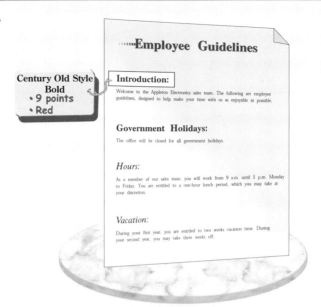

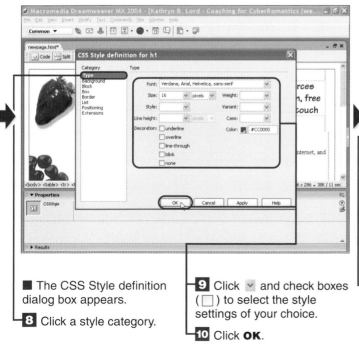

■ The CSS Style definition dialog box appears.

8 Click a style category.

9 Click ☑ and check boxes (☐) to select the style settings of your choice.

10 Click **OK**.

■ Dreamweaver adds the new style to any content formatted with the redefined tag.

■ In this example, the Heading 1 is redefined to use a different font face, color, and size.

■ You can also apply the style by selecting content on the page and selecting the Heading 1 format.

CREATE A CUSTOM STYLE

You can define specific style attributes as a custom style. You can then apply that style to text or other elements on your Web page.

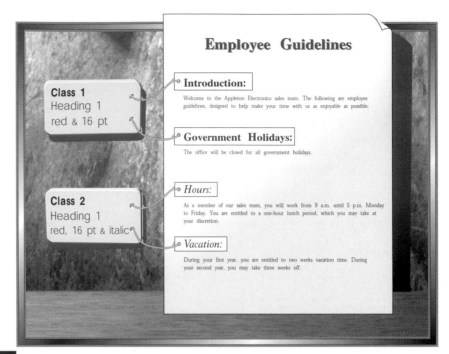

Employee Guidelines

Class 1
Heading 1
red & 16 pt

Introduction:
Welcome to the Appleton Electronics sales team. The following are employee guidelines, designed to help make your time with us as enjoyable as possible.

Government Holidays:
The office will be closed for all government holidays.

Class 2
Heading 1
red, 16 pt & italic

Hours:
As a member of our sales team, you will work from 9 a.m. until 5 p.m. Monday to Friday. You are entitled to a one-hour lunch period, which you may take at your discretion.

Vacation:
During your first year, you are entitled to two weeks vacation time. During your second year, you may take three weeks off.

CREATE A CUSTOM STYLE

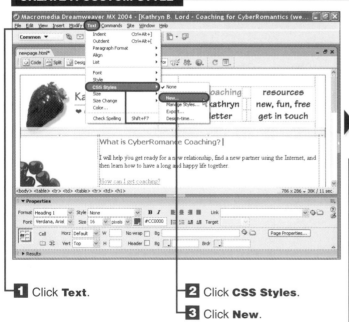

1 Click **Text**.

2 Click **CSS Styles**.

3 Click **New**.

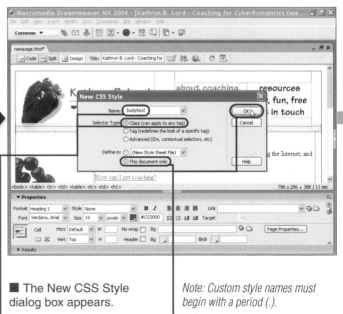

■ The New CSS Style dialog box appears.

4 Click the **Class (can apply to any tag)** option (○ changes to ●).

5 Type a name for the style.

Note: Custom style names must begin with a period (.).

6 Click the **This Document Only** option (○ changes to ●).

Note: To create style sheets for more than one document, see page 218.

7 Click **OK**.

How does customizing an HTML tag differ from creating a custom style?

Customizing an HTML tag links a style to an existing HTML tag. The new style affects every instance of that tag. For example, if you customize your paragraph tags as green, every paragraph in your page will be green. With custom styles, you can apply styles that are independent of HTML tags.

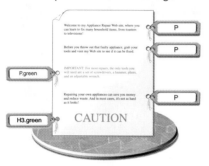

Is it better to customize HTML or create my own styles?

The advantage to redefining HTML tags is that you or your page designers will not have to keep track of many styles. On the other hand, will there be times when you need to use the HTML tag without the style? If so, custom styles may be a better solution.

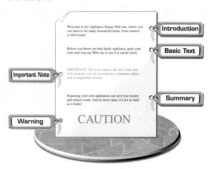

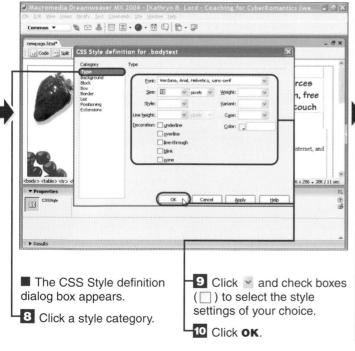

■ The CSS Style definition dialog box appears.

8 Click a style category.

9 Click ![dropdown] and check boxes (☐) to select the style settings of your choice.

10 Click **OK**.

11 Click **Window**.

12 Click **CSS Styles** to open the CSS Styles panel.

■ The new style appears in the CSS Styles panel.

■ In this example, a font style setting is created.

■ You can apply the new style to new or existing content.

Note: To apply a style, see page 212.

APPLY A STYLE

Applying a style sheet to elements on your Web page enables you to make changes to the color, font, size, background, and other characteristics of content on your page without using standard HTML.

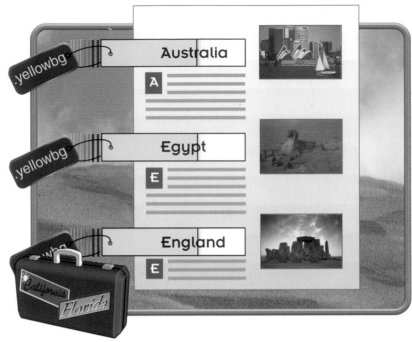

APPLY A STYLE TO AN ELEMENT

Note: To create a new custom style, see page 210.

1 Click and drag to select the text or other element to which you want to apply the style.

2 In the Properties inspector, click the Style ▾.

3 Click the name of a style.

■ Dreamweaver applies the style.

■ In this example, a font style is applied.

**What are some type-based
features that I can apply with style
sheets which I cannot with HTML?**

With style sheets, you can specify
a numeric value for font weight,
enabling you to apply varying
degrees of boldness, instead of
just a single boldness setting as
with HTML. You can also define
type size in absolute units, such
as pixels, points, picas, inches,
centimeters, or millimeters, or in
relative units, such as ems, exs, or
percentage. Keep in mind that
these features work only with
certain fonts and will not display in
all browsers.

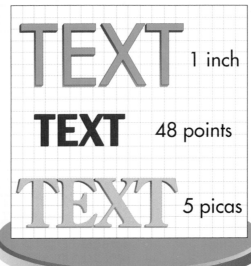

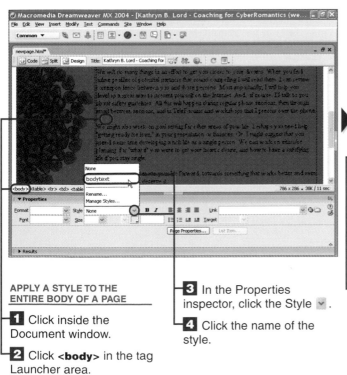

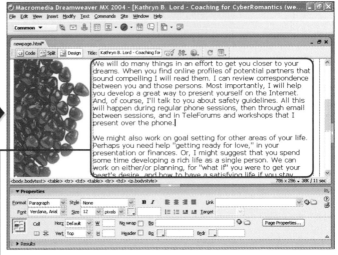

**APPLY A STYLE TO THE
ENTIRE BODY OF A PAGE**

1 Click inside the
Document window.

2 Click **<body>** in the tag
Launcher area.

3 In the Properties
inspector, click the Style ▾ .

4 Click the name of the
style.

■ Dreamweaver applies
the style sheet class to the
entire body of the page in
the Document window.

■ In this example, a font
style is applied, thereby,
changing the font face
of all text on the page.

EDIT A STYLE

You can edit style sheet definitions and automatically apply the changes across all of the text or other elements to which you have applied the style on your site.

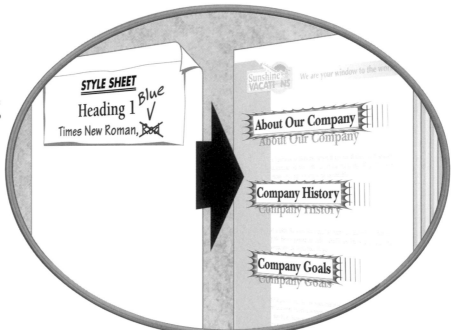

EDIT A STYLE

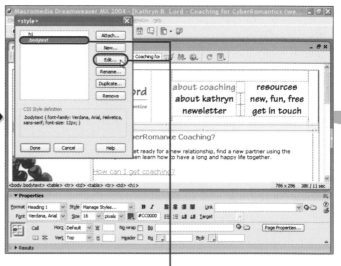

1 In the Properties inspector, click the Style ⌄.

2 Click **Manage Styles**.

■ The CSS Styles panel opens and displays the styles available to that page.

3 Click the style you want to edit.

4 Click **Edit**.

How are CSS styles implemented in HTML code?

You can implement CSS styles in one of three ways by adding the `<CLASS>` attribute, the `<SPAN>` tag, or the `<DIV>` tag. First, you can simply add the `<CLASS>` attribute to any existing HTML tag. Whatever is affected by that tag uses the style specified by the class. The `<SPAN>` tag allows you to implement a style independently of any HTML on the page and without affecting the page layout. The `<DIV>` tag actually defines blocks of content, which then take on the style attributes defined in the `<DIV>` tag. `<DIV>` tags are very powerful and can actually be used for absolute positioning, much like layers, and can even replace HTML tables. For more on layers, see Chapter 13.

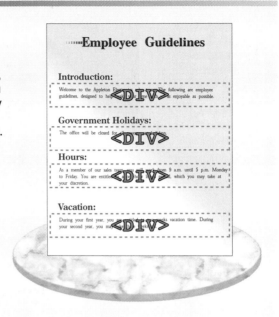

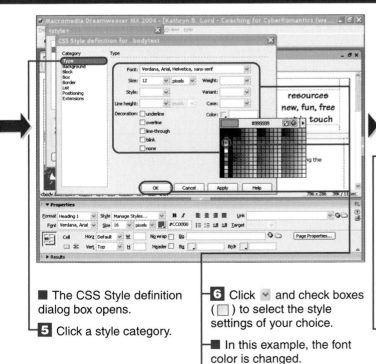

■ The CSS Style definition dialog box opens.

5 Click a style category.

6 Click ⌄ and check boxes (☐) to select the style settings of your choice.

■ In this example, the font color is changed.

7 Click **OK**.

■ Dreamweaver saves the style sheet changes.

8 Click **Done**.

■ In this example, the font color is changed when the new style definition is applied.

CREATE CUSTOM LINK STYLES

You can use style sheet *selectors* to customize the links on your page. Selectors enable you to customize your links in ways that you cannot with HTML, such as removing the underline from linked text.

CREATE CUSTOM LINK STYLES

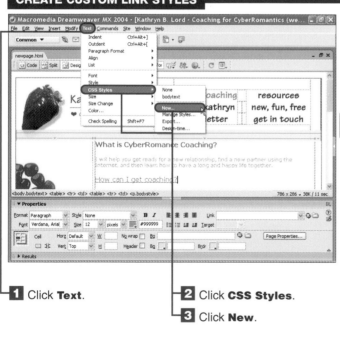

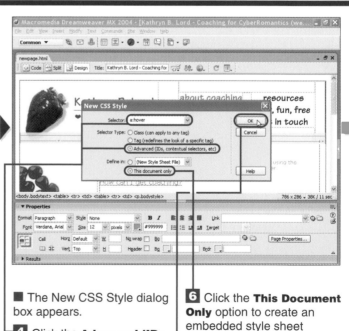

1 Click **Text**.

2 Click **CSS Styles**.

3 Click **New**.

■ The New CSS Style dialog box appears.

4 Click the **Advanced (IDs, contextual selectors, etc)** option (○ changes to ◉).

5 Click ✓ and select a selector.

6 Click the **This Document Only** option to create an embedded style sheet (○ changes to ◉).

Note: To create style sheets for more than one document, see page 218.

7 Click **OK**.

216

Below are some of the flowers you'll
find on my Dictionary of Flowers site:

`<div align="center">`

What are some non-text based features that I can implement with style sheets?

Probably the most exciting thing you can do with cascading style sheets is position elements precisely on the page. Style sheets give you freedom from traditional, and imprecise, layout methods like HTML tables. The `<DIV>` tag, when used in an HTML document, defines an area on the page in which you can position it with alignment attributes, and more precisely by specifying an actual pixel location in the page. It is too soon to leave tables behind completely, because there still is not good browser support for CSS positioning.

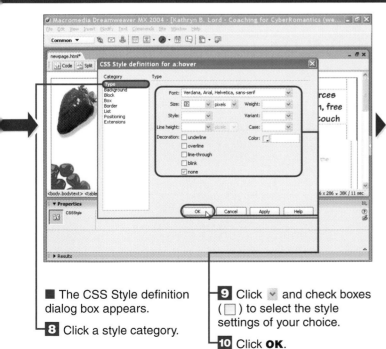

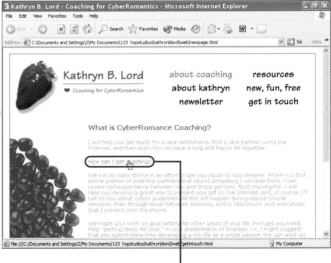

■ The CSS Style definition dialog box appears.

8 Click a style category.

9 Click ⌄ and check boxes (☐) to select the style settings of your choice.

10 Click **OK**.

11 Preview the page in a Web browser.

Note: To preview a page in Web browsers, see page 26.

■ Dreamweaver applies the style changes to the link.

■ In this example, the linked question is not underlined, even though it is a link.

CREATE AN EXTERNAL STYLE SHEET

External style sheets enable you to define a set of style sheet rules and apply them to many different pages — even pages on different Web sites. With this capability, you can keep a consistent look and feel across many pages and streamline style updates.

STYLE SHEET
Heading 1
Times Roman Bold

About Our Company

Company History

Company Goals

CREATE AN EXTERNAL STYLE SHEET

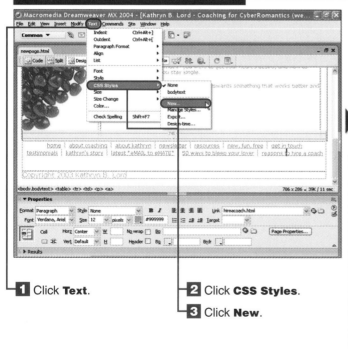

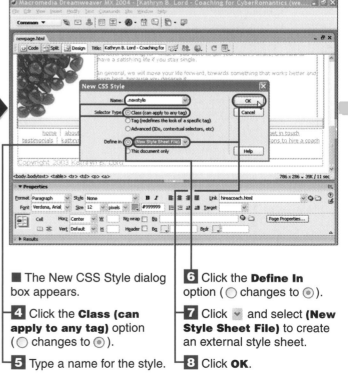

1 Click **Text**.

2 Click **CSS Styles**.

3 Click **New**.

■ The New CSS Style dialog box appears.

4 Click the **Class (can apply to any tag)** option (○ changes to ◉).

5 Type a name for the style.

6 Click the **Define In** option (○ changes to ◉).

7 Click ⌄ and select **(New Style Sheet File)** to create an external style sheet.

8 Click **OK**.

Note: Class names must begin with a period (.).

How can I export an internal style sheet?

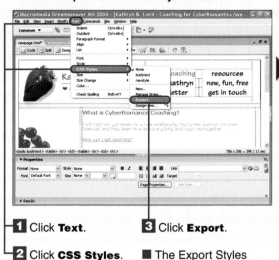

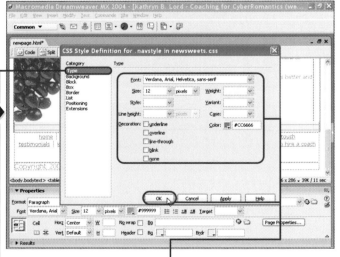

1 Click **Text**.

2 Click **CSS Styles**.

3 Click **Export**.

■ The Export Styles As CSS File dialog box appears.

4 Click ⌄ and select a location to save the CSS file.

5 Type a name for the file.

6 Click **Save**.

■ Dreamweaver exports the internal styles to the new external style sheet, which you can then apply to other pages.

Note: To apply the style sheet to a new page, see page 212.

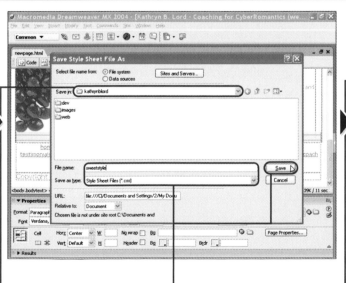

■ The Save Style Sheet File As dialog box appears.

9 Click ⌄ and select the folder in which you want to store the external style sheet.

Note: Store the external style sheet somewhere inside your local site folder.

Note: To define a local site, see page 20.

10 Type a name for the style sheet and select a **.css** extension.

11 Click **Save**.

■ The CSS Style Definition dialog box appears.

12 Click a style category.

13 Click ⌄ and check boxes (☐) to select the style settings of your choice.

14 Click **OK**.

■ Dreamweaver saves the style to the external style sheet.

219

ATTACH AN EXTERNAL STYLE SHEET

You can format text from the Properties inspector Style ⌄, which allows you to apply complicated styles with a single click.

ATTACH AN EXTERNAL STYLE SHEET

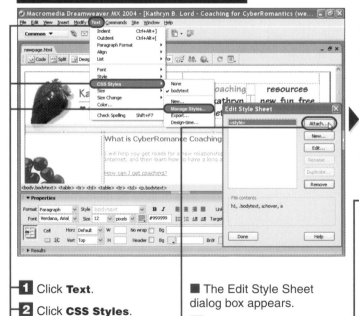

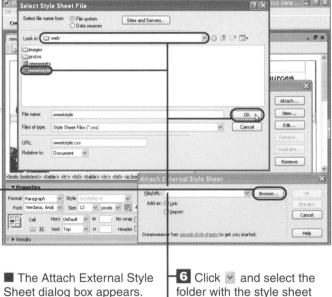

1 Click **Text**.

2 Click **CSS Styles**.

3 Click **Manage Styles**.

■ The Edit Style Sheet dialog box appears.

4 Click **Attach**.

■ The Attach External Style Sheet dialog box appears.

5 Click **Browse**.

■ The Select Style Sheet File dialog box appears.

6 Click ⌄ and select the folder with the style sheet you want to use.

7 Click the style sheet.

8 Click **OK**.

How can I add more styles to an external style sheet?

To add more styles to an existing external style sheet, you can follow the steps to create a custom style on page 210, or follow the steps to customize an HTML tag on page 208, but define the style in the existing external style sheet. You can add styles to an external style sheet at any point during production, even months after the site was first published. In addition, you can make changes or additions while you work on any page that is currently attached to the external style sheet.

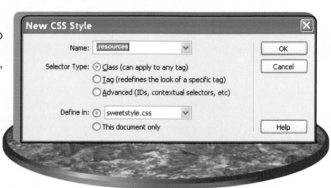

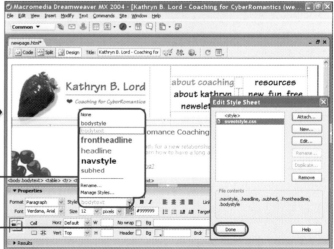

■ The Select Style Sheet File dialog box closes.

9 Click **OK** to close the Attach External Style Sheet dialog box.

■ The style sheet is attached to the current document.

10 Click **Done** to close the Edit Style Sheet dialog box.

■ The new styles are visible in the Style ⌄ in the Properties inspector.

Note: To apply styles to content in a document, see page 212.

EDIT AN EXTERNAL STYLE SHEET

You can include hundreds of styles in a single external sheet, allowing you to continue to add to the sheet as your site grows and changes or adds sections.

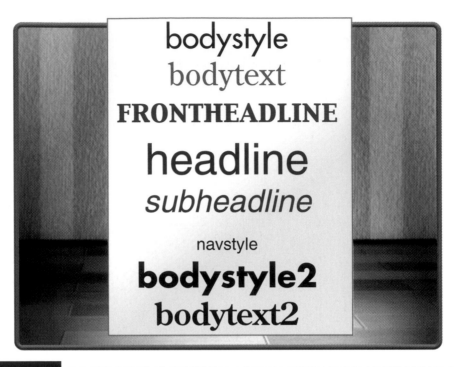

bodystyle

bodytext

FRONTHEADLINE

headline

subheadline

navstyle

bodystyle2

bodytext2

EDIT AN EXTERNAL STYLE SHEET

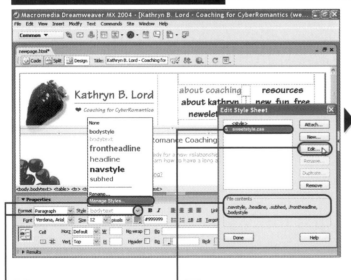

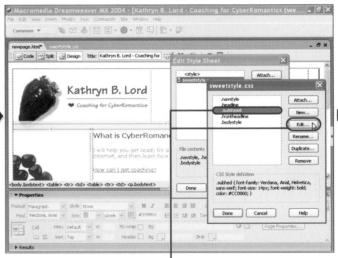

1 In the Properties inspector, click the Style ▾.

2 Click **Manage Styles**.

■ The Edit Style Sheet dialog box appears.

3 Click a style sheet from the list.

■ The contents of the style sheet appear at the bottom of the dialog box.

4 Click **Edit**.

■ The style sheet dialog box appears with a list of all the styles that it contains.

5 Click the style you want to edit.

6 Click **Edit**.

What should I worry about when I use CSS?

The benefits to using cascading style sheets are enormous, and they mostly outweigh the small problems that come with their implementation. This does not mean you can ignore those problems completely. First, watch out for browser support. Some CSS specifications simply are not completely reliable across browsers, so always test your pages to make sure you like what you are getting. Secondly, the user pays the price for increased design control that you get in your pages. If you are using text CSS controls to set your font size in pixels and points, the users will no longer be able to increase the text size when they browse. This may mean decreased usability, depending on your audience.

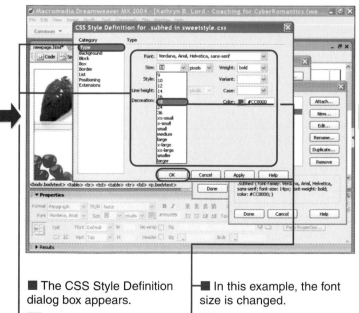

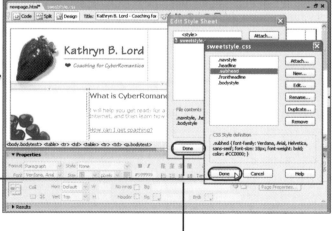

■ The CSS Style Definition dialog box appears.

7 Click a style category.

8 Click ⌄ and select the style settings of your choice.

■ In this example, the font size is changed.

9 Click **OK**.

■ Dreamweaver saves the style to the external style sheet.

10 Repeat steps **5** to **9** for each style you want to edit.

11 Click **Done** to close the style sheet dialog box.

12 Click **Done** to close the Edit Style Sheet dialog box.

Ancient Treasure:

See the most recen
discoveries in the
world of archaeol

CUSTOMER INFORMATION

NAME: **J. Anderso**

ADDRESS: **322 W**

CITY:

STAT

IP CODE **47777-8844**

VALIDATED

CHAPTER 13

Using Layers to Increase User Interaction

In addition to other layout tools, Dreamweaver lets you quickly implement stackable layers and interactivity. This chapter shows you how to have more design control and increase user interaction.

Introduction to Layers 226

Create a Layer with Content 228

Resize and Reposition Layers............230

Change the Stacking Order of
   Layers...232

Drag a Layer 233

Show and Hide Layers Behavior 234

Create a Nested Layer 236

INTRODUCTION TO LAYERS

You can use advance Dreamweaver tools to create layers by stacking them on top of each other as a precise layout tool. You can also add scripting with Dreamweaver behaviors to increase your Web site's interactivity.

Layer Basics

Layers are discrete blocks of content that you can precisely position on the page, make moveable by the user, and make invisible. Most significantly, you can stack layers on top of each other. Layers can contain any kind of content, including text, graphics, tables — even other layers. It is important to test your layers across browsers to make sure your pages look the way you want them to look.

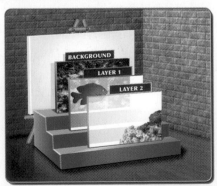

Nested Layers

Layers can contain other nested layers, which create areas of content that stay linked together on a page for better control during production of Web pages. Nested, or child, layers can inherit the properties of their parent layers, including visibility or invisibility. You can also nest layers within other nested layers.

Behavior Basics

Behaviors are cause-and-effect events that you can insert into your Web pages. Creative behaviors can make pictures on a Web page change or a new browser window open when a user clicks or positions the mouse over an object. Logical behaviors tell people what Web browser they are using, or remind them to fill in their names in your site's questionnaire form.

Behind the Scenes

Dreamweaver behaviors insert brief programs called *scripts* into your Web pages. Dreamweaver creates these scripts in a language called *JavaScript*; however, many available behaviors rely on other technologies such as ActiveX and SSI. JavaScript is by far the most accepted and widely used browser-side programming language due to wide browser acceptance and its powerful capabilities.

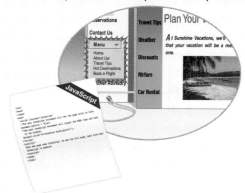

Behaviors and Browsers

Behaviors vary in complexity and are written in various ways to ensure compatibility with older browsers. Both Internet Explorer and Netscape Navigator adopted the majority of DHTML and JavaScript technologies after version 4. However, each browser's result may still vary. Dreamweaver lets you disable behaviors that may not work in older browsers.

Check Browser Versions

Designing a page that works equally well in all browsers generally means that you have to refrain from using the latest Web-design technologies available. Some of the features in this chapter are not available for older browser versions. While you can create two versions of your site — one for current browsers and one for older browsers — Dreamweaver can automatically redirect users to the page appropriate for their browser. Most Webmasters do not want the added work of maintaining two versions of their sites. More commonly, you can use a behavior that lets people know they need to upgrade their browser for the best possible experience.

CREATE A LAYER WITH CONTENT

Layers are scalable rectangles inside of which you can place text and pictures, similar to tables. However, layers can float above the body of a document. You can move layers wherever you want with pixel-perfect precision. If you have worked with the layer feature of Adobe Photoshop, you will find that layers are very similar.

Layers do not follow normal HTML flow. You can sit layers on top of page content and place anywhere on a page. Layers can overlap other layers.

CREATE A LAYER

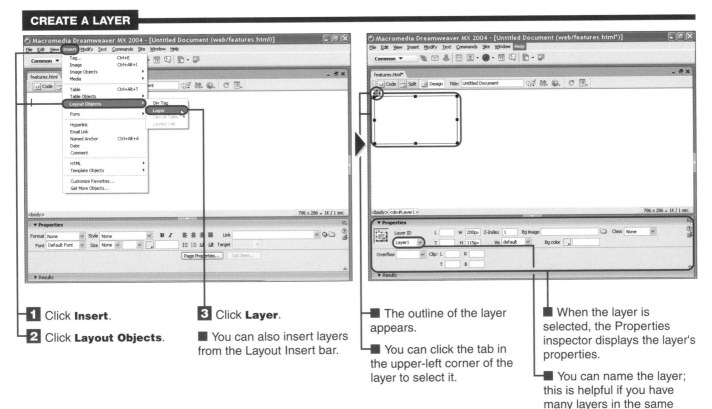

1 Click **Insert**.

2 Click **Layout Objects**.

3 Click **Layer**.

■ You can also insert layers from the Layout Insert bar.

■ The outline of the layer appears.

■ You can click the tab in the upper-left corner of the layer to select it.

■ When the layer is selected, the Properties inspector displays the layer's properties.

■ You can name the layer; this is helpful if you have many layers in the same page.

Should I use layers instead of HTML tables?

Layers are very powerful layout tools that offer a page designer better control over the placement of content on a Web page. Layers are not fully supported by all browsers; therefore, many Web designers continue to use tables. It is important to know what kind of browser and the version your visitors are using when deciding whether to use layers or tables.

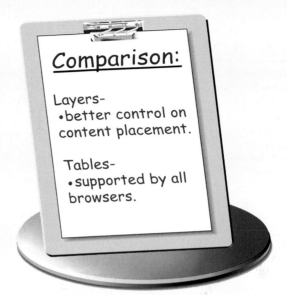

Comparison:

Layers-
•better control on
content placement.

Tables-
•supported by all
browsers.

ADD CONTENT TO A LAYER

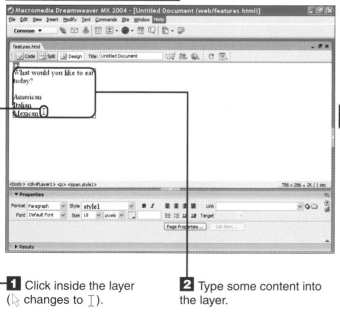

1 Click inside the layer
(⬧ changes to I).

2 Type some content into the layer.

■ You can also add an image by clicking the Insert Image button (🖻).

■ In this example, the text and image are inside the layer.

■ You can perform the same actions within a layer as within the document body, such as format text, align text, and insert tables.

Note: To format text, see Chapter 5. To insert and format tables, see Chapter 8.

RESIZE AND REPOSITION LAYERS

When you create a new layer, you can adjust its position and dimensions to make it fit attractively with the rest of the content on your page. Do not forget to look at your page in a browser, because the positioning may be different from the Dreamweaver document window.

RESIZE A LAYER

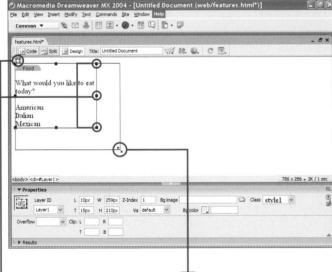

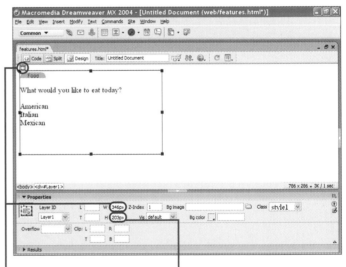

RESIZE WITH THE CURSOR

1 Click the tab in the upper-left corner of the layer to select it.

■ Square, black handles appear around the edges of the layer.

2 Click and drag one of the handles.

■ Dreamweaver resizes the layer to the new size.

RESIZE THE WIDTH AND HEIGHT ATTRIBUTES

1 Click the tab in the upper-left corner of the layer to select it.

■ The layer's properties appear in the Properties inspector.

2 Type a new measurement into the W (Width) field.

3 Press Enter (Return).

■ Dreamweaver changes the layer's width.

4 Repeat steps **1** to **3**, but in step **2**, type a new measurement in the H (Height) field.

■ You can also type **in** for inches or **cm** for centimeters.

How can I change the visibility of a layer?

To change a layer's visibility, select a layer and then click the Vis 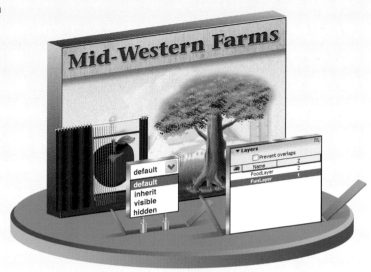 in the Properties inspector. You can make a layer visible or invisible, or if it is a nested layer, it can inherit its characteristic from its *parent*, which is the enclosing layer. There is also a visibility column available in the Layers panel. Click next to the layer name in the visibility column to adjust. The open eye (👁) means the layer is visible; the closed eye (👁) means the layer is invisible. If no icon is showing, visibility is set to the default, and the layer will appear visible or inherit its visibility.

REPOSITION A LAYER

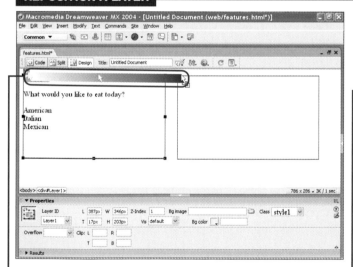

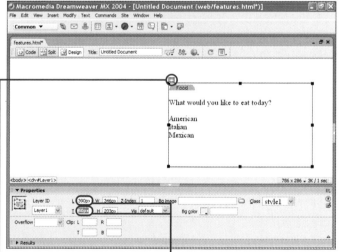

REPOSITION WITH THE CURSOR

1 Click and drag the tab in the upper-left corner of the layer to move it to a new position.

■ Dreamweaver moves the layer to the new position.

RESIZE WITH LEFT AND TOP ATTRIBUTES

1 Click the tab in the upper-left corner of the layer to select it.

■ The layer properties appear in the Properties inspector.

2 Type the new distance from the top of the window in the T field.

■ Dreamweaver applies the new positioning to the layer.

3 Repeat steps **1** and **2**, but in step **2**, type the new distance in the L field.

CHANGE THE STACKING ORDER OF LAYERS

You can change the
stacking order of
layers on a page,
affecting how they
overlap one another.
You can then hide
parts of some layers
under other layers.

Autumn Leaves,
Falling Leaves

Falling Leaves

CHANGE THE STACKING ORDER OF LAYERS

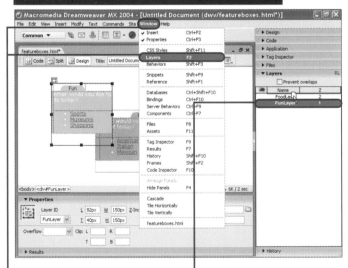

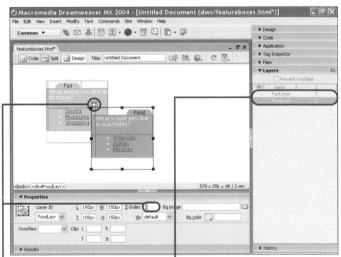

**CHANGE ORDER IN
LAYERS PANEL**

*Note: The Food layer covers a
portion of the Fun layer.*

1 Click **Window**.

2 Click **Layers**.

■ The Layers panel appears.

3 Click and drag the
layer name above or
below another layer
(↕ changes to ↕).

■ Dreamweaver changes the
stacking order of the layers.
Note the difference in Z-Index
values in the Layers panel.

**CHANGE ORDER WITH
Z-INDEX ATTRIBUTE**

1 Click the tab in the
upper-left corner of the layer
to select one of the layers.

2 Type a new number in
the Z-Index field.

■ Layers with greater Z-
Index values are placed
higher in the stack.

■ Dreamweaver changes
the stacking order of the
layers.

Using Dreamweaver behaviors and layers, you can enable site visitors to pick up and move elements around your Web page. It helps to name layers when you start to work with behaviors.

DRAG A LAYER

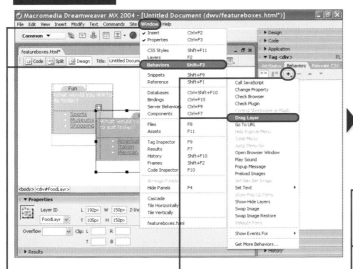

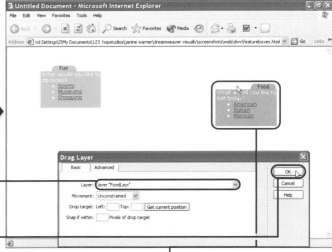

1 Click **Window**.

2 Click **Behaviors**.

■ The Behaviors tab opens in the Tag panel.

3 Click ⊞.

4 Click **Drag Layer**.

■ The Drag Layer dialog box appears.

5 Click ⌄ and select a layer.

6 Click **OK**.

7 Preview the file in a Web browser.

Note: To preview a Web page in a browser, see page 26.

■ You can move the layer around the Web page by clicking and dragging it.

233

SHOW AND HIDE LAYERS BEHAVIOR

You can add interactivity to your Web pages by creating *buttons* that interact with your layers. You can use behaviors to show and hide these animate layers.

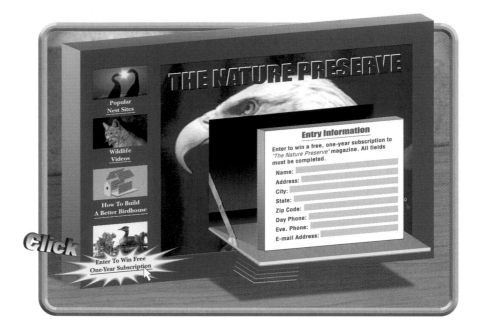

HIDE A VISIBLE LAYER

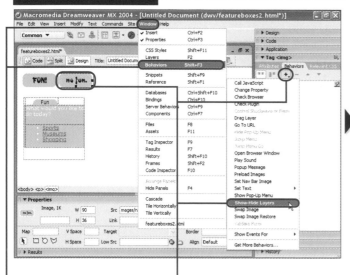

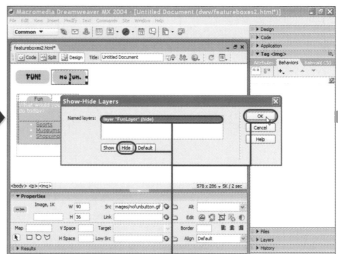

■ In this example, a graphic is used as a button to hide a layer.

1 Click **Window**.

2 Click **Behaviors**.

■ The Behaviors tab opens in the Tag panel.

3 Click the graphic.

4 Click ⊞.

5 Click **Show-Hide Layers**.

Note: Dreamweaver prevents you from choosing behaviors unless your target browser supports them. While Netscape does support layers, older versions are not fully compatible with this Show-Hide Layer behavior.

■ The Show-Hide Layers dialog box appears.

6 Click the layer.

7 Click **Hide**.

8 Click **OK**.

What are some practical uses for showing and hiding layers?

Many sites use these types of behaviors to create Windows-style navigational menus that expand in a tree-like structure over content. You can also use this technique to display a large amount of content on one page, simply by showing one layer while simultaneously hiding other layers. Because the person never has to leave the page, you can literally create a small Web site on one page!

SHOW A HIDDEN LAYER

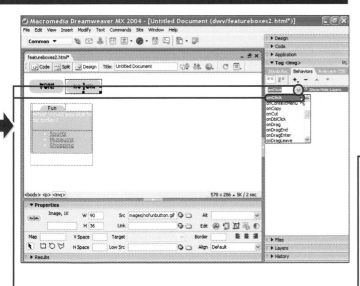

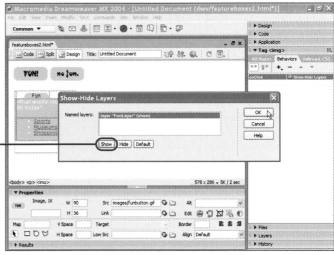

-**9** Click ⌄.

-**10** Click **onClick** from the drop-down menu.

■ The behavior is now associated with the action. In this example, clicking the graphic hides the layer.

Note: The layer remains hidden after the behavior executes until you create another behavior that makes it visible again or until you reload the page.

-**1** Repeat steps **3** to **10**, but select **Show** instead of Hide in step **7**.

■ The behavior is now associated with the action. In this example, clicking the graphic shows the layer.

CREATE A NESTED LAYER

Nested layers are often called child layers, and the layers that contain them are parents. They act as a unit on the page. If the parent layer moves, the child goes with it. You can move the child layer independently of the parent, but the layers will always stay linked.

CREATE A NESTED LAYER

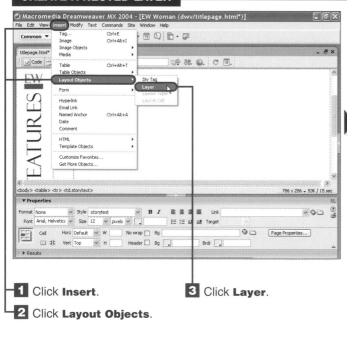

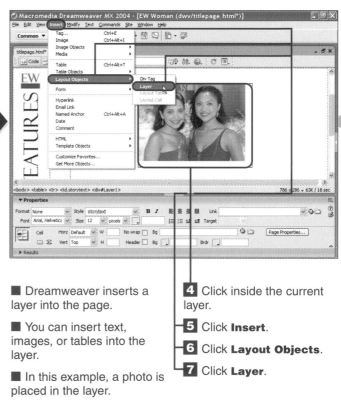

1 Click **Insert**.

2 Click **Layout Objects**.

3 Click **Layer**.

■ Dreamweaver inserts a layer into the page.

■ You can insert text, images, or tables into the layer.

■ In this example, a photo is placed in the layer.

4 Click inside the current layer.

5 Click **Insert**.

6 Click **Layout Objects**.

7 Click **Layer**.

Can I unnest a nested layer?

Yes, you can take a nested
layer out of its parent layer.
Click Window and then
Layers to open the Layers
panel. Click the nested layer
and drag it above the parent
layer. The layer is no longer
nested.

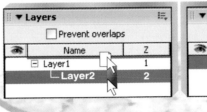

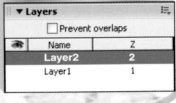

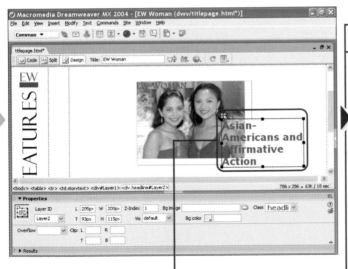

■ Dreamweaver inserts a
nested layer into the first
layer.

■ You can insert text,
images, or tables into the
layer.

■ In this example, text is
placed in the layer.

8 Click and drag to position
the layer on the page.

9 Click **Window**.

10 Click **Layers**.

■ The Layers panel opens.

■ Both layers appear. The
└ indicates that Layer2 is
nested inside Layer1.

CHAPTER 14

Publishing a Web Site

You can publish your completed Web pages on a server to allow the world to view them. This chapter shows you how to publish your Web site and keep it up-to-date with Dreamweaver.

Publish Your Web Site......................240

Use the Site Window 241

Test Your Work in Different
    Browsers 242

Organize Your Files and Folders 244

Set Up a Remote Site 246

Connect to a Remote Site 248

Upload Files to a Web Server 250

Download Files from a Web
    Server...252

Synchronize Your Local and
    Remote Sites 254

Woman's Web Page

WOMAN

she's a little bit East, a little bit West

CONTENTS   FEATURES   BEAUTY   HEALTH   RELATIONSHIPS   EWMAN   WORK
SALTY DISH   EWCLOSET   WATCH FOR   REVIEW CORNER   HOROSCOPE   ARCHIVES

OCTOBER 2003

FEATURES

The Asian Face Of Breast Cancer
Increasing rates, but invisible in the
battle.

A Daughter's Story
In the moment of realization,
daughters of breast cancer victims
say their whole perspective changed.

This is Better
Revisiting a post 9-11 hate crime.
The effects on the family and the
community.

Meena Alexander: A Perennial

PUBLISH YOUR WEB SITE

To make the Web pages that you have built in Dreamweaver accessible on the Web, you must transfer them to a Web server. A *Web server* is an Internet-connected computer running special software that enables the computer to serve files to Web browsers. Dreamweaver includes tools that enable you to connect and transfer pages to a Web server.

Steps for Publishing Your Web Site

Publishing your site content using Dreamweaver involves the following steps:

1 Specify where on your computer the site files are kept.

Note: To define a local site, see page 20.

2 Specify the Web server to which you want to publish your files.

Note: To define a remote site, see page 246.

Note: Most people publish their Web pages on servers maintained by their Internet service provider (ISP), a hosting company, or their company or school.

3 Connect to the Web server and transfer the files.

Note: The Site window gives you a user-friendly interface for organizing your files and transferring them to the remote site.

After uploading your site, you can update it by editing the copies of the site files on your computer (the local site) and then transferring those copies to the Web server (the remote site).

With the Site window, you can view the organization of all files in your site. You can also upload local files to the remote site and download remote files to the local site through the Files panel. You can access the Site window by clicking the Expand/Collapse button in the Files panel. For more information about the Files panel, see Chapter 3.

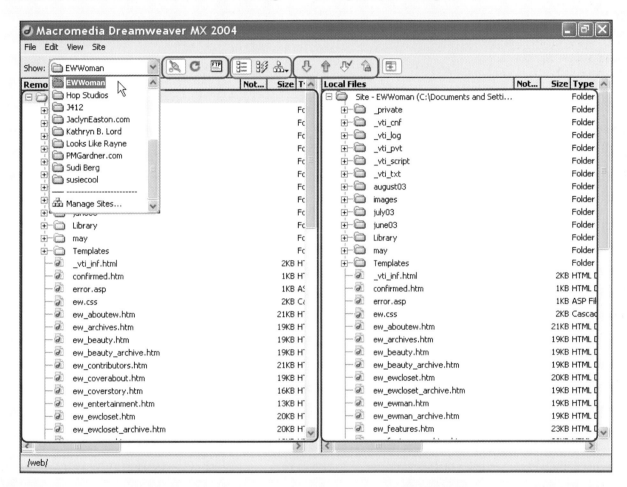

Remote Site

The left pane displays the contents of your site as it exists on the remote Web server. To define a remote site, see page 246.

Site Window View

You can click 📋 or 🗺️ to switch between viewing your site as a list of files or as a site map. For more on using the site map view, see page 258. You can click 📝 to access a Testing Server.

Site Menu

Lets you select from the different sites you have defined in Dreamweaver. For more on defining sites in Dreamweaver, see page 20.

File Transfer

Buttons enable you to connect to your remote site, refresh the file list, upload files to the remote server, download files to the local site, and view the FTP log.

Local Site

The right pane displays the content of your site as it exists on your local computer. To define a local site, see page 20.

TEST YOUR WORK IN DIFFERENT BROWSERS

There are still big differences between how HTML pages display in different browsers and different browser versions. You can preview an HTML page in any browser that is installed on your computer.

TEST YOUR WORK IN DIFFERENT BROWSERS

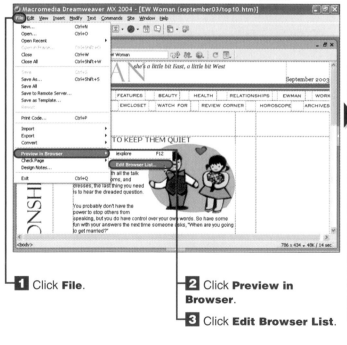

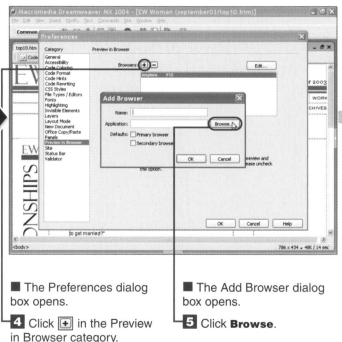

1 Click **File**.

2 Click **Preview in Browser**.

3 Click **Edit Browser List**.

■ The Preferences dialog box opens.

4 Click ⊞ in the Preview in Browser category.

■ The Add Browser dialog box opens.

5 Click **Browse**.

**Where can I download older
versions of browsers that
are still in use?**

There are several browser
archives on the Web,
but one of the best is at
http://browsers.evolt.org/,
which has a comprehensive
listing of current and
discontinued browsers
for all kinds of operating
systems and versions.

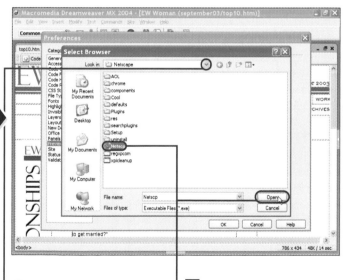

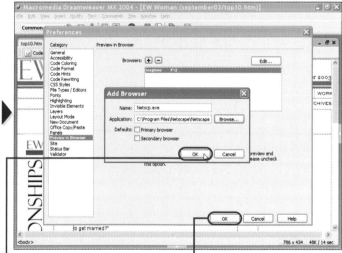

■ The Select Browser dialog
box opens.

6 Click ⌄ and select
the folder that contains a
browser application.

7 Click the browser
application you want to add.

8 Click **Open**.

■ The Select Browser dialog
box closes.

9 Click **OK** to add the
browser.

■ The Add Browser dialog
box closes.

10 Repeat steps **4** to **9** to
add additional browsers.

11 Click **OK**.

■ The Preferences dialog
box closes.

■ You can now use the 🖭
icon in the Document toolbar
to preview an HTML page in
any browsers you have
added.

ORGANIZE YOUR FILES AND FOLDERS

You can use the Site window to organize the elements that make up your local and remote sites. With this window, you can create and delete files and folders, as well as move files between folders.

Creating subfolders to organize files of a similar type can be useful if you have a large Web site.

ORGANIZE YOUR FILES AND FOLDERS

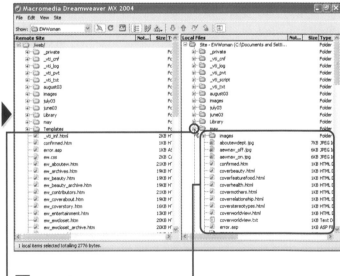

REARRANGE SITE FILES

1 Click ⊞ in the Files panel to expand the Site window.

2 Click ⊞ to view the files in a subfolder (⊞ changes to ⊟).

■ The folder contents display.

■ You can click ⊟ to close the subfolder.

What happens to links when I move files?

When you move files into and out of folders, you will need to update the hyperlinks and images referenced on those pages, because document-relative references become invalid. Dreamweaver keeps track of any affected code when you rearrange files and can update it for you when you move a file. This capability can save you time and prevent your site links from breaking.

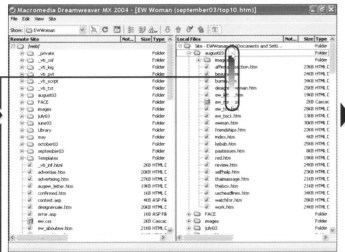

3 Click and drag a file from the local site folder into a subfolder (▷ changes to 🖑).

■ A prompt appears asking if you want to update your links.

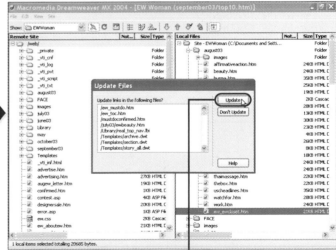

4 Click **Update** to keep your local site links from breaking.

SET UP A REMOTE SITE

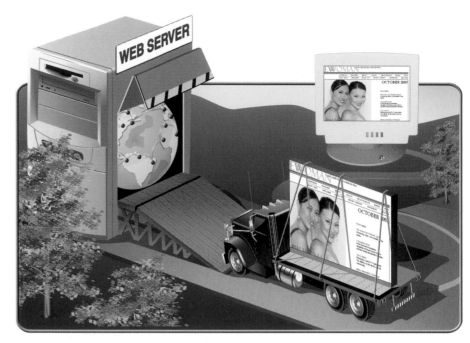

The *remote site* is a place where the files of your site are made available to the rest of the world. You set up a remote site by specifying a directory on a Web server where your site will be hosted.

SET UP A REMOTE SITE

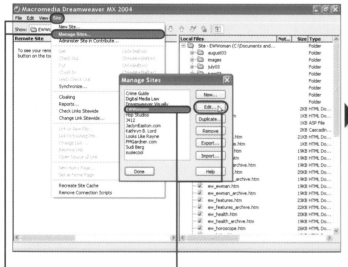

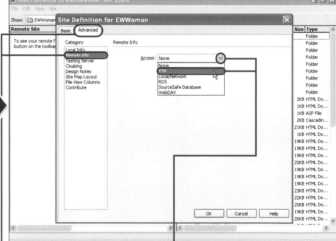

1 In the Site window, click **Site**.

2 Click **Manage Sites**.

■ The Manage Sites dialog box appears.

3 Click a site name from the list.

4 Click **Edit**.

■ The Site Definition dialog box appears.

5 Click the **Advanced** tab.

6 Click **Remote Info**.

7 Click ⌄ to select an access method.

8 Click **FTP**.

Note: FTP is the most common way for Web designers to connect to their Web servers. The other options are only used in special situations.

**What happens if I change my
Internet service provider (ISP)
and need to move my site to a
different server?**

You need to change your
remote site settings to enable
Dreamweaver to connect to
your new ISP server. Your local
site settings can stay the same.
Make sure you keep your local
files current and backed up
before you change servers.

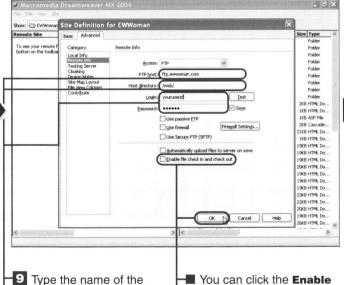

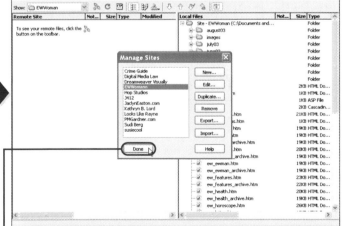

9 Type the name of the
FTP host (Web server).

10 Type your directory path
of the site on the Web
server.

11 Type your login name
and password.

■ You can click the **Enable
file check in and check
out** option if you will work
on the site collaboratively
(☐ changes to ☑).

12 Click **OK**.

■ The Site Definition dialog
box closes.

13 Click **Done**.

■ The remote site is now
set up.

CONNECT TO A REMOTE SITE

You can connect to the Web server that hosts your remote site and transfer files between it and Dreamweaver. Dreamweaver connects to the Web server by a process known as *File Transfer Protocol,* or *FTP.*

CONNECT TO A REMOTE SITE

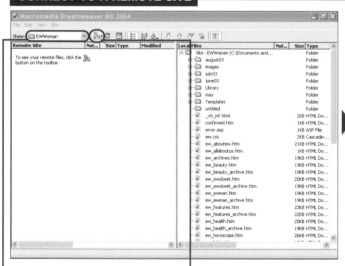

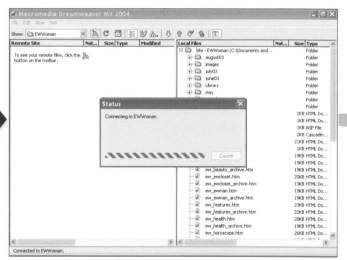

1 In the Site window, click ☑ and select your Web site.

2 Click the Connect button () to connect to the Web server.

■ Dreamweaver attempts to connect to the remote site.

Note: Dreamweaver displays an alert box if it cannot connect to the site. If you have trouble connecting, double-check the host information you entered for the remote site.

How do I keep Dreamweaver from prematurely disconnecting from the Web server?

You can click **Edit**, **Preferences**, and then **Site**. You can adjust the FTP transfer options to change the time that Dreamweaver lets pass between commands before it logs you off the server — the default is 30 minutes. Note that Web servers also have a similar setting on their end. Therefore, the server, not Dreamweaver, may sometimes log you off.

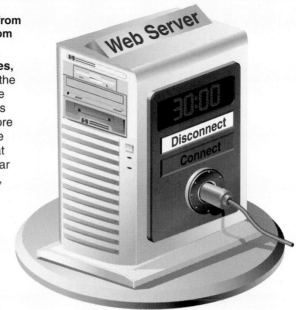

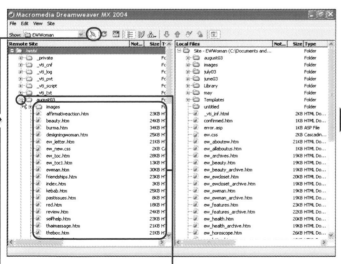

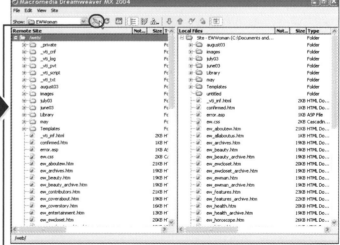

■ Dreamweaver displays the contents of the remote site's host directory.

■ The Disconnect button ([⚒]) changes to the Connect button ([⚒]), indicating a successful connection.

3 Click [+] to view the content of a directory on the Web server ([+] changes to [−]).

■ Dreamweaver displays the contents of the directory.

4 Click [⚒] to disconnect from the Web server.

■ Dreamweaver disconnects from the Web server.

■ If you do not transfer any files for 30 minutes, Dreamweaver automatically disconnects from a Web server.

UPLOAD FILES TO A WEB SERVER

You can upload site files from Dreamweaver to your remote site to make the files available to others on the Web.

UPLOAD FILES TO A WEB SERVER

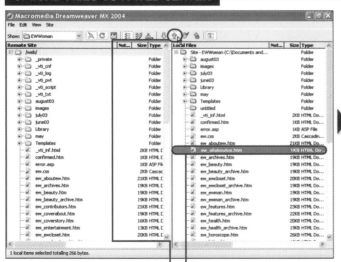

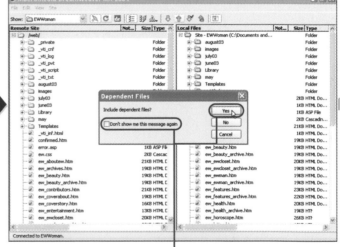

1 Connect to the Web server through the Site window.

Note: To connect to the Web server, see page 248.

2 Click the file you want to upload.

3 Click 🔼.

*Note: You can also right-click the file and select **Put** from the menu that appears.*

■ An alert box appears asking if you want to include dependent files.

Note: Dependent files are images and other files associated with a particular page. If you are uploading a page that displays images, those images are dependent files.

4 Click **Yes** or **No**.

■ You can click the option box to avoid the alert box in the future (☐ changes to ☑).

How do I stop a file transfer in progress?

You can click **Cancel** from the Status window that appears while a transfer is in progress. You can also press Esc.

How can I delete a file off the Web server?

With the Site window open, connect to the Web server. When the list of files appears in the left pane, click the file you want to delete and then press Delete. Dreamweaver will ask if you really want to delete the selected file. Click **OK**. You can also delete multiple files and folders.

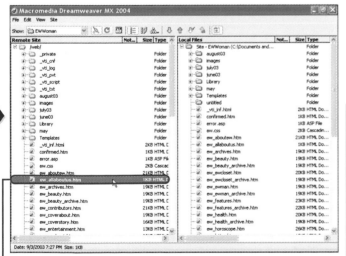

■ The file transfers from your computer to the Web.

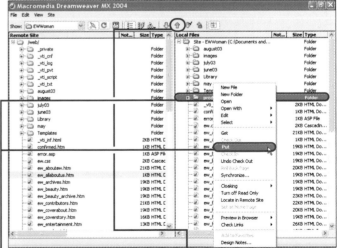

UPLOAD A FOLDER

1 In the right pane, right-click the folder you want to upload.

2 Click **Put** from the menu that appears.

■ You can also click the folder and then click 🔼.

■ Dreamweaver transfers the folder and its contents from your computer to the Web server.

DOWNLOAD FILES FROM A WEB SERVER

You can download files from your remote site in Dreamweaver if you need to retrieve to make changes or updates to pages on the Web server.

DOWNLOAD FILES FROM A WEB SERVER

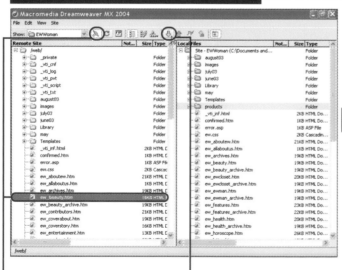

1 Click ![icon].

Note: To connect to a remote site, see page 248.

2 Click the file you want to download.

3 Click ![icon].

*Note: You can also right-click the file in the remote site and select **Get** from the menu that appears.*

■ An alert box appears asking if you want to include dependent files.

Note: Dependent files are images and other files associated with a particular page. If you are downloading a page that displays images, those images are dependent files.

4 Click **Yes** or **No**.

■ You can click the option box to avoid the alert box in the future (☐ changes to ☑).

Where does Dreamweaver log errors that occur during transfer?

Dreamweaver logs all transfer activity, including errors, in a file-transfer log. You can view it by clicking **Window**, **Results**, and then **FTP Log**. The FTP Log panel appears at the bottom of the screen.

Can I use my Web site to store files on which I am working?

If a file is on the Web, the public can see it. When pages are under construction and should not be seen, do not put them up on your Web site, even temporarily. Someone may see it, and there is the possibility that a search engine will index and cache it.

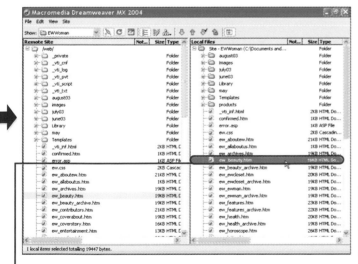

■ The file transfers from the Web server to your computer.

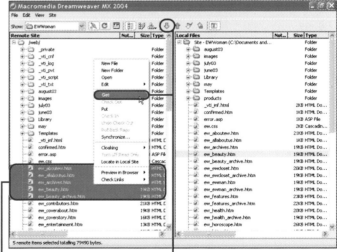

DOWNLOAD MULTIPLE FILES

1 Press and hold `Ctrl` (`Shift`) and click to select the files you want to download.

2 Right-click the selection.

3 Click **Get** from the menu that appears.

■ You can select the files and then click 🔽.

■ The files transfer from your Web server to your computer.

SYNCHRONIZE YOUR LOCAL AND REMOTE SITES

Dreamweaver can synchronize files between your local and remote sites so that both sites have an identical set of the most recent files. This can be useful if other people are editing the files on the remote site, and you need to update your local copies of those files.

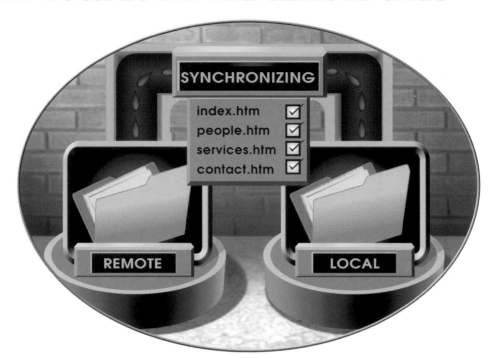

SYNCHRONIZE YOUR LOCAL AND REMOTE SITES

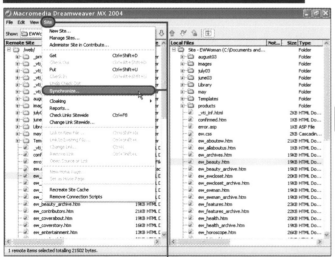

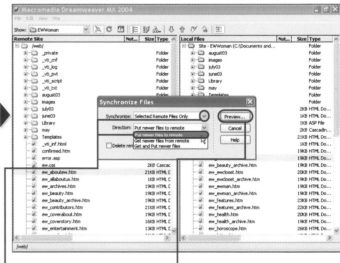

Note: To use the site window, see page 241.

1 In the Site window, click **Site**.

2 Click **Synchronize**.

■ The Synchronize Files dialog box appears.

3 Click ⌄ and select the files you want to synchronize.

4 Click ⌄ and select a direction where you want to copy the files.

■ You can place the newest copies on both the remote and local sites by selecting the **Get and Put newer files** option.

5 Click **Preview**.

Are there other FTP tools besides those available from Dreamweaver?

Dreamweaver offers the convenience of transferring files without having to open other programs. However, it uses many system resources and can slow down some machines significantly. There are many good alternatives available. On a PC, a good program to try is WS_FTP. On a Macintosh, Transmit is an excellent tool. You can download evaluation copies of either program from www.download.com. Other alternatives for transferring files via FTP include CuteFTP, LeechFTP, and CoffeeCup Direct FTP.

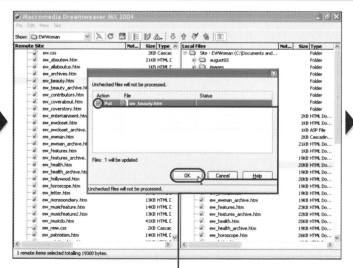

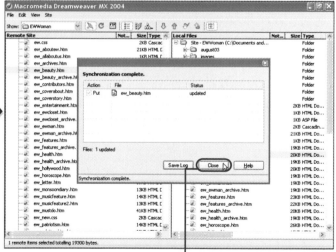

■ Dreamweaver compares the sites and then lists the files for transfer based on your selections in steps **3** to **4**.

6 Click to uncheck any files that you do not want to transfer (☑ changes to ☐).

7 Click **OK**.

■ The files are transferred and the Synchronize dialog box updates.

8 Click **Close**.

■ The local and remote sites are now synchronized.

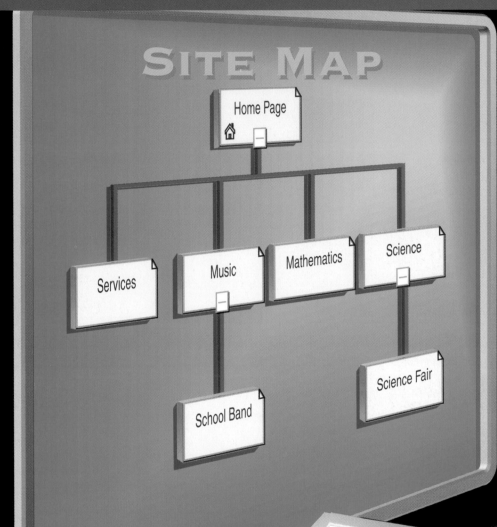

CHAPTER 15

Maintaining a Web Site

Keeping all the features of a Web site working and its content fresh can be as much work as creating the site. Dreamweaver's site maintenance tools make updating faster and easier.

View the Site Map 258

Manage Site Assets 260

Add Content with the Assets Panel 262

Specify Favorite Assets 264

Check a Page In or Out 266

Make Design Notes 268

Run a Site Report 270

Change a Link Sitewide 271

Find and Replace Text......................272

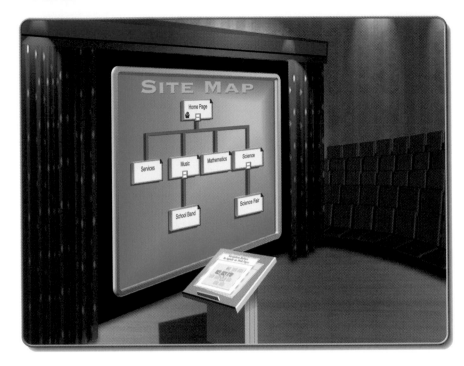

The Site Map View enables you to see your site in a flowchart form with lines representing links connecting the document icons. This view highlights pages that have broken internal links, which can help you maintain your site.

VIEW THE SITE MAP

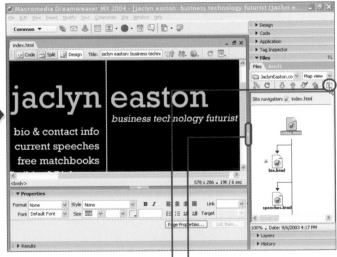

Note: You must set up a site for the file window features to function. To set up a site using the Files panel, see page 20.

1 Click **Window**.

2 Click **Files**.

■ The Files panel opens.

3 Click ⌄.

4 Click **Map View**.

■ A site map appears in the Files panel. By default, the site map displays the site structure two levels deep beginning from the home page.

5 Click and drag the side of the Files panel to expand it to fill the screen.

6 Click the Expand/Collapse button (⊞) in the Site panel to split the screen.

How do I fix a broken link in the site map?

A broken chain icon in the site map means the link to a page is broken. You can fix a broken link by right-clicking the destination page and then clicking **Change Link** from the menu that appears. Links can break because a destination page is renamed or deleted.

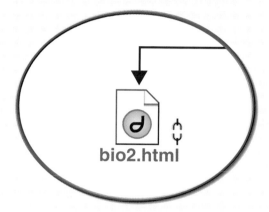

bio2.html

How can I make changes to the layout of the site map?

From the Site Window, click **View** and then **Layout**. The Site Definition window appears and displays the Site Map Layout options. You can select the home page, determine the number of columns and rows to display, determine whether to identify files by their names or titles, and choose whether to view hidden and dependent files.

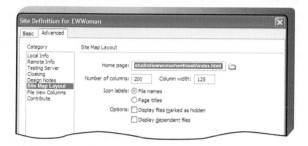

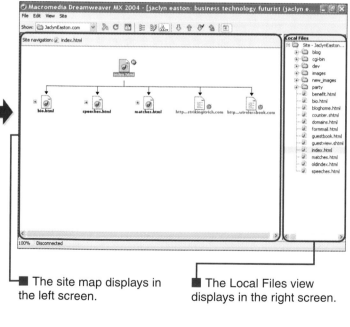

■ The site map displays in the left screen.

■ The Local Files view displays in the right screen.

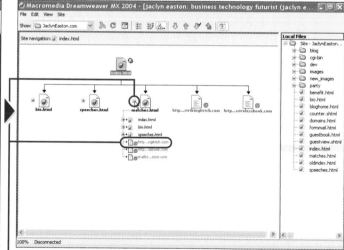

7 To view files below the second level, click ⊞.

■ External links are marked with an External Link icon (⬚@).

■ To save the site map as a BMP image that you can print or view in an image editor, click **File** and then **Save Site Map**.

MANAGE SITE ASSETS

You can view and
manage important
elements that appear in
the pages of your site
with the Assets panel.

MANAGE SITE ASSETS

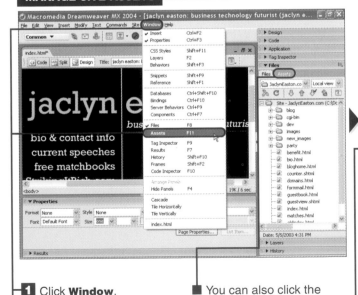

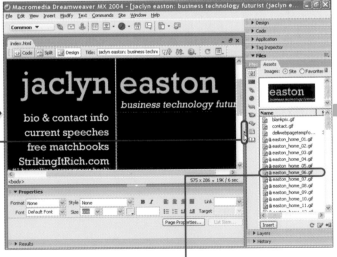

1 Click **Window**.

2 Click **Assets**.

■ You can also click the
Assets tab in the Files panel
to open the Assets panel.

■ The Assets panel
appears, displaying objects
from the selected category.

3 Click and drag the side
of the Assets panel to
expand it.

4 Click the name of any
asset to preview it in the
Assets panel.

How are assets organized?

Items in the Assets panel are organized into
the following categories:

ASSETS BUTTON CATEGORIES	
🖼	GIF, JPG, and PNG images
▦	Text, background, link, and style-sheet colors
🔗	Accessible external Web addresses
⊙	Flash-based multimedia
▥	Shockwave-based multimedia
📽	QuickTime and MPEG movies
📑	External JavaScript or VBScript files
📄	Page layout templates
📖	Library of reusable page elements

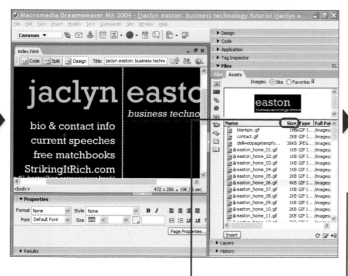

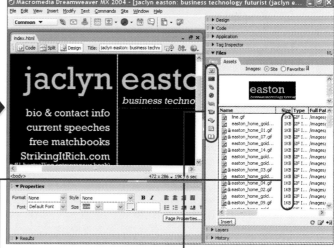

■ The panel assumes the
new dimensions and the
selected asset is previewed.

5 Click a column heading.

■ The assets are sorted
by the contents under the
selected column heading in
ascending order. You can
click the column again to
sort in descending order.

■ To view other assets, click
a different category button.

ADD CONTENT WITH THE ASSETS PANEL

You can add frequently used content to your site directly from the Assets panel. This technique can be more efficient than using a menu command or the Insert panel.

ADD CONTENT BY USING THE ASSETS PANEL

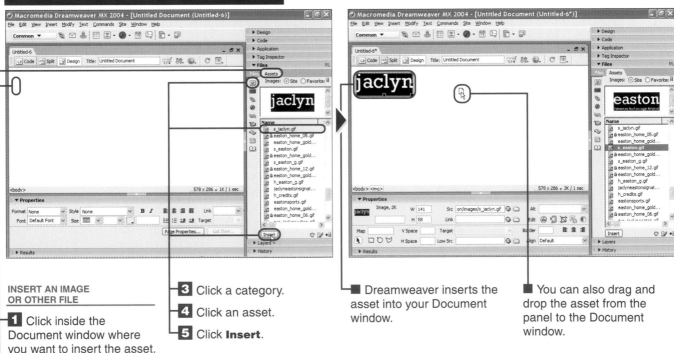

INSERT AN IMAGE OR OTHER FILE

1 Click inside the Document window where you want to insert the asset.

2 Click the **Assets** tab to open the Assets panel.

3 Click a category.

4 Click an asset.

5 Click **Insert**.

■ Dreamweaver inserts the asset into your Document window.

■ You can also drag and drop the asset from the panel to the Document window.

How do I copy assets from one site to another?

Click one or more items in the Assets panel, and then right-click the selected asset(s). From the menu that appears, click **Copy to Site** and then click a site to which you want to copy. The assets appear in the Favorites list under the same category in the other site.

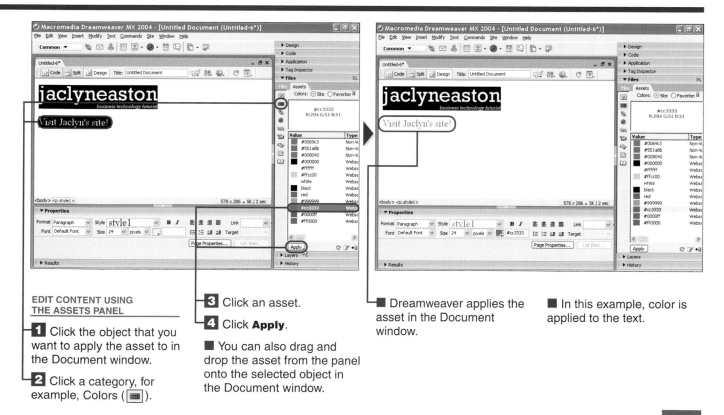

EDIT CONTENT USING THE ASSETS PANEL

1 Click the object that you want to apply the asset to in the Document window.

2 Click a category, for example, Colors (▦).

3 Click an asset.

4 Click **Apply**.

■ You can also drag and drop the asset from the panel onto the selected object in the Document window.

■ Dreamweaver applies the asset in the Document window.

■ In this example, color is applied to the text.

SPECIFY FAVORITE ASSETS

To make your assets lists more manageable, you can organize assets that you use often into a Favorites list inside each asset category.

SPECIFY FAVORITE ASSETS

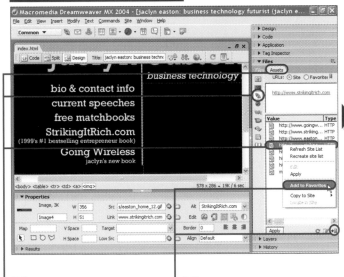

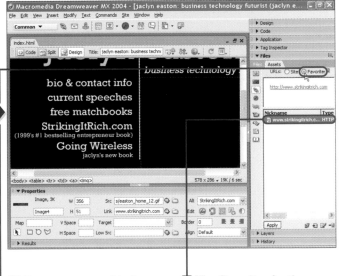

1 Click the **Assets** tab to open the Assets panel.

2 Click a category.

3 Click an asset.

4 Right-click the selected asset, and click **Add to Favorites** from the menu that appears.

■ You can also click 🔲.

■ Dreamweaver adds the asset to the category favorites list.

5 Click the **Favorites** option (○ changes to ◉).

■ The Favorites for the category appears.

How do I remove an item from the Assets panel entirely?

You need to delete the item from your local site folder. You can right-click (+click) the item in the Files panel and then click **Edit** and **Delete** from the menu that appears. When you return to the Assets panel and click the Refresh button (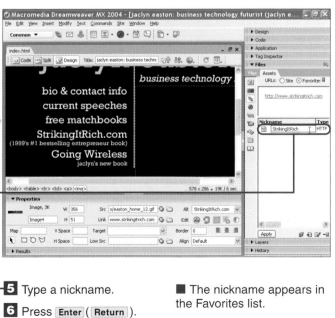), the asset is gone. You can also delete from the Site panel by clicking  from the Files panel and then following the same steps described above.

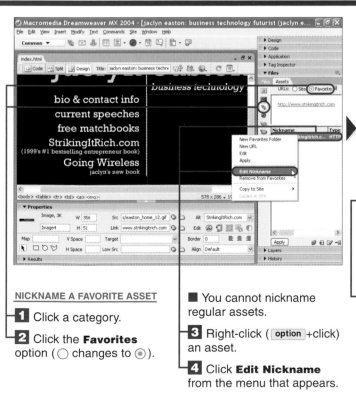

NICKNAME A FAVORITE ASSET

1 Click a category.

2 Click the **Favorites** option (○ changes to ⊙).

■ You cannot nickname regular assets.

3 Right-click (option +click) an asset.

4 Click **Edit Nickname** from the menu that appears.

5 Type a nickname.

6 Press Enter (Return).

■ The nickname appears in the Favorites list.

CHECK A PAGE IN OR OUT

Dreamweaver provides a Check In/Check Out system that keeps track of files when a team is working on a Web site. When one person checks out a page from the Web server, others cannot access the same file.

When the Check In/Check Out system is off, multiple people can edit the same file at once.

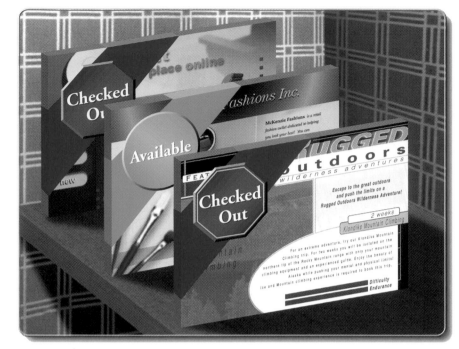

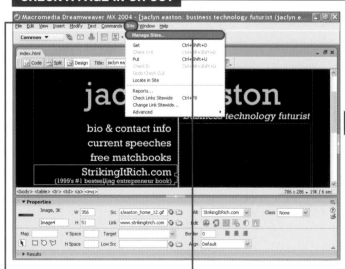

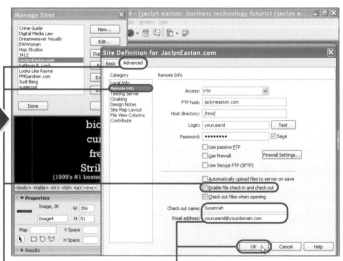

ENABLE CHECK IN/CHECK OUT

Note: You will need to specify the remote settings to use the Check In/Out to function. To set up a remote site, see page 246.

1 Click **Site**.

2 Click **Manage Sites** to open the Manage Sites dialog box.

3 Click to select the name of the site on which you want to work.

4 Click **Edit**.

■ The Site Definition dialog box opens.

5 Click the **Advanced** tab.

6 Click **Remote Info**.

7 Click the **Enable file check in and check out** option (☐ changes to ☑).

8 Type your name and e-mail address.

9 Click **OK**.

10 Click **Done** in the Manage Sites dialog box.

■ Check In/Check Out is now enabled.

How is a file marked as checked out?

When you check out a file, Dreamweaver creates a temporary LCK file that is stored in the remote site folder while the page is checked out. The file contains information about who has checked the file out. Dreamweaver does not display the LCK files in the file list, but you can see them if you access your remote site with a non-Dreamweaver FTP program.

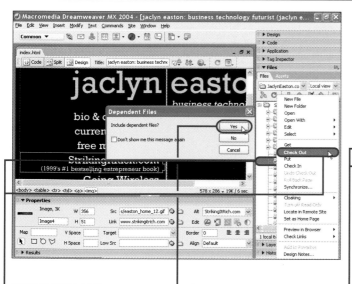

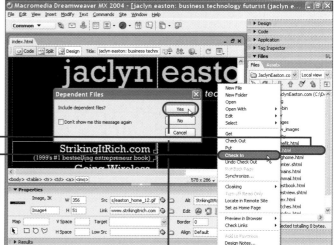

CHECK OUT A FILE

1 Click a file in the Files panel that is not checked out to select it and then right-click it.

2 Click **Check Out**.

■ A prompt appears asking if you want to include dependent files.

3 Click **Yes** if you want to check them out.

■ The page is marked as checked out.

CHECK IN A FILE

1 Click a file that is checked out by you to select it and then right-click it.

2 Click **Check In**.

■ A prompt appears asking if you want to include dependent files.

3 Click **Yes** if you want to check them in.

■ The page is marked as checked in.

MAKE DESIGN NOTES

If you are working on a site collaboratively, Design Notes can enable you to add information about the development status of a file. You can attach information to your Web pages with Design Notes, such as editing history and an author name.

MAKE DESIGN NOTES

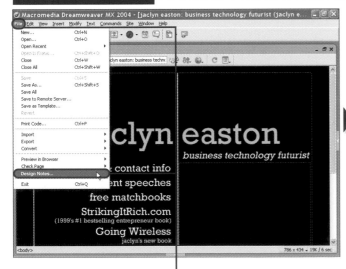

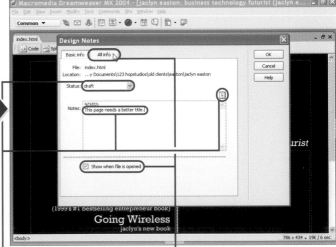

■ Design Notes are on by default when you create a site. You can turn them off in your site definition settings by clicking **Site** and then **Manage Sites**.

1 Open the page to which you want to attach Design Notes.

2 Click **File**.

3 Click **Design Notes**.

■ The Design Notes dialog box appears.

4 Click and select a status for the page.

5 Type a note.

■ You can click to enter the current date in the Notes field.

■ You can click the **Show when file is opened** option (changes to) to automatically show Design Notes when a file opens.

6 Click the **All info** tab.

How can I view Design Notes?

You can view Design Notes in two ways. First, files with a Design Note will have a yellow bubble (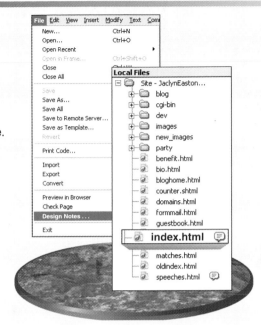) in the Site Window. Double-click to open the Design Note. Alternatively, you can open any file with an attached Design Note and then click **File** and **Design Notes** to open the Design Note.

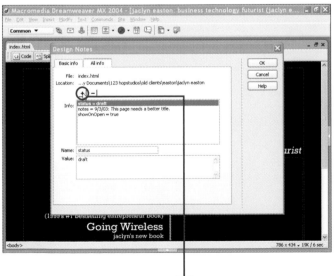

■ The All info options display.

7 To enter new information into Design Notes, click ➕.

8 Type a name and value pair.

■ The added information appears in the Info section.

■ You can delete information by clicking it in the Info section and then clicking ➖.

9 Click **OK**.

■ Dreamweaver makes the Design Note.

Running a site report can help you pinpoint problems in your site, such as redundant HTML code in your pages and missing descriptive information as image alt text and page titles. It is a good idea to test your site by running a report before you upload it to a Web server.

RUN A SITE REPORT

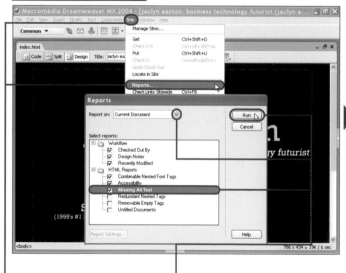

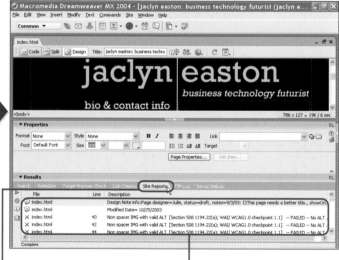

1 Click **Site**.

2 Click **Reports**.

■ The Reports dialog box opens.

3 Click the Report On ▼ and select to run a report on the entire site or selected files.

4 Click the reports you want to run.

5 Click **Run**.

■ Dreamweaver creates a report and displays it in the Results panel.

6 Click any tab across the top of the Results panel to display the report.

■ Details appear in the Results panel.

You can search and replace all the hyperlinks on your site that point to a specific address. This is helpful when a page is renamed or deleted and links to it need updating.

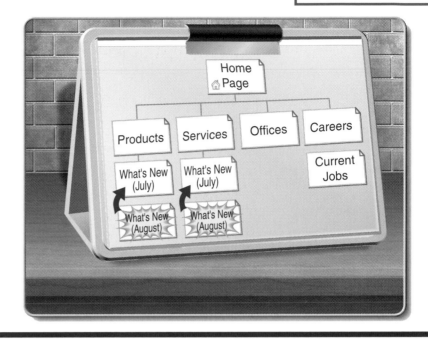

CHANGE A LINK SITEWIDE

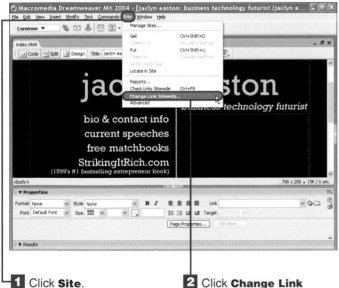

1 Click **Site**.

2 Click **Change Link Sitewide**.

■ The Change Link Sitewide dialog box appears.

3 Type the old hyperlink destination you want to change.

4 Type the new hyperlink destination.

■ The hyperlinks must start with a **/** and be a mailto: (e-mail) link, or a full URL.

5 Click **OK**.

■ Dreamweaver finds and replaces all instances of the old destination. A dialog box asks you to confirm the changes.

FIND AND REPLACE TEXT

The Find and Replace feature is a powerful tool for making changes to text elements that repeat across many pages. You can find and replace text on your Web page, your source code, or specific HTML tags in your pages.

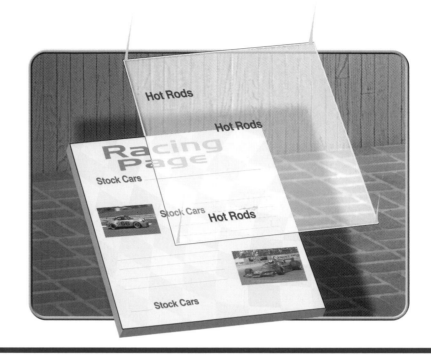

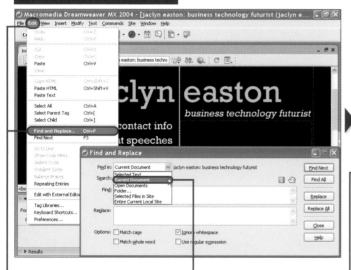

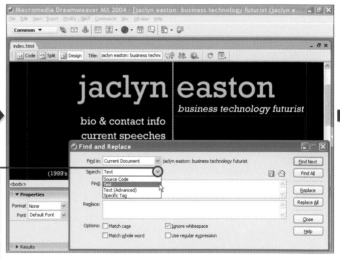

1 Click **Edit**.

2 Click **Find and Replace**.

■ The Find and Replace dialog box appears.

3 Click 🔽 and select whether you want to search the entire site or only selected files.

■ You can select multiple files to search by Ctrl + clicking (Shift +clicking) the filenames in the Site window before you click **Edit** and then **Find and Replace**.

4 Click 🔽 and select the type of text you want to search.

■ For example, you can select **Text (Advanced)** to find text that is inside a specific tag.

Can I use find and replace to alter an HTML attribute?

You can replace attributes to achieve many things. You can change the alignment of the contents of a table (change `align="center"` to `align="right"` in `<td>` tags), change the color of specific text in your page (change `color="green"` to `color="red"` in `<font>` tags), or change the page background color across your site (change `bgcolor="black"` to `bgcolor="white"` in `<body>` tags).

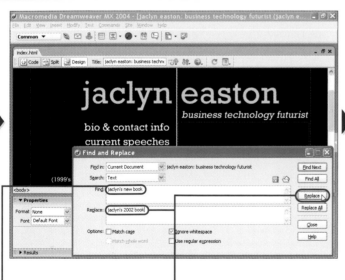

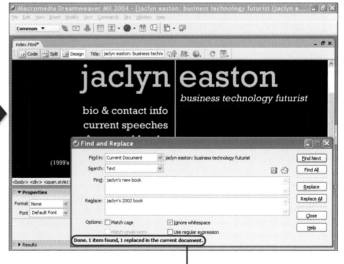

5 Type the text you want to search for in the Find field.

■ When searching, you can click **Find Next** to find instances of your query one at a time.

6 Type the replacement text in the Replace field.

7 Click **Replace** to replace one at a time.

■ You can also click **Replace All** to replace all automatically.

■ An alert box may appear asking if you want to replace text in documents that are not open. Click **Yes**.

■ Dreamweaver replaces the text, and the details appear in the bottom of the Find and Replace dialog box.

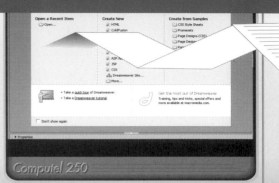

CHAPTER 16

Building a Database-Driven Web Site

If you are an advanced Dreamweaver user who understands databases, you can read this chapter to learn how to use server behaviors to create powerful dynamic Web sites.

The Power of Dynamic Web Sites......276

Install a Testing Server 278

Create a Database Connection 282

Configure a Dynamic Web Site 286

Create a Recordset..........................288

Add a Record 292

Update a Record 293

Add Recordset Paging 294

Create a Site Search 296

THE POWER OF DYNAMIC WEB SITES

Dynamic Web sites use a database to store all kinds of information, and then make the data accessible in various ways. The Web sites that you visit for news, weather, e-mail, forums, and shopping are all examples of how powerful dynamic Web technologies can be.

Database-Driven Web Sites

Dynamic web pages communicate with a database to display and store content on demand. You can store thousands of pages of information and images in a database. You can then create a handful of dynamic web pages that allow you to browse or search that content. This is much more efficient than creating a thousand individual HTML pages!

Growth and Maintenance Friendly

Dynamic Web sites are built to handle ever-changing content. For example, e-commerce sites typically consist of a few dynamic pages capable of displaying any item in a database, because databases are easier to edit than Web pages. They are also more adaptable — you can sort, find, delete, and add information faster in a database than manually browsing through individual Web pages. With the help of dynamic Web pages, people visiting your site can perform those same tasks.

Get People Involved

Databases are not just about storing content. They can also collect and share data on demand. Web sites like eBay, Yahoo!, Amazon.com, and many others like them are powered by complex databases. Dynamic Web sites enable you to display and receive information from anyone who participates in dynamic areas of your site.

INSTALL A TESTING SERVER

A *Testing Server*, also called an *Application Server*, is software that enables a computer to receive connections from Web browsers. This software supports technologies such as ASP, PHP, and ColdFusion, which act as the liaison between your database and your Web pages.

Note: This section assumes that you are running Windows XP Professional. You may need your Windows XP installation disk to install IIS. If IIS is not available for your version of Windows, you can download Personal Web Server from www.microsoft.com.

INSTALL A TESTING SERVER

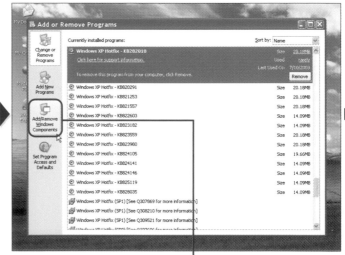

1 Click **Start**.

2 Click **Settings**.

3 Click **Control Panel** to open the Control Panel.

4 Click **Add or Remove Programs**.

■ The Add or Remove dialog box appears.

5 Click the **Add/Remove Windows Components** button.

Why does Windows need the installation CD?

Windows is made up of thousands of individual files and programs. In order to save space on your computer's hard drive, Windows copies only the files that it needs when it is originally installed. When you install a Windows component, like Internet Information Services, Windows sometimes needs to copy these files from the CD and put them on your computer's hard drive.

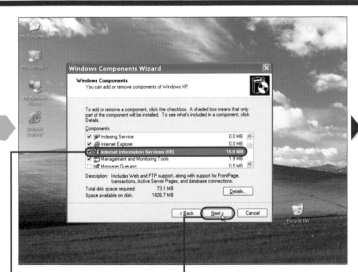

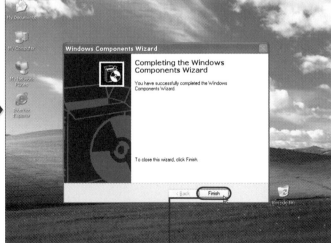

6 Click **Internet Information Services (IIS)** (☐ changes to ☑). If Internet Information Services (IIS) is already checked, click Cancel and skip to step **15**.

7 Click **Next**.

■ A progress screen lets you know how the installation is going.

Note: You may receive a prompt asking you to insert your Windows Installation CD into the CD-ROM drive. If you do receive this prompt, please complete this step.

■ The Windows Component Wizard completion dialog box appears.

8 Click **Finish**.

CONTINUED

INSTALL A TESTING SERVER

Windows XP Professional
ships with Internet
Information Server (IIS),
an Application Server
that processes Active
Server Pages (ASP) and
makes it easy to create
dynamic pages.

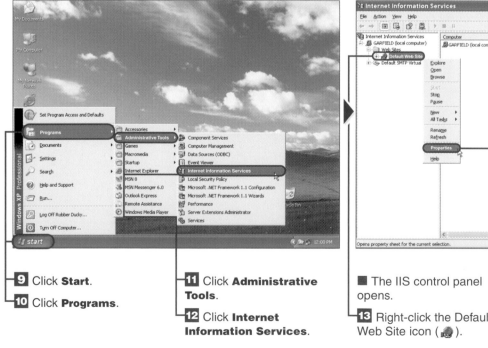

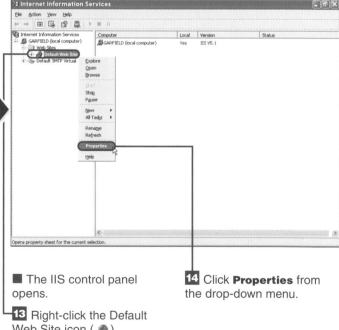

9 Click **Start**.

10 Click **Programs**.

11 Click **Administrative Tools**.

12 Click **Internet Information Services**.

■ The IIS control panel opens.

13 Right-click the Default Web Site icon ( ).

14 Click **Properties** from the drop-down menu.

**What is a server-side programming
language? Is HTML a server-side
programming language?**

HTML is a *markup* language, meaning that its
primary use is to display content. However, it
was built to connect with other technologies.
Server-side programming languages such as
ASP, PHP, JSP, and ColdFusion make
database communication possible.
Dreamweaver MX's server
behaviors write server-side
programming code for you.

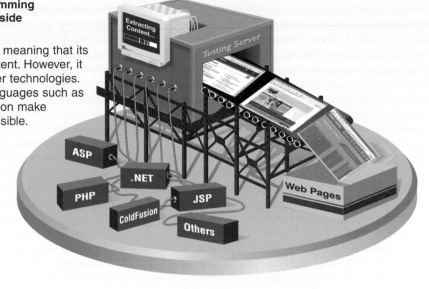

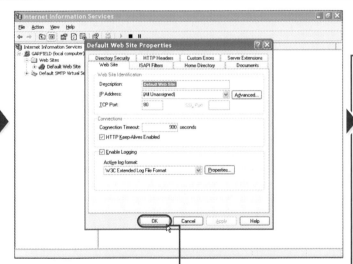

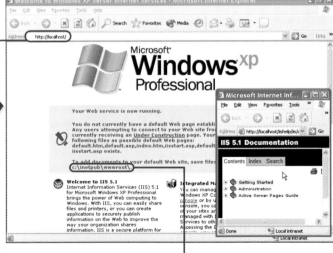

■ The Default Web Site
Properties dialog box
appears.

■ IIS allows you to control
various Web site settings,
such as public folder
browsing. For more
information on IIS, visit
www.microsoft.com.

15 Click **OK** to close the
window.

16 Open your Web browser.

17 Type **http://localhost/**.

■ The default Testing Server
page displays, telling you the
server was installed
correctly.

■ This page also tells you
where to move your Web
site. The path is usually at
c:\inetpub\wwwroot.

CREATE A DATABASE CONNECTION

A data source name, or DSN, is used to store database connection settings. Acting as a bookmark, it allows you to conveniently connect to your database from applications without defining a database's settings every time. You must first create a database before defining a DSN.

Note: This example uses a simple database created with Microsoft Access 2000, a popular database program for Windows.

CREATE A DATABASE CONNECTION

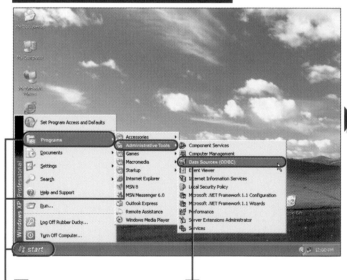

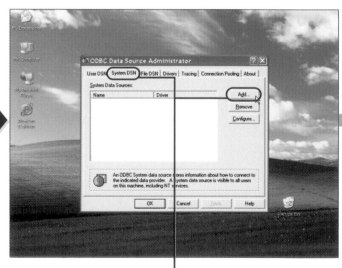

1 Click **Start**.

2 Click **Programs**.

3 Click **Administrative Tools**.

4 Click **Data Sources (ODBC)**.

Note: Windows XP hides folders that you do not regularly use. Click ☒ to expand hidden items.

■ The ODBC Data Source Administrator dialog box appears.

5 Click the **System DSN** tab.

6 Click **Add**.

What is the difference between a System DSN, a User DSN, and a file DSN?

All three types of DSN store the same type of database connectivity information. You use a System DSN when you want every user on the PC to have access. A user DSN only allows specific computer users to access it, usually the user who creates it. Both System and User DSN store the information inside the Registry. A file DSN creates a DSN file, storing the information inside this text file instead of the registry.

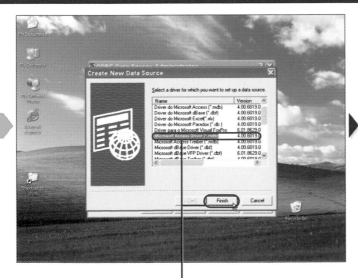

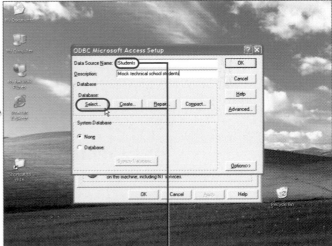

■ The Create New Data Source dialog box appears with a list of database drivers.

7 Click **Microsoft Access Driver**.

8 Click **Finish**.

■ The ODBC Microsoft Access Setup dialog box appears.

9 Type a unique, descriptive name for your database.

10 Click **Select**.

CONTINUED

CREATE A DATABASE CONNECTION

If your Application Server is running on a Windows system, you can use a DSN to connect your dynamic Web pages to a database.

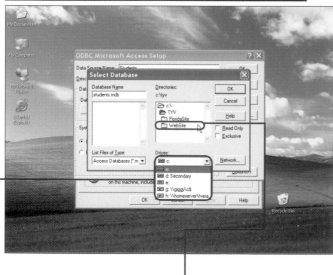

■ The Select Database dialog appears.

11 Click here and select the drive the database is on.

12 Click the folder in which the database is located.

13 Click the desired MDB file.

14 Click **OK**.

How can I connect to a database without creating a DSN?

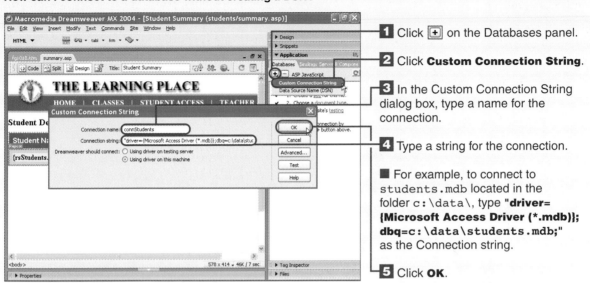

1 Click ⊞ on the Databases panel.

2 Click **Custom Connection String**.

3 In the Custom Connection String dialog box, type a name for the connection.

4 Type a string for the connection.

■ For example, to connect to students.mdb located in the folder c:\data\, type **"driver= {Microsoft Access Driver (*.mdb)}; dbq=c:\data\students.mdb;"** as the Connection string.

5 Click **OK**.

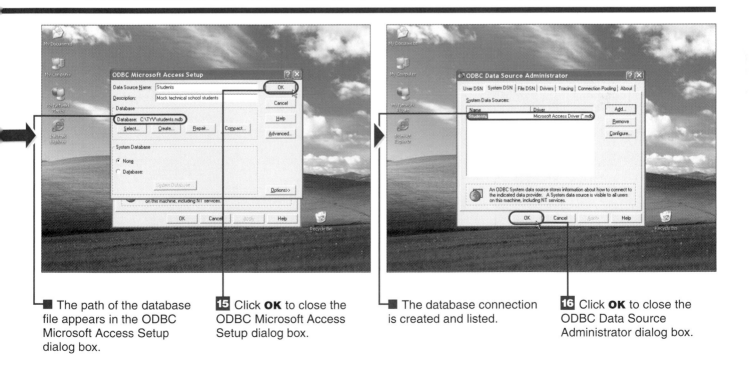

■ The path of the database file appears in the ODBC Microsoft Access Setup dialog box.

15 Click **OK** to close the ODBC Microsoft Access Setup dialog box.

■ The database connection is created and listed.

16 Click **OK** to close the ODBC Data Source Administrator dialog box.

CONFIGURE A DYNAMIC WEB SITE

Dynamic Web pages do not display database content when opened directly from the Web browser. Thus, you have to configure Dreamweaver to use your Testing Server. These features create a seamless authoring environment for you.

CONFIGURE A DYNAMIC WEB SITE

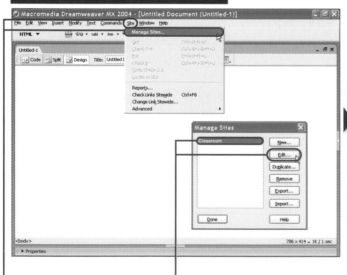

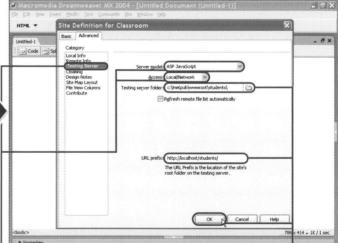

ASSOCIATE THE TESTING SERVER

1 Click **Site**.

2 Click **Manage Sites**.

■ The Manage Sites dialog box appears.

3 Click a site.

4 Click **Edit.**

Note: You must either move all the contents of your site into your Testing Server area (usually a folder inside c:\inetpub\wwwroot), or configure IIS to point to its current folder. For more about the testing server, see page 278.

5 Click **Testing Server**.

6 Click ⌄ and select **ASP JavaScript**.

7 Click ⌄ and select **Local/Network**.

8 Click 📁 and select where your site is located on your computer.

9 Type the path to your local site folder starting with the URL prefix of **http://localhost/**.

10 Click **OK**.

Can I open dynamic Web pages directly through my browser instead of installing a Testing Server?

No. Web browsers are not capable of understanding server-side programming languages. Instead of displaying a dynamic Web page, the Web browser displays the programming code that makes up such a page. Think of the Testing Server as a person who translates the results of this code into HTML, a language your Web browser understands.

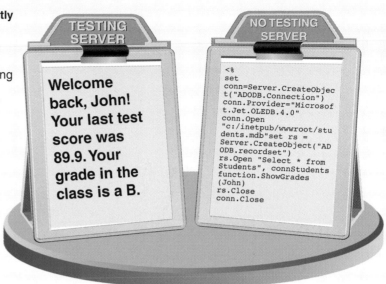

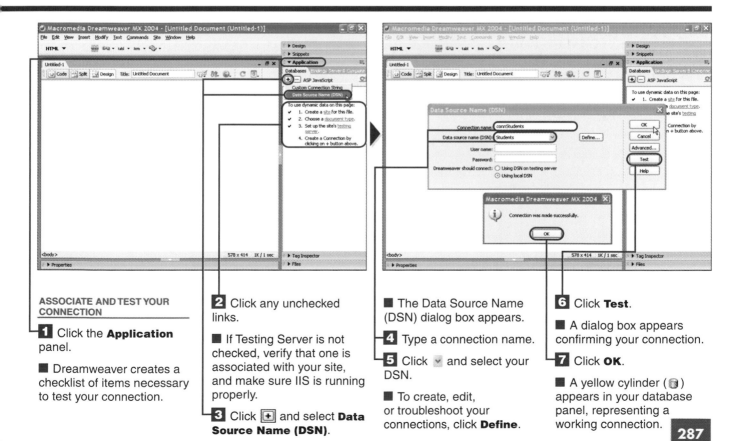

ASSOCIATE AND TEST YOUR CONNECTION

1 Click the **Application** panel.

■ Dreamweaver creates a checklist of items necessary to test your connection.

2 Click any unchecked links.

■ If Testing Server is not checked, verify that one is associated with your site, and make sure IIS is running properly.

3 Click ➕ and select **Data Source Name (DSN)**.

■ The Data Source Name (DSN) dialog box appears.

4 Type a connection name.

5 Click ⌄ and select your DSN.

■ To create, edit, or troubleshoot your connections, click **Define**.

6 Click **Test**.

■ A dialog box appears confirming your connection.

7 Click **OK**.

■ A yellow cylinder (🗄) appears in your database panel, representing a working connection.

CREATE A RECORDSET

A *recordset* is a virtual group of items that you can request retrieval of from a database. You can then manipulate and/or display this selection of data on the Web page. A recordset can contain one or more items in it.

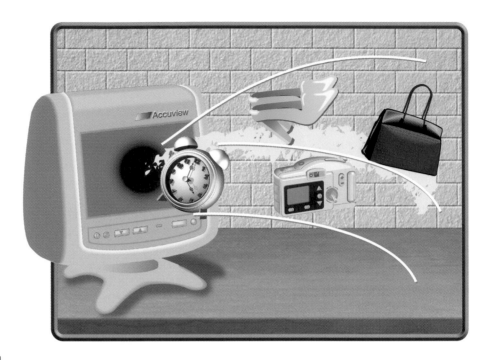

CREATE A RECORDSET

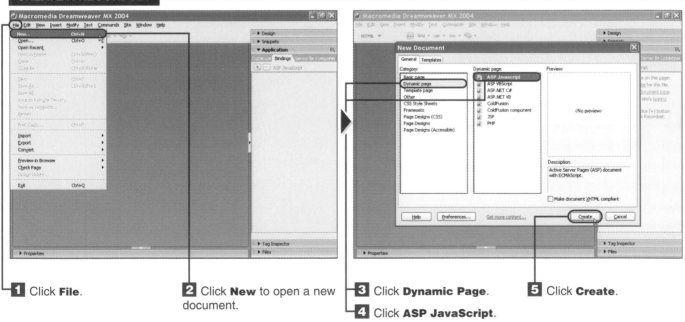

1 Click **File**.

2 Click **New** to open a new document.

3 Click **Dynamic Page**.

4 Click **ASP JavaScript**.

5 Click **Create**.

Does it matter if I choose ASP VBScript or ASP JavaScript for new Dynamic Web pages?

No, it does not make a difference. Dreamweaver inserts code, JavaScript, or VBScript to create your dynamic Web pages. The only time that it makes a difference is if you want to make changes to the code that Dreamweaver inserts. If this is the case, you should choose the scripting language with which you are more familiar. For more information about scripting in ASP pages, visit www.microsoft.com/scripting/ or www.4guysfromrolla.com/.

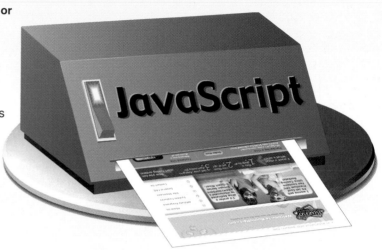

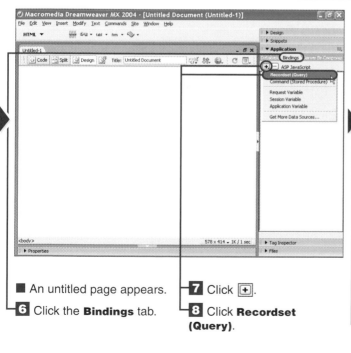

■ An untitled page appears.

6 Click the **Bindings** tab.

7 Click ⊞.

8 Click **Recordset (Query)**.

■ The Recordset dialog box appears.

9 Type a name for your recordset.

10 Click ∨.

11 Click a connection.

Note: Your connection is the DSN you assigned to this site. To configure a dynamic Web site, see page 286.

CREATE A RECORDSET

A *recordset* serves as a temporary mediator between the databases where the information is stored and the dynamic Web page application.

RECORDSET

CREATE A RECORDSET (CONTINUED)

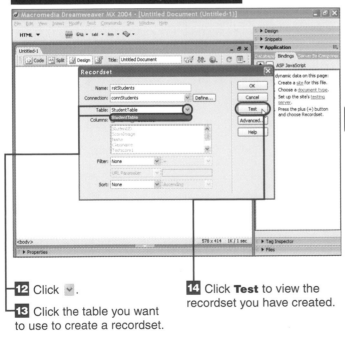

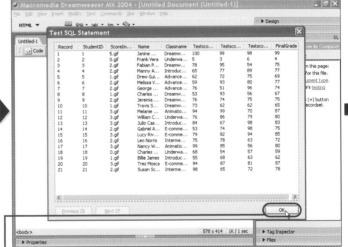

12 Click ⌄.

13 Click the table you want to use to create a recordset.

14 Click **Test** to view the recordset you have created.

■ The Test SQL Statement dialog box appears.

15 Click **OK** to close the test screen.

■ Filtering and sorting are optional. If you choose not to set either menu, your recordset will display everything in the table as it appears in the database.

How do I organize database
content on a Web page?

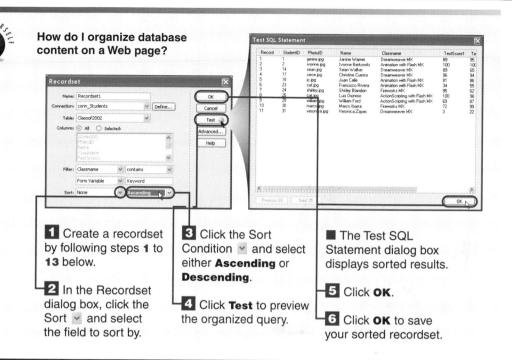

1 Create a recordset
by following steps **1** to
13 below.

2 In the Recordset
dialog box, click the
Sort ⌄ and select
the field to sort by.

3 Click the Sort
Condition ⌄ and select
either **Ascending** or
Descending.

4 Click **Test** to preview
the organized query.

■ The Test SQL
Statement dialog box
displays sorted results.

5 Click **OK**.

6 Click **OK** to save
your sorted recordset.

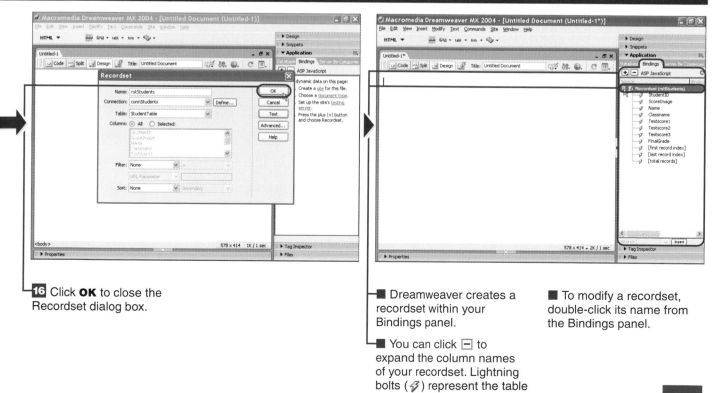

16 Click **OK** to close the
Recordset dialog box.

■ Dreamweaver creates a
recordset within your
Bindings panel.

■ You can click ⊟ to
expand the column names
of your recordset. Lightning
bolts (⚡) represent the table
columns in your recordset.

■ To modify a recordset,
double-click its name from
the Bindings panel.

ADD A RECORD

Instead of entering information into your database with desktop software, you can create your own Web page forms that enable you to input content into your database using a Web browser.

Your new records have been added to the database.

Computel 250

ADD A RECORD

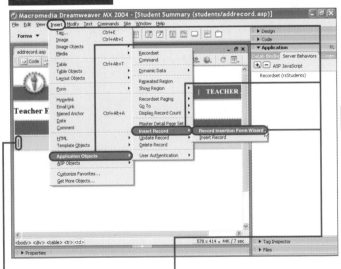

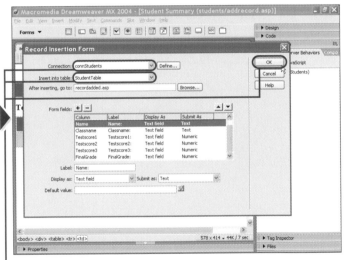

1 Create a recordset containing the tables to which you want to add a record.

Note: To create a recordset, see page 288.

2 Click your mouse where you want to insert the form.

3 Click **Insert**.

4 Click **Application Objects**.

5 Click **Insert Record**.

6 Click **Record Insertion Form Wizard**.

■ The Record Insertion Form dialog box appears.

7 Click ⌄ and select your connection.

8 Click ⌄ and select your table.

9 Click **OK**.

■ A completed form with highlighted fields and assigned server behaviors appears.

10 Open your Web browser and test the page in your Testing Server.

Similar to the Record
Insertion Form object,
this server object creates
a form that lets you view
content from a database
in form fields, modify
them on the page, and
submit your changes
back to the database.

UPDATE A RECORD

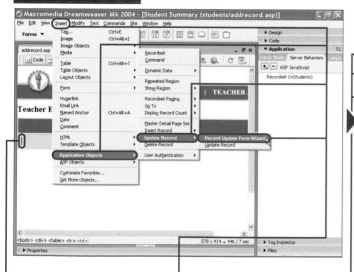

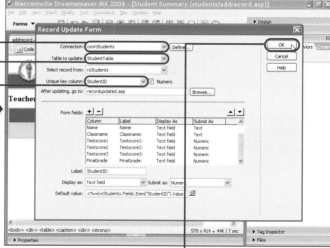

1 Create a recordset
containing the tables to
which you want to add a
record.

2 Click your mouse
where you want to insert the
form.

3 Click **Insert**.

4 Click **Application
Objects**.

5 Click **Update Record**.

6 Click **Record Update
Form Wizard**.

■ The Record Update Form
dialog box appears.

7 Click ▾ and select a
connection.

8 Click ▾ and select your
table.

9 Click ▾ and select a
unique key for the table.

10 Click **OK**.

■ A highlighted form and
submit button appear.

11 Open your Web browser
and test the page in your
Testing Server.

■ The first record for
updating appears.

ADD RECORDSET PAGING

Recordset Paging

You can display a desired amount of information per page with the server behavior Recordset Paging. Most search engines, for example, limit their pages to 20 results per page. You can use dynamic links or buttons to navigate to the rest of the content.

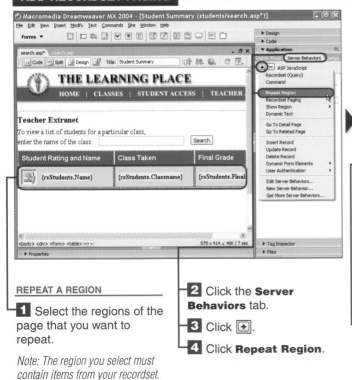

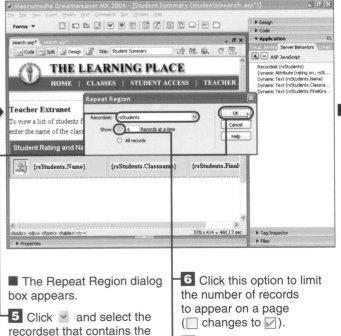

REPEAT A REGION

1 Select the regions of the page that you want to repeat.

Note: The region you select must contain items from your recordset.

2 Click the **Server Behaviors** tab.

3 Click ⊞.

4 Click **Repeat Region**.

■ The Repeat Region dialog box appears.

5 Click ⌄ and select the recordset that contains the data you want to repeat.

6 Click this option to limit the number of records to appear on a page (☐ changes to ☑).

7 Click **OK**.

294

How can I protect my add/update record forms from hackers?

First, save all the data-entry screens in an obscurely named area of your Web site. Next, utilize simple password authentication. IIS lets you modify a folder's properties to have directory security. Finally, install an SSL certificate so that passwords sent to unlock this directory cannot be intercepted. To purchase a certificate and learn more about SSL, visit www.thawte.com and www.verisign.com.

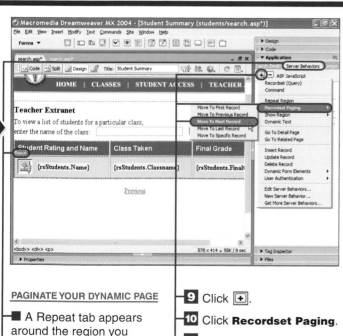

PAGINATE YOUR DYNAMIC PAGE

■ A Repeat tab appears around the region you specified.

8 Click the **Server Behaviors** tab.

9 Click ⊞.

10 Click **Recordset Paging**.

11 Click a paging behavior from the menu.

■ The most commonly used paging behaviors are next and previous.

■ A highlighted text link appears on your page.

12 Preview the page in a Web browser.

13 Click the links you created to browse your database.

■ The Show Region enables you to hide your navigational links by clicking the **Next** button or link, then clicking **Show Region** from the Server Behaviors panel, and then clicking **Show If Not Last Record**.

CREATE A SITE SEARCH

You can create a *site search* to quickly and easily enable Web site visitors to locate records in a database. Creating a site search essentially combines several sections of this chapter. You must create the search form, define the search parameters in a recordset, and then lay out where the search results will appear with the Repeated Region server behavior.

CREATE A SITE SEARCH

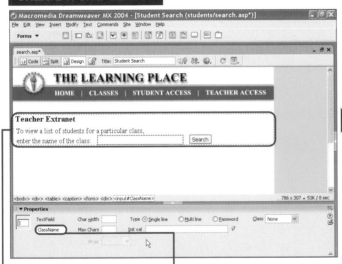

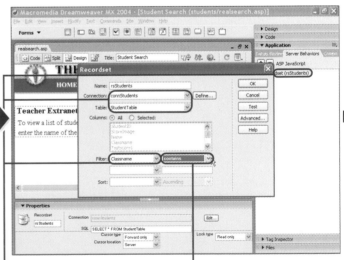

1 Create a new dynamic page using ASP JavaScript technology.

Note: To create a recordset, see page 288.

2 Create a form with a text field and a Submit button.

■ The form method should be post by default.

Note: To create a form, see page 173.

3 Type a name for your text field.

4 Click **Recordset**.

5 Click ⊻ and select the table and connection for your site search.

6 Click ⊻ and select the column in the database that matches the field with which you will search.

7 Click ⊻ and select how the filter should behave.

■ You can select **contains** for flexible searching and select = for exact matches.

**How do I create a site search that indexes my site's
Web pages like a search engine?**

There are no page indexing features packaged with
Dreamweaver MX. However, there are third-party
extensions you can install, plus manual indexing
methods. Visit http://exchange.macromedia.com and
search on the term *search*. Atomz Search and Deva
Tools are among the best third-party indexing
extensions. To create your own index, add a table in
your database that contains URLs and keywords
about your pages, and then create a site search that
looks at those keywords. Your repeated region can
then display the URLs to those relevant pages in
your database just as a search engine would.

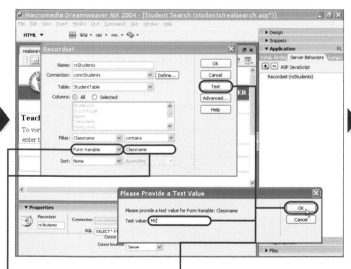

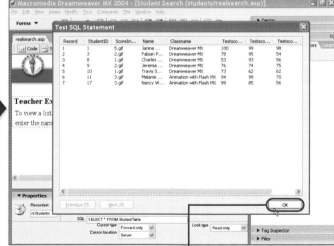

8 Click ⌄ and select
Form Variable as your filter
style.

9 Type the name of your
text field as the filter style
variable, using the name
of the field you created in
step **3**.

10 Click **Test** to open the
Test Value dialog box.

11 Type a search term that
is in the specified area of
your database.

12 Click **OK**.

■ The Test SQL Statement
dialog box displays filtered
results. In this example, the
test value was the word MX.

13 Click **OK** to close the
Test SQL dialog box.

14 Click **OK** in the
Recordset dialog box to save
your filtered recordset.

CONTINUED

CREATE A SITE SEARCH

A site search is made possible by formulating a recordset with a dynamic value set by a site user. The form allows the web site visitor to input what the recordset filters. The user submits the form, the server behaviors perform the filter script, and the filtered data is returned as a recordset to display on the Web page.

CREATE A SITE SEARCH (CONTINUED)

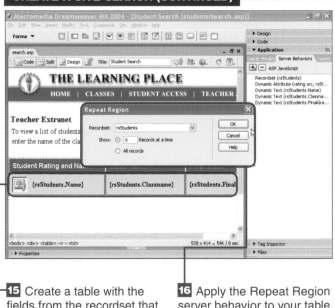

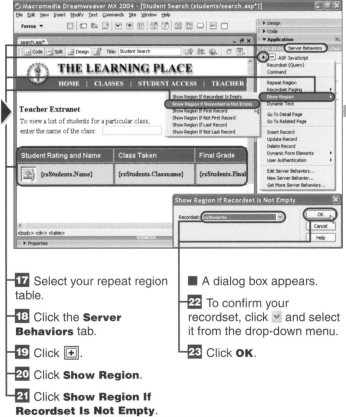

15 Create a table with the fields from the recordset that you want to display as search results.

16 Apply the Repeat Region server behavior to your table.

Note: To repeat a region, see page 294.

17 Select your repeat region table.

18 Click the **Server Behaviors** tab.

19 Click ⊞.

20 Click **Show Region**.

21 Click **Show Region If Recordset Is Not Empty**.

■ A dialog box appears.

22 To confirm your recordset, click ⌄ and select it from the drop-down menu.

23 Click **OK**.

How can I create a site search for a photo gallery?

A photo gallery site search relies on keywords associated with a photo, which you must enter into a database along with the path to the image. First, set up a column in the database and enter keywords associated with each image. Next, follow the steps from Add a Dynamic Image to set your gallery search results region. Lastly, follow the concepts in the Site Search task, setting the recordset filter to search your keyword column in your database.

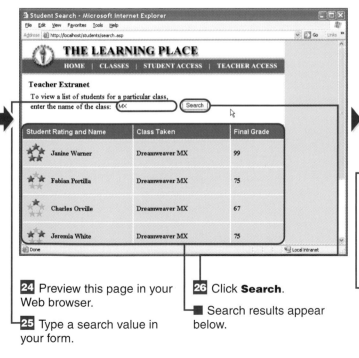

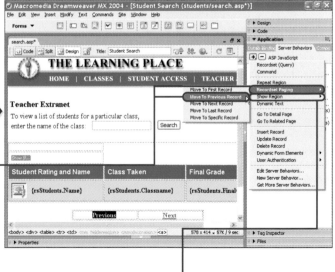

24 Preview this page in your Web browser.

25 Type a search value in your form.

26 Click **Search**.

■ Search results appear below.

■ You can apply the Recordset Paging server behavior to aid in navigating through a long list of search results.

Note: To apply the Recordset Paging server behavior, see page 294.

■ Remember to apply the appropriate **Show Region** behaviors to your Next and Previous links. Otherwise, both these links will show up before a search is performed.

INDEX

Special Characters

< > (angle brackets), 44

A

<a> tag, 50
align
    cell content, 137
    images, 84–85
    paragraphs, 62–63
    tables, 136
    text, 51
align attribute, 51
angle brackets (< >), 44
animation. *See* multimedia
Application Server, install, 278–281
ASP JavaScript *versus* ASP VBScript, 289
assets
    copy, 263
    manage, 260–263
    organize, 37
    remove, 265
    specify favorites, 264–265
Assets panel, 37, 262–263
audience for your site, 9

B

<b> tag, 50
background
    cell, 133
    color, 96
    images, 94–95
    tables, 132–133
banner ads. *See* multimedia
basic document structure, 48
bgcolor attribute, 48
block format, 49
<body> tag, 48
bold text, 50
borders
    frames, 166–167
    tables
        thickness, 135
        turn off, 129

 tag, 49
broken links
    check for, 111
    fix, 259
    moved files, 245
    report on, 123
browser. *See* Web browsers
bulleted lists, 66–67
buttons
    layers, 234–235
    radio, 178–179
    Reset, 183
    Submit, 183

C

captions, 131, 195
cartoons. *See* multimedia
Cascading Style Sheets. *See* CSS

case sensitivity, HTML tags, 45
cells, table
    align content, 137
    background, 133
    insert/delete, 138–139, 147
    pad, 134
    rearrange, 146–147
    resize, 142
    space, 135
    split/merge, 140–141
centered images, 85
certificates, 295
check boxes, 176–177
    See also lists (form)
    See also menus (form)
    See also radio buttons
<CLASS> attribute, 215
Clean Up HTML command, 52–53
Code Inspector, 45
Code View mode, 46–47
color
    fonts, 73–75
    hexadecimal codes, 75
    links, 124–125
color attribute, 50
columns, delete, 138–139
command history. *See* History panel
commands, 38–39. *See also entries for specific* commands
create
    CSS, 210–211
    custom commands, 38
    forms, 173
    headings, 60–61
    layers, 228–229
    library items, 188–189
    links, 120
    a page with frames, 160–161
    paragraphs, 62–63
    templates, 196–197
    Web pages, 22
crop images, 86–87. *See also* resize, images
Crop tool, 86–87
CSS (Cascading Style Sheets)
    See also forms
    See also frames
    See also library items
    See also tables
    See also templates
    apply to a page, 212–213
    apply to multiple pages *See* external style sheets
    browser compatibility, 207, 223
    create, 210–211
    edit, 214–215
    embedded, 207
    export internal sheets, 219
    external
        add styles to, 221
        attach, 220–221
        create, 218–219
        definition, 207
        edit, 222–223
    format text, 206, 212–213
    global Web page style, 206

HTML code for, 215
HTML style, 207
introduction, 206–207
link styles, 216–217
position page elements, 217
redefine HTML tags, 208–209, 211
selectors, 216–217

D

data source name (DSN), 282–285
database-driven sites
    add records, 292
    ASP JavaScript *versus* ASP VBScript, 289
    configure, 286–287
    database connection, 282–285
    definition, 276
    DSN, 282–285
    HTML, 281
    index Web pages, 297
    install a Testing Server, 278–281
    installation CD, 279
    introduction, 276–277
    organize Web page content, 291
    passwords, 295
    photo galleries, 299
    recordset paging, 294–295
    recordsets, 287–291
    security, 295
    server-side programming language, 281
    site search, 296–299
    SSL certificates, 295
    update records, 293
    in Web browsers, 287
delete
    cells, 138–139, 147
    columns, 138–139
    files from Web servers, 251
    frames, 162
    rows, 138–139
    tables, 147
design notes, 268–269
Design View mode, 46–47
Detach from Original command, 195
detach library items, 194–195
<DIV> tag, 215, 217
Document window
    customize, 30–31
    format content, 33–34
    Macintosh, 13
    PC, 12
documents. *See* HTML; Web pages
download
    files from Web servers, 252–253, 255
    older versions of Web browsers, 243
    speed, 83
    stop, 251
drag layers, 233
Dreamweaver
    definition, 4
    exit, 15
    help, 16–17
    hide panels, 14
    screen descriptions *See* user interface
    show panels, 14

DSN (data source name), 282–285
dynamic Web sites. *See* database-driven sites

E

edit
    CSS, 214–215
    find and replace text, 272–273
    HTML, 45, 273
    images, 87
    inserted library items, 191–195
    single frame in a frameset, 155
    templates, 202–203
editable template attributes, 203
editable template regions, 198–199
elements of your site. *See* assets; *entries for specific assets*
e-mail links, 122
embedded CSS, 207
error correction, 41, 53. *See also* History panel
error logs, Web servers, 252
exit Dreamweaver, 15
exporting internal style sheets, 219
external style sheets
    add styles to, 221
    attach, 220–221
    create, 218–219
    definition, 207
    edit, 222–223

F

favorite assets, specify, 264–265
favorite features, reuse, 31. *See also* CSS; library items; templates
file DSN, 283
File panel, 120
File Transfer Protocol (FTP), 248–249, 255
files
    formats, 81
    moved, and broken links, 245
    organize, 244–245
        and image display, 21
        importance of, 21
        and links, 21, 109
        recommended location, 25
    store *See* organize, files
    temporary, from page preview, 27
    view organization, 241
Flash files, 98–99
Font menu, 71
<font> tag, 50
fonts. *See also* CSS; text
    browser compatibility, 33
    color, 73–75
    face, 70–71
    on the Font menu, 71
    multiple per page, 33
    per-page settings, 74–75
    sans-serif, 71
    serif, 71
    size, 72, 74–75
    specification, 50
form handler, 172–173
format page content, 32–34
        See also CSS
        See also forms
        See also frames

See also library items
See also tables
See also templates
format text
    See CSS
    See fonts
    See specific text elements
    See text
forms
    See also CSS
    See also frames
    See also layers
    See also tables
    check boxes, 176–177
    create, 173
    introduction, 172
    lists, 180–181
    menus, 180–181
    passwords, 182
    radio buttons, 178–179
    Reset button, 183
    Submit button, 183
    text fields, 174–175
    user-selected options
        See check boxes
        See lists (form)
        See menus
        See radio buttons
    as Web page element, 7
frames. *See also* forms; tables
    add content, 160–161
    borders, 166–167
    change attributes, 158–159
    create a new page, 160–161
    delete, 162
    divide a page, 156
    introduction, 152
    link to a page, 161
    link to another frame, 163–165
    name, 163
    nested, 157
    resize
        change attributes, 158–159
        drag borders, 159
        prohibit, 169
    scroll bars, 168
    as Web page element, 7
framesets
    edit a single frame, 155
    predefined, 153
    save, 154–155
FTP (File Transfer Protocol), 248–249, 255

G

GIF format, 81
graphics. *See* images; multimedia

H

`<h1>...<h6>` tags, 49
head content, 54–55
`<head>` tag, 48

headings
    create, 60–61
    HTML tags for, 49
    levels, 61
help
    Dreamweaver, 16–17
    HTML tags, 56–57
hide
    Dreamweaver panels, 14
    layers, 234–235
History panel
    command history, 35
    custom commands, 38–39
    definition, 31
home page, 4
host Web sites, 9
`href` attribute, 51
HTML (Hypertext Markup Language). *See also* tags
    automatic generation, 45
    code for CSS, 215
    Code Inspector, 45
    Code View mode, 46–47
    database-driven sites, 281
    definition, 5, 44
    Design View mode, 46–47
    direct access to, 45
    edit, 45, 273
    error correction, 41, 53
    head content, 54–55
    line numbers, 47
    optimize, 52–53
    preview results, 46–47
    Quick Tag Editor, 45
    server-side programming language, 281
    wrap lines, 47
`<html>` tag, 48
hyperlinks. *See* links
Hypertext Markup Language. *See* HTML

I

`<i>` tag, 50
image maps, 118–119
images. *See also* multimedia
    align, 84–85
    alternate text, 97
    background, 94–95
    background color, 96
    captions, 131, 195
    centered, 85
    crop, 86–87 *See also* resize
    download speed, 83
    edit, 87
    file formats, 81
    and file organization, 21
    GIF format, 81
    HTML code for, 50
    insert in Web page, 80–81
    invisible, 149
    JPEG format, 81
    links from, 111–113, 118–119
    navigation bars, 104–105
    resample, 90–91
    resize, 88–89 *See also* crop

rollover, 102–103
source specification, 51
space around, 92–93
table space, 149
trim *See* crop; resize
as Web page element, 6
wrap text around, 82–83
`<img>` tag, 50
import from other documents, 76–77
import text, 76–77
indent paragraphs, 65
information gathering. *See* forms
Insert bar (panel)
insert an e-mail link, 34
Macintosh, 13
PC, 12
installation CD, 279
interactive U.S. map, 119
interactivity. *See* database-driven sites; forms; layers
invisible
frame borders, 166–167
images, 149
layers, 231
italic text, 50

J

JavaScript *versus* VBScript, 289
JPEG format, 81

L

layers. *See also* forms
browser compatibility, 227
buttons, 234–235
create, with content, 228–229
drag, 233
introduction, 226–227
nested, 226, 236–237
parent, 231
reposition, 230–231
resize, 230–231
show/hide, 234–235
stacking order, 232
versus tables, 229
unnested, 237
visibility, 231
layout tools
See CSS
See forms
See frames
See layers
See library items
See tables
See templates
levels of headings, 61
`<li>` tag, 49
library items. *See also* CSS; templates
create, 188–189
detach for edit, 194–195
edit inserted item, 191–195
insert in Web page, 190–191
introduction, 186
in templates, 199
update a Web site, 192–193
view, 187

line breaks, 49, 64
line numbers, 47
links
anchor, 50
to another file type, 116–117
broken
check for, 111
fix, 259
moved files, 245
report on, 123
change sitewide, 271
color, 124–125
create, 120
customize with CSS, 216–217
destination, 51
e-mail, 122
file organization, 109
and file organization, 21
frame to a page, 161
frame to another frame, 163–165
HTML tags, 50–51
image maps, 118–119
from images, 111–113, 118–119
insert an e-mail link, 34
interactive U.S. map, 119
to non-HTML documents, 116–117
open in new window, 121
to other sites, 110–111
within a page, 114–115
to pages in same site, 108–109
remove underline, 216
test, 111, 123
as Web page element, 7
when files move, 245
list items, 49
lists (document)
bulleted, 66–67
ordered, 49, 66–67
unordered, 49, 66–67
lists (form), 180–181
See also check boxes
See also menus (form)
See also radio buttons
Lorem ipsum dolor, 57

M

Macintosh interface
Document window, 13
Insert bar (panel), 13
interface, 13
menus, 13
panels, 13
Properties inspector, 13
start, 10–11
toolbar, 13
maintain Web sites
add content, 262–263
assets
copy, 263
manage, 260–263
removing, 265
specifying favorites, 264–265
check pages in/out, 266–267

INDEX

design notes, 268–269
find and replace text, 272–273
links
    change sitewide, 271
    fix broken, 259
site flow chart, 258–259
site map, 258–259
site reports, 270
menus (Dreamweaver), 12–13
menus (form), 180–181
    See also check boxes
    See also lists (form)
    See also radio buttons
merge cells, 140–141
`<meta>` tag, 48
metatags, 48
multimedia. *See also* images
    Flash files, 98–99
    HTML tags for, 99
    insert in Web page, 98–101
    video clips, 100–101

N

name frames, 163
navigation bars, 104–105
nested frames, 157
nested layers, 226, 236–237
non-English text, 69

O

`<object>` tag, 99
`<ol>` tag, 49
open panels, 36–37
optimize HTML code, 52–53
ordered lists, 66–67
organize
    assets, 37
    files
        and image display, 21
        importance of, 21
        and links, 21
        recommended location, 25

P

`<p>` tag, 49, 63
pad cells, 134
pages under construction, store, 253
panels
    Macintosh, 13
    open, 36–37
    PC, 12
    rearrange, 36–37
paragraphs
    align, 62–63
    create, 62–63
    HTML tag, 49, 63
    indent, 65
    width, 63
`<param>` tag, 99
parent layers, 231
passwords
    database-driven sites, 295
    forms, 182

PC interface
    Document window, 12
    Insert bar (panel), 12
    interface, 12
    menus, 12
    panels, 12
    Properties inspector, 12
    start, 10
    toolbar, 12
photo galleries, 299
pictures. *See* images; multimedia
plan Web sites
    gather content, 9
    site maps, 8
    sketch organization of, 8
    sticky notes, as planning tools, 8
    target audience, 9
    visualize size and scope, 8
    Web server host, 9
position page elements, 217
`<pre>` tag, 49
predefined framesets, 153
preferences, set, 40–41
Preferences dialog box, 40–41
preformatted text, 49
preview
    HTML results, 46–47
    Web pages, 26–27
Preview in Browser command, 26–27
Properties inspector
    format content with, 32–33
    Macintosh, 13
    PC, 12
publish Web sites
    organize files and folders, 244–245
    premature server disconnect, 249
    procedure for, 240
    remote site
        connect to, 248–249
        set up, 246–247
    synchronize local and remote sites, 254–255
    test browser compatibility, 242–243
    view file organization, 241
    Web servers
        delete files from, 251
        download files from, 252–253, 255
        error logs, 252
        pages under construction, 253
        premature disconnection, 249
        stop a file transfer, 251
        upload files to, 250–251, 255

Q

Quick Tag Editor, 45
quotations, 65

R

radio buttons, 178–179
    See also check boxes
    See also lists (form)
    See also menus (form)

rearrange
     cells, 146–147
     panels, 36–37
     table content, 139
recordset paging, 294–295
recordsets, 287–291
remote site
     connect to, 248–249
     set up, 246–247
     synchronize to local, 254–255
rename custom commands, 39
resample images, 90–91
Resampling tool, 90–91
Reset buttons, 183
resize
     cells, 142
     frames
          change attributes, 158–159
          drag borders, 159
          prohibit, 169
     images, 88–89
     layers, 230–231
     tables, 143, 148–149
reuse favorite features, 31. *See also* CSS; library items; templates
rollover images, 102–103
rows, delete, 138–139

S

sans-serif fonts, 71
save
     framesets, 154–155
     Web pages, 24–25
scroll bars, 168
security
     database-driven sites, 295
     forms, 182
     passwords, 182, 295
     SSL certificates, 295
selectors (CSS), 216–217
serif fonts, 71
server. *See* Web servers
server-side programming language, 281
show
     Dreamweaver panels, 14
     layers, 234–235
site search, 296–299
Site window, 241
size
     fonts, 72, 74–75
     text, varies across computers, 61
     Web pages, 83
size attribute, 50
space
     cells, 135
     images, 92–93
spacer images, 149
<SPAN> tag, 215
special characters, 68–69
split cells, 140–141
spreadsheets. *See* tables
src attribute, 51
SSL certificates, 295
stacking order, layers, 232
start Dreamweaver, 10–11

sticky notes, as planning tools, 8
store files. *See* organize, files
style sheets. *See* CSS
Submit buttons, 183
surveys. *See* forms
System DSN, 283

T

table spacer images, 149
tables. *See also* forms; frames
     align, 136
     background, 132–133
     borders
          thickness, 135
          turn off, 129
     cells
          align content, 137
          background, 133
          insert/delete, 138–139, 147
          pad, 134
          rearrange, 146–147
          resize, 142
          space, 135
          split/merge, 140–141
     columns, delete, 138–139
     content
          format, 129
          insert, 130–131
          move, 139
          position, 145
     fit to browser window, 148–149
     image captions, 131, 195
     insert in Web pages, 128–129
     insert/delete, 147
     versus layers, 229
     rearrange, 146–147
     resize, 143, 148–149
     rows, delete, 138–139
     space images, 149
     undo actions, 139
     as Web page element, 7
     Web page layout, 144–145
     width, 148–149
     wrap text around, 136
tags. *See also* HTML
     < > (angle brackets), 44
     <a>, 50
     align attribute, 51
     align text, 51
     <b>, 50
     basic document structure, 48
     bgcolor attribute, 48
     block format, 49
     <body>, 48
     bold text, 50

, 49
     case sensitivity, 45
     color attribute, 50
     definition, 44
     <DIV>, 215, 217
     document body, 48
     document head, 48
     document title, 48
     empty, 53

`<font>`, 50
font specification, 50
`<h1...h6>`, 49
`<head>`, 48
headings, 49
help for, 56–57
`href` attribute, 51
`<html>`, 48
`<i>`, 50
image source, 51
images, 50–51
`<img>`, 50
italic text, 50
`<li>`, 49
line break, 49
link anchor, 50
link destination, 51
links, 51
list items, 49
`<meta>`, 48
multimedia, 99
`<object>`, 99
`<ol>`, 49
ordered lists, 49
`<p>`, 49
paragraphs, 49
`<param>`, 99
`<pre>`, 49
preformatted text, 49
prewritten snippets, 56–57
redefine with CSS, 207, 208–209, 211
reference information, 56–57
searchable metatags, 48
size attribute, 50
`<SPAN>`, 215
src attribute, 51
syntax, 45
text color, 48, 50
text format, 50
text size, 50
`<title>`, 48
`<ul>`, 49
unordered lists, 49
target audience, 9
templates. *See also* CSS; library items
    content types, 197
    create, 196–197
    create a page from, 200–201
    detach a page from, 201
    edit, 202–203
    editable attributes, 203
    editable regions, 198–199
    introduction, 186
    library items in, 199
    store, 203
    update a Web site, 202–203
    view, 187
Templates folder, 203
test links, 111, 123
Testing Server, install, 278–281
text. *See also* fonts
    align, 51
    bold, 50

color, 48, 50
CSS, 206, 212–213
format, 50
headings
    create, 60–61
    HTML tags for, 49
    levels, 61
import from other documents, 76–77
italic, 50
line breaks, 64
list items, 49
lists
    bulleted, 66–67
    ordered, 49, 66–67
    unordered, 49, 66–67
non-English, 69
paragraphs
    align, 62–63
    create, 62–63
    HTML tag, 49, 63
    indent, 65
    width, 63
preformatted, 49
quotations, 65
size, 50
    varies across computers, 61
special characters, 68–69
as Web page element, 6
text fields, forms, 174–175
text wrap
    around images, 82–83
    around tables, 136
    HTML documents, 47
`<title>` tag, 48
titles, add to Web pages, 23
toolbar, 12–13
trim images, 86–87. *See also* resize, images

U

`<ul>` tag, 49
undo, 139. *See also* History panel
unnested layers, 237
unordered lists, 66–67
upload
    files to Web servers, 250–251, 255
    stop, 251
U.S. map, link example, 119
User DSN, 283
user feedback. *See* forms
user interface
    Assets panel, 37
    customize, 40–41
    Document window
        customize, 30–31
        format content, 33–34
        Macintosh, 13
        PC, 12
    History panel
        command history, 35
        custom commands, 38–39
        definition, 31

Insert bar (panel)
  insert an e-mail link, 34
  Macintosh, 13
  PC, 12
Macintosh
  interface, 13
  menus, 13
  panels, 13
  start, 10–11
  toolbar, 13
panels *See also entries for specific panels*
  open, 36–37
  rearrange, 36–37
PC
  interface, 12
  menus, 12
  panels, 12
  start, 10
  toolbar, 12
Preferences dialog box, 40–41
Properties inspector
  format content with, 32–33
  Macintosh, 13
  PC, 12
reuse favorite features, 31 *See also* CSS; library items; templates
set preferences, 40–41
user-selected options
  See check boxes
  See lists (form)
  See menus
  See radio buttons

V

VBScript *versus* JavaScript, 289
video clips, 100–101
visibility
  frame borders, 166–167
  images, 149
  layers, 231

W

Web, definition, 4
Web browsers
  compatibility
    CSS (Cascading Style Sheets), 207, 223
    database-driven sites, 287
    fonts, 33
    layers, 227
    tables, 148–149
    test, 242–243
  definition, 5
  download older versions, 243
  preview Web pages, 26–27
Web pages
  add titles, 23
  body, 48
  check in/out, 266–267
  create, 22
  create from templates, 200–201
  detach from templates, 201
  download speed, 83
  global style *See* CSS
  head, 48

headings, 49
ideal size, 83
index, 297
insert images, 80–81
insert library items, 190–191
insert tables in, 128–129
layout
  See CSS (Cascading Style Sheets)
  See forms
  See frames
  See library items
  See tables
  See templates
parts of, 6–7 *See also* assets; *entries for specific parts*
preview, 26–27
reuse common elements *See* library items; templates
save, 24–25
title, 48
Web servers
  definition, 5
  delete files from, 251
  download files from, 252–253, 255
  error logs, 252
  pages under construction, 253
  premature disconnection, 249
  stop a file transfer, 251
  transfer Web pages to *See* publish Web sites
  upload files to, 250–251, 255
Web sites
  definition, 4
  dynamic *See* database-driven sites
  flow chart, 258–259
  interactivity *See* database-driven sites; forms; layers
  maintenance *See* maintain Web sites
  making available *See* publish Web sites
  plan
    gather content, 9
    site maps, 8
    sketch organization of, 8
    sticky notes, as planning tools, 8
    target audience, 9
    visualize size and scope, 8
    Web server host, 9
  search engine rankings, 55
  set up
    add titles to Web pages, 23
    create new Web pages, 22
    define a local site, 20–21
    organize files, 21, 25
    preview Web pages, 26–27
    save Web pages, 24–25
  site map, 258–259
  site reports, 270
  transfer to Web servers *See* publish Web sites
  update library items, 192–193
  update templates, 202–203
windows (Dreamweaver). *See* panels
World Wide Web. *See* Web
wrap
  lines, HTML documents, 47
  text
    around images, 82–83
    around tables, 136
    HTML documents, 47

You know the basics. Now it's time to go beyond.

Let the Top 100 Simplified series show you how—now!

The newest member of Wiley's popular Visual family brings you 100 shortcuts, tips, and tricks in every book, presented in the award-winning format Visual readers love. In no time, you'll be working smarter.

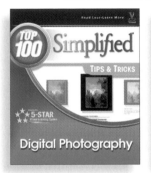
Digital Photography

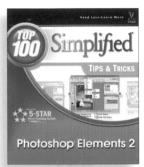
Photoshop Elements 2

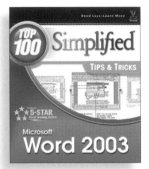
Word 2003

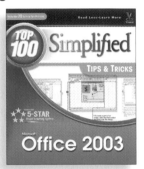
Office 2003

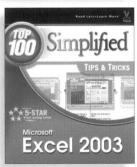
Excel 2003

HTML

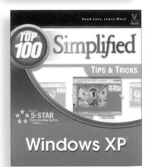
Windows XP

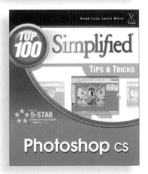
Photoshop CS

More tools for visual learners

| Just the essentials | Beginning computer skills for novice users | Beginning to intermediate instruction | Deeper coverage plus additional tools | Professional level instruction |

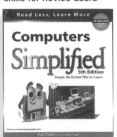

Visit us at wiley.com/compbooks

WILEY
Now you know.